Teaching Writing in High School and College

Conversations and Collaborations

Edited by

Thomas C. Thompson
The Citadel, Charleston, South Carolina

National Council of Teachers of English
1111 W. Kenyon Road, Urbana, Illinois 61801-1096

Staff Editor: Bonny Graham

Interior Design: Doug Burnett

Cover Design: Evelyn C. Shapiro

Cover Photograph: Karen DeWig

NCTE Stock Number: 09756-3050

Library of Congress Cataloging-in-Publication Data

Teaching writing in high school and college : conversations and collaborations / edited by Thomas C. Thompson.
    p. cm.
Includes bibliographical references.
    ISBN 0-8141-0975-6 (pbk.)
  1. English language—Composition and exercises—Study and teaching (Secondary) 2. English language—Rhetoric—Study and teaching. 3.
Report writing—Study and teaching (Secondary) 4. Report writing—Study and teaching (Higher) I. Thompson, Thomas C., 1958–
    PE1404 .T487 2002
    808' .042'0711—dc21
                                                                    2002003050

In memory of Richard Straub
1956–2002

Contents

Preface

Committee meetings. We generally abhor them; when possible, we avoid them. Yet I recently attended a series of committee meetings that, though sometimes contentious and even rancorous, ultimately proved useful—both to the individuals on the committee and to the college as a whole. We came together from our various departments to discuss the college's core curriculum and how best to assess it. Regardless of the specific topics we discussed, however, the fact that the discussion included people from different departments—people with different perspectives, different methodologies, and different concerns—increased our chances of learning something useful about those topics. By including voices from different disciplines, we increased our knowledge base. Fortunately, the barriers that normally prevent such interdisciplinary discussions are relatively easy to overcome: we need only walk from our various corners of campus to a common room; aside from the physical distance between our departments, we all stand on fairly common ground.

When the conversations cross grade levels rather than departments, however, the barriers change. The public seems to accord differing degrees of professionalism to teachers depending on the grade level at which they teach. As Richard Brantley and Diana Brantley note in Chapter 14, "A professor works hard for an initial credential, usually a doctorate, and tenure, but then it is assumed that each professor is a professional who can maintain currency in the field. . . . [High school teachers, however,] must continually update their certification and receive 'inservice' instruction on topics from ESOL to IDEA and other alphabet soup" (p. 217).

Further, the public seems to place a different responsibility on high school teachers than on their college counterparts. While college students, for example, are generally held responsible for their own grades, at the high school level it's the teachers, not the students, who are commonly held responsible for students' grades. In Chapter 3, Marguerite Quintelli-Neary even mentions a situation in which a principal "informed his faculty that actual teachers' names would appear next to students' standardized test scores," presumably so everyone would know which teachers were doing their jobs properly—and which weren't. In fact, if student scores are low enough and fail to improve over the course of several years, the state of South Carolina, for instance, can fire all the teachers and take over the school. Such a situation seems unimaginable in a college setting, where, as Wendy Strachan notes in Chapter 9, "success or failure . . . is attributed not to the teacher but to the learner" (p. 138).

Besides the differences in public perception, the teachers themselves live in different worlds, depending on the grade level they teach. When I taught high school, for example, I subscribed to *English Journal,* but I never even looked at *College English.* With no travel budget and no time off to travel anyway, I didn't attend conferences. When I moved (or "moved up") to college, I switched my journal subscription; I now travel to the annual convention of NCTE or CCCC or to some other professional conference at least once each year as a matter of course. This morning the departmental secretary took care of some correspondence relating to this book—a luxury I certainly would not have had were I still teaching high school. (But then, I wouldn't have tried to publish a book while I was still teaching high school, either.) I used to be a "teacher"; now I'm a "professor."

Somehow, teaching college is an entirely different world from teaching high school. Yet the students I face in August were sitting in high school classrooms in May. Have they changed *that* much in three months? Their work doesn't seem to have improved significantly in quality. Maybe, then, teachers from high school and college would do well to talk with each other about their common (or different) goals and challenges. The authors of Chapter 13 argue that the conversations should include teachers from all grade levels—elementary through college.

But to talk, we have to come together. Hence, this collection offers models for ways we can come together across grade levels, both to talk and to work together. It also offers conversations between teachers from different grade levels about the common challenges we face when we try to teach students to write.

My hope is that by offering these models and conversations this book will encourage and inspire readers to engage in cross-grade conversations and collaborations. The more we talk together and work together, the more successful we will be in the classroom.

I Trading Places

One of the most obvious ways to find out "how the other half lives" is to go into one of the "other" classrooms—and teach there. Chapter 1 records Don Daiker's reflections on his experience of taking a break from the university to teach high school for a semester. Not surprisingly, his experience increased his respect for high school teachers and changed the way he now teaches future teachers.

While Don's experience might be too impractical (for high school teachers) or too intimidating (for college professors) for some teachers to implement, a team approach might be more realistic for many. Chapter 2 describes such a project: Ron Fortune, Claire Lamonica, and Janice Neuleib each team-taught with someone from another grade level. A high school teacher and a college professor, for example, taught one semester at a high school and then a second semester at a college. The initial two-semester exchange led to additional collaborations and conversations that now include teachers across the state.

Both projects—going solo and team-teaching—offer teachers the kind of understanding possible only through immersion in a different classroom culture.

1 Scriptless in High School: Teaching Dreams of a College Professor

Don Daiker
Miami University of Ohio

During the 1995 spring semester, after thirty-two years of college teaching, Don became a high school teacher for the first time in his life. . . .

It was guilt that drove me to high school teaching. I had been teaching inservice teachers for a decade in the summer institute of the Ohio Writing Project, and for five years I had taught a required course for preservice English language arts teachers with the imposing title "Backgrounds to Composition Theory and Research." Judging from student comments and course evaluations, both classes seemed moderately successful, but I felt more and more as if my ideas and suggestions had less and less relevance to what actually happens in high school and middle school classrooms. I felt increasingly like a fraud or, at best, an impostor.

So, prodded by a high school colleague who kept asking, "Are you going to do it? Are you really going to do it?," I applied to Miami University for a faculty improvement leave that would allow me to spend a full semester teaching at Princeton High School in Cincinnati. I chose Princeton for several reasons: I knew and admired several teachers there; I could reach the high school from my Oxford home in thirty-five minutes; and, most important, Princeton was noted for the diversity of its student body. In creating the Princeton School District, the state of Ohio had put together one of its wealthiest (Glendale) with one of its poorest (Lincoln Heights) districts: the high school was 45 percent African American and 5 percent Asian American.

At Princeton High School, there are four class levels: international baccalaureate (IB), advanced placement (AP), college preparatory (CP), and basic. Because I did not want to spend my semester away from college working with the kinds of students who would be attending Miami a year or two later, I purposely asked to teach college prep and basic classes. I was assigned two tenth-grade basic English classes and two twelfth-grade college prep English classes. I did not understand then, as I do now, that teaching at least one advanced placement class would have given me a more balanced and more positive high school teaching experience.

I prepared as carefully as I knew how for teaching high school; I never thought it would be less than a challenge and struggle. To prepare, I observed classes at Princeton for weeks before I became the teacher of record. Sitting at the back of the classroom, I carefully watched both teachers and students in order to learn how to change my pedagogy as I moved from university to secondary teaching. I visited other classes at various levels in Cincinnati and Dayton schools, especially those taught by Ohio Writing Project associates who had won awards for their teaching. I interviewed half a dozen middle and high school teachers, asking for their advice, their recommendations, their do's and don'ts. I reread Tom Romano's *Clearing the Way: Working with Teenage Writers,* still the best book I know on high school teaching, and I reviewed Nancie Atwell's *In the Middle: New Understandings about Writing, Reading, and Learning,* Linda Rief's *Seeking Diversity: Language Arts with Adolescents,* and Donald Graves's *Writing: Teachers and Children at Work.* I read more than a dozen books of adolescent fiction, books such as Walter Dean Myers's *Hoops,* Bette Greene's *Summer of My German Soldier,* Robert Lipsyte's *The Contender,* Gary Paulsen's *Nightjohn,* and Lois Lowry's *Number the Stars.* I tried to be ready.

From January through June of 1995, I taught four classes at Princeton High School. My additional duties varied from week to week, but I also performed cafeteria duty, worked in the attendance office, and supervised study halls. All in all, my four months at Princeton High School constituted the most challenging and difficult teaching assignment I have ever undertaken. Despite thirty years of experience in teaching writing, literature, and education courses at Miami University, I always felt inadequate and unprepared in my high school classrooms. There were some small victories, but many more defeats. Those defeats and inadequacies were registered clearly and powerfully in a series of dreams that visited me in the months following my Princeton experience.

Interestingly, I hardly dreamed at all while I was teaching at Princeton; I don't think I had the time or energy to dream. But afterward I did dream, and in all my dreams, it seems clear to me, I was re-experiencing my difficult days at Princeton High School.

This was a dream I had on August 19, 1995, while my family and I were vacationing at North Litchfield Beach, South Carolina:

It's intermission during a production of Tennessee Williams's A Streetcar Named Desire *(my all-time favorite play). I am an actor in the play, but I have no idea where it is being produced, and I don't seem to know anyone else in the cast or in the audience: both are blanks, outside the scope of my dream. I have a major part in the play, although I'm not sure exactly what it is. I know that my part is not as large and prominent as Stanley Kowalski's but I know that it is larger and more prominent than Harold Mitchell's. [That there is no such part as Harold Mitchell in the play does not seem to bother me; it's no more confusing a fact than others that present themselves to me.] It's inter-mission, and I'm looking for a script because I realize that I don't know my lines—any of them—for the second half of the play. I ask everyone I see back-stage (no one is individualized here) for a copy of the script, but no one has a copy: each person I ask looks about him- or herself for a second or so and then says, "Sorry." I'm almost panicked, but then I remember that somehow I got through the first half of the play without screwing up too badly; at least I guess I did, for although I can't remember what happened during the first act, no one is yelling at me or criticizing me; no one seems worried at all. Indeed, harmony reigns backstage except for my dilemma. I continue asking for a script, and a couple of people give scripts to me—but one script is for a Shakespeare play and another is for Ibsen's* The Enemy of the People. *They're not right! Last thing I know I've gone outside the theater and I'm looking for a script on the sidewalk in front of the theater: it's daylight, people are passing by, I'm look-ing down, and I can't find what I need.*

A month later, now safely back at Miami University teaching courses in college composition, American literature, and the short story, I am visited by two related dreams:

I'm driving alone in my car heading to Princeton High School along Highway 27, the route I had always taken from Oxford to Princeton, minding my own business. I look up to see flashing red lights in my rearview mirror, and sud-denly there's a cop behind me motioning me to pull over. "I can't have been speeding," I say to myself and look down at my speedometer to see if I have been exceeding the 35 mph speed limit. My dream ends without my learning how fast I've been traveling.

I've just bought a new suit at Lazarus department store in Cincinnati, and I've had it altered. I'm wearing it for the first time—I'm going to a concert or wedding, some dress-up affair. I put on the slacks, and they seem long. "Well, maybe they'll fit better with my shoes on," I think, although without much hope. Nope—with shoes on they're still way too long. I try to blame the store and the alterations clerk, but I know within that it's my fault. I must have done something wrong during the measurement session—I know I did—but I can't put my finger on exactly what it was.

These two September dreams are succeeded by a pair of October dreams that clarify even further that Princeton High School is their subject:

I'm trying to get to Princeton High School, but I can't get there. The whole time I'm telling myself, "I'll make it, I'll get there," even though another, equally compelling voice says, "You'll never make it; you'll never make it." For some reason, I'm trying to get to school by bus. But even then I get off to a late start. I'm not even sure where to exit from the bus. But eventually I pull the buzzer and get off at a place that seems familiar. But once I'm off the bus, everything seems strange, and I don't even know which direction to walk. At one point, I'm not sure which of two directions to follow, so I ask a passerby; he points in a third direction, and I start off that way. I say to myself that I'm lucky this is exam day at Princeton because I can arrive later than usual without being late.

New scene: Apparently it's the end of the school day. I have no idea how to get home. I don't even know if I brought a car with me. For a long time I wander aimlessly around the parking lot. Maybe I took a bus to school? But I don't even know where the bus stop is. Somehow I find myself in a car; I come to what should be a familiar intersection, and I don't know which of four directions to follow. I just sit motionless in my stopped car as the dream ends.

My final two Princeton dreams—the last I have had—each occurred in conjunction with the 1995 National Council of Teachers of English Annual Convention that was held during the third week of November, five months after my last high school class. The first dream took place on my first night in San Diego and the second on the night after I returned to Oxford:

I'm back in Princeton, in my own classroom—507 or whatever it is. I can't see much in the classroom; the students don't have names. The key point is that I'm having trouble with time: I don't know when this period is over and when this class ends. And for some reason I don't ask the students. [Why not? They know. And I know that they know, don't I?] There's a student who's giving me a hard time—I'm not sure how, probably by smarting off. He is fairly heavy and looks a little like Josh Penzone, one of my college students this semester in English 304. When he does something out of line—talks back, disobeys, something—I respond and cut him down verbally. [I have no idea exactly what I said.] At any rate, when I see that he is close to tears, I try to make it up to him, wishing the class would end but not sure when the period will be over.

I have been asked by the principal to speak at the Princeton High School graduation. I know that I am not the central graduation speaker: I am to speak only two to three pages' worth. But I work hard on my speech, and I bring the pages with me to the ceremony. But graduation ceremonies do not take place outside, as you might think; they take place inside in something that looks very much like a church, almost like the baccalaureate graduation service I attended at Rutgers University in 1959. Not only that, but my whole family is there, including my wife Vicky—and our four kids are small, as if it were twenty years ago. I feel pretty good as the ceremonies begin, but ten or fifteen minutes into it I think I'll just check my folder to make sure my speech copy is there. I can't find it. I begin to get nervous. It's hard to sort through all my papers in a pew, especially because the kids are moving around and getting in my way. If I set the papers down beside me on the pew, Stephen would be likely to mess them up. I haven't completely panicked yet because I know there will be a halftime intermission; then I can really look for my speech notes. But halftime comes, and although I take every single item out of my folder, the speech notes are nowhere to be found. I ask myself if I can't do the speech from memory—after all, I often talk with few or no notes—but I can't remember a single thing I have planned to say. And then my dream ends.

Taken together, these seven dreams clearly summarize my emotional response to teaching at Princeton High School. As my first and last dreams suggest, I saw myself as essentially scriptless in the classroom. Although I had thought myself in possession of the necessary material—I did get through the first half of *A Streetcar Named Desire* and I had finished writing my graduation address—there came a time in each dream when I had absolutely nothing to say, when I was utterly clueless, when silence and then oblivion became my only response. What all seven dreams have in common is the absence of resources, especially knowledge, to do what needs to be done: to perform on stage, to find out how fast I am driving, to fit my clothes correctly, to get to and from Princeton High School, to figure out class periods, and to address the graduates. These are all dreams of inadequacy and failure.

And my dreams spoke the truth: I often felt inadequate as a high school teacher. I audiotaped the following message as I drove home on a Friday afternoon in May during my fourth month at Princeton:

> It's been an interesting week—pleasure combined with despair. Yesterday, riding back and forth to school, I had the overwhelming sense that my whole approach to teaching was wrong, that somehow I had failed to understand a cardinal principle of learning (I'm still not sure what it is!) and that no matter how long I tried or how hard I struggled I would never "get it": my classes would continue to be mere sophisticated forms of baby-sitting rather than forums for genuine learning. [May 6, 1995]

Much of my despair stemmed from my inability to deal with the kinds of discipline problems I had never encountered in my college classrooms. Not once at Miami University had a student physically threatened me. But one morning at Princeton, when I had repeatedly asked a senior to move the desk he kept purposely banging into a classmate's, he looked directly into my eyes and said, "If you don't get out of my face, I'm going to break your jaw and split you in half." It was about that time that the school nurse told me that my blood pressure, never before a problem, had reached the point where I should consult my physician. It was also about that time that Vicky said to me, not completely in jest, "If you ever try a stunt like this high school teaching again, you may want to look for a new wife at the same time." Teaching high school may have damaged my relationships and physical health as well as my self-image as a competent teacher.

Yet the audiotape refers not only to "despair" but also to "pleasure." And although my subconscious told me through dreams that I had failed miserably as a high school English teacher, I nevertheless had the sense during those four months that I had achieved some success. Indeed, there were moments and even hours when being a high school teacher was rewarding and even gratifying. After all, each of my four classes had produced a class publication that included an edited piece of writing by virtually every student. We had survived, albeit barely, a trip to the Cincinnati Museum of Natural History at historic Union Terminal. Almost every student had seen at least one major piece of writing through the full writing process, including a peer conference. Almost every student had read, more or less steadily, at least one book of his or her choice, and several had read two or three. We had dutifully read, discussed, acted out, and written about *Of Mice and Men* in sophomore English and *Macbeth* in senior English. There was even an instance or two of real breakthrough, none more heartening than that of Mike Delmonico (not the student's real name).

When Mike arrives in my third-bell sophomore English class, he looks like an emaciated rodent—skinny and with thin, ratty hair all over his head and face. He has come to Ohio from Staten Island, New York, because both his parents have died, one of AIDS and the other from a drug overdose. Because Mike has no clue what book to choose for his independent reading project, I loan him a copy of S. E. Hinton's *The Outsiders* during the second week of the quarter. During class reading time, Mike almost always has his book with him, and each day he diligently fills out his reading log. But, if he is really reading at all, he reads very, very slowly. At last, during the next to last week of the quarter, he finishes *The Outsiders*, ambles to the front of the room, mutters, "Here's your book back" without making eye contact, and tosses the book into the book basket with what I take to be a contemptuous look on his face. "Oh, well," I say to myself. "That was a waste of time."

I grab my stuff and am walking down the back hallway to my next class when I'm warmly greeted by Marta, one of the counselors, who asks, "Do you have just a minute?" Of course I don't have a minute—I never have a minute between classes—but I say, "Sure." Inside her office, she says, "I just got a telephone call from Mike's guardians, and they are so excited! *The Outsiders* is the first book Mike has ever read in his life. Last night, they said, Mike was so eager to finish his book that he didn't want to come to dinner. When they insisted that he come, he left before dessert to finish it in his room. They couldn't be more pleased. I thought you'd like to know."

One of the scripts I've constructed from my high school teaching experience is that it takes practice to discern when students like Mike are genuinely enthusiastic about their reading and writing, since it's usually not cool, especially in basic classes, to evince enthusiasm for schoolwork. Mike did not know how to say "Thank you" or "That book was great" or "I really liked *The Outsiders*," but he did know that his next book would be Forrest Carter's *The Education of Little Tree*, which he grabbed from the book cart and immediately began to read next class.

Still, it was not this modest success—there were others—that resonated most deeply for me. It was all those times when I lacked a script for dealing with students who wouldn't stop talking, or refused to change seats when requested, or neglected to do their homework, or insisted on taking a nap at their desk. These students somehow dominated my psyche even when they were in the minority. Perhaps it was because of my vulnerability in the face of such intransigence that I resorted to calling myself "Dr. Daiker" at Princeton as I never did at Miami University. All my handouts and notices were prominently labeled "Dr.

Daiker," whereas my Miami syllabi list me only as "Don Daiker" or just plain "Don." At Princeton, by contrast, I needed the protection and prestige of "Dr. Daiker" to make me a little less vulnerable: it was a kind of armor against the slings and arrows of student resistance.

Of course, I would have felt less vulnerable had I been able to follow the standard advice proffered to all new teachers: "Leave your ego at the door—because if you bring it inside with you, it will surely be bruised." My problem was that I just didn't know what else to do with my ego except bring it with me. That's one of the lessons I take with me from my high school teaching experience: the necessity of not taking student resistance or misconduct too personally, because it can eat you alive if you do. As one of my favorite high school teachers told me, "Your college students may treat you like a prima donna, Don, but high school students will not be impressed by your degree, your publications, or your experience. Get used to it."

An even more important gain for me is a tremendous increase in respect and admiration for high school teachers—and not simply because they work harder than we college professors, either. No, it's more than that. Teaching high school requires not only more effort but also a more comprehensive self-offering, a fuller giving of the self, a tapping of more and different kinds of energies. High school teachers have to be wiser than college teachers. High school teaching demands more of a total response, requires that you use not only your brains (which is usually enough for college teachers) but your heart and emotions and common sense and good psychology as well. As John Gaughan demonstrates in his powerful and practical *Reinventing English: Teaching in the Contact Zone,* high school teaching calls for a more holistic, comprehensive, human approach than college teaching. It calls for more diverse talents, more interpersonal skills, more resourcefulness. To be an effective high school teacher, you have to be wiser in the ways of the world.

Paradoxically, the high school environment makes wisdom hard to come by because there is so little time during the school day, lengthy as it is, to think and reflect. The normal demands of the day—hall duty between classes, attendance reports, calls to parents, discipline problems, rushed lunches—conspire to make reflection difficult and to encourage unthinking responses even to complex issues. A year after teaching at Princeton I was encouraging inservice teachers to distribute a statement of goals to their students. To illustrate my point, I handed out copies of the goals statement I had distributed a year earlier to my tenth-grade students. Reading over my statement, I saw that it announced that during the last week of class I would ask my students to think about their individual course goals and to tell me in writing what progress they had made in achieving them. I only then realized that in the welter and chaos of teaching I had completely forgotten to ask for student responses. We didn't do any reflecting on goals at all. But even had I remembered, would there have been time—in the rush to complete our papers on *Of Mice and Men*—to do the goals reflection I had anticipated? Probably not. High school teaching, especially in the language arts, is time- and self-consuming in ways that few outsiders realize. No wonder so many beginning teachers never make it to year two. In my education courses at Miami, I encourage prospective teachers to become thoughtful and reflective practitioners, but I know now that it's hard to reflect while you're trying to survive. When you're just trying to keep your head above water, it's not easy to notice or care about the sky above.

Having survived just one semester of high school teaching, I may have become a more effective teacher. Certainly the course I teach for prospective writing teachers has become more practical, more reality based. To take one instance, prospective teachers in my class now conduct teacher research in the form of a writing exchange with high school students. Each of my students is matched with one or two seniors at Cincinnati's Madeira High School. The relationship begins with my students writing a personal letter to their high school partner(s) explaining the program and introducing themselves. Two or three times during the semester, my students receive a paper, together with the assignment, from their partner. My students' assignment is to read the papers and respond in writing, taking special care to consider their decisions about how to respond in terms of their credo—their evolving beliefs about teaching and learning. As part of the exchange, high school students are asked to assess the usefulness and effectiveness of the responses they receive. From this two-way exchange with high school students, the prospective teachers in my class write a research report on responding to student writing that becomes a significant part of their final course portfolio.

Would I recommend that my university colleagues committed to teacher education try a stint of high school teaching? Yes, I would. Despite my own difficulties, I have absolutely no regrets. Just this semester I built on my earlier Princeton experience by creating a weeklong teaching exchange with a colleague at Sycamore High School in suburban Cincinnati. For three days here at Miami, Beth Rimer taught my class for prospective teachers, and for five days I taught her three sections of sophomore English and one section of senior English. It was an enjoyable and instructive experience for both of us and, I believe, for our students as well.

But I have several suggestions for college professors who contemplate moving up to the challenges of high school teaching:

1. The earlier in your career, the better. I may have started a bit late at age fifty-seven.

2. Try to teach first semester rather than second: it's easier to establish positive relationships with students at the beginning rather than the middle of a yearlong course.

3. Try not to teach a second-semester class of graduating seniors, especially if your course is not required for graduation.

4. Try for balance in your teaching schedule. Make sure you're working with at least some of the school's best and most highly motivated students.

5. Try for a reduced teaching load. I taught four courses at Princeton instead of the usual five and it still nearly killed me, in part because of my continuing university responsibilities: committee assignments, letters of recommendation, thesis advising, and the like.

6. Lower your expectations—not for your students but for yourself.

7. Try to do what student teachers do: teach your first few classes with an experienced high school teacher as your observer and mentor. Meet afterward to have your teaching critiqued and to ask hard questions about class management and course content. What a difference there is between sitting at the back and standing at the front of a class!

8. Try to be prepared for the roller-coaster ride of your career. Hang on for dear life!

In the final pages of "Spring" from *Walden*, a celebration of life as experiment and renewal, Henry David Thoreau writes, "We need the tonic of wildness." Without wildness, Thoreau says, without the "unexplored forests and meadows" that surround us, "our village life would stagnate" (255). I went from Miami University to Princeton High School because I wished not to stagnate but to experience a different and perhaps wilder kind of teaching and learning. I was not disappointed.

Work Cited

Thoreau, Henry David. *The Variorum Walden*. Ed. Walter Harding. New York: Twayne, 1962.

2 A Teacher Exchange That Changed Teachers

Ron Fortune
Illinois State University

Claire Lamonica
Illinois State University

Janice Neuleib
Illinois State University

*When six teachers from different levels work in each other's classrooms,
changes occur—and continue to influence their teaching years later.*

Illinois State University's English department has long been committed to interactive work with teachers of English throughout the state.
ISU has a history of "articulation" with (in the manner of one joint in
the body being articulated with another) and connections to teachers.
These connections have sought to improve the teaching of English
through better understanding of how college connects to high school
and high school to the junior, middle, and elementary schools. This kind
of articulation fits with the basic tenets of the National Writing Project,
which stresses that *teachers* must teach teachers, rather than professo-
rial "experts" telling educators how schools should function and what
classrooms should do. When university faculty meet and work with
teachers on their own terms in their own worlds, these interactions
emphasize that everyone is learning from everyone else.

To describe all the history of this articulation at ISU would be
beyond the scope of this essay; thus one particular project will illustrate
the kinds of projects that are ongoing in this program. This project involved an extensive teacher exchange between a high school, a community college, and the university. Readers may find that this project
provides an outline for similar work and suggestions for improvement
on the original model.

In 1964, Illinois State University's English department began to
host a spring conference for high school English teachers, calling the
meeting the Heads of Illinois Secondary English Departments (HISED).
The spring meeting consistently attracts between two and three hun-

dred teachers a year, and each year it continues to offer teachers a chance to meet, talk, listen, and plan. HISED became a vital part of the English department's yearly activities. This conference quickly led to work with teachers around the state on a variety of projects. In 1983 the articulation effort at ISU led to faculty involvement with a state task force that was formed to investigate student writing skills in the state. The committee included several schoolteachers as well as faculty members from ISU and culminated in a special issue of the *Illinois English Bulletin,* an NCTE affiliate journal, which stressed the need for teachers and university faculty to work together to improve instruction (Neuleib 1983). The outcome of that recommendation for ISU was an NEH grant that detailed a new kind of college-school articulation.

The Teaching Exchange

In 1982 Ron Fortune proposed an NEH grant that would build on the work of the state task force and on the experiences Jan Neuleib had had while teaching a writing class in a local high school. Ron proposed an NEH project that would put university professors and high school and community college teachers in the classroom together. Everyone in the project co-taught in both his or her own classrooms and in one another's classrooms. The account of the grant and its outcomes is chronicled in Ron and Jan's essay in the 1986 MLA volume *School-College Collaborative Programs in English;* the purpose of the essay here is to give specific advice on how others might replicate and elaborate on that experience. The plan for the grant included the college teachers working with three high school teachers and one community college teacher, one each teaching high school sophomores, juniors, seniors, and first-year community college students. In the first semester, the high school teachers and community college teacher co-taught in Ron's and Jan's first-year university composition courses. The process was then reversed the following semester. Thus two teachers participated every day in every classroom.

In the summer before the project began, the four teachers (Patsy Fortune from University High School, the sophomore teacher; Kay Parker from Normal Community High School, the junior teacher; Linda Lienhart from Bloomington High School, the senior teacher; and Edwina Jordan from Illinois Central College, the first-year community college teacher) met with the two college professors (Ron and Jan) to plan lessons, practices, and general approaches to this new kind of classroom. The group agreed that each teacher would be the lead teacher in his or her own classroom but that students would understand that both teachers were to be involved in all classroom activities.

In the fall of 1983, the high school and community college teachers came to the composition classrooms of ISU. Writing instruction was changing radically in those early days. A move toward computer technology was about to take place at ISU, and a strong emphasis on argument and revision in the writing classroom was being implemented. The high school teachers and community college teacher brought preconceptions about the differences between their students and the university students into the composition classrooms. For the most part, the teachers were not surprised by the lack of change between high school and the first semester of college, but they also noted that students were more likely to take responsibility for their work and to initiate requests for help both in and outside of the classroom.

Through their experiences in the ISU composition classrooms, the secondary teachers and community college teacher learned exactly what their students would be facing in a four-year college first-year writing course. When they went back to their own classrooms, they no longer approached their students with their own memories of college or with an image of college writing gleaned from college texts or from college writing-class materials. They took back to their students a firsthand account of what university writing would be like. They also could pick and choose among the practices they had helped implement in the university composition courses to enrich their high school and community college classrooms.

In the spring of 1984, Jan began to teach with Patsy and Kay at their high schools one hour a day at each school, five days a week. Ron taught with Linda and Edwina at their schools. Ron and Jan were sponsored by the NEH grant for two classes each and supported for travel in order to meet the teaching demands of the exchange. Classroom management worked smoothly, both teachers in each classroom emphasizing a student-centered classroom with teachers and students working in groups for both writing and literature instruction. The sophomore and senior high school classes and the first-year community college classes were writing courses, whereas the junior class was a Shakespeare course with heavy emphasis on writing.

Jan had taught high school in the sixties, but Ron had never taught at the secondary level. The students' exuberance and energy may have been the greatest shock for both of these longtime college professors. At the time of the exchange, Jan had been teaching for nearly twenty years and Ron for over ten. Both had long forgotten the feel of a high school class. Jan once commented that she awakened each morning to pray that Patsy would never be ill, leaving her alone with the sophomores. These students exploded each day with questions, comments, and new ideas—a great experience, but a noise level far beyond that of a college class.

That spring many new lessons developed. The concept of "process" was just emerging in the college composition field, but in high school it was pretty much unheard of, and group work was not the norm. This project gave all the teachers a chance to ask students to revise and rethink their work. Students worked together in groups to accomplish these tasks and found that they developed new attitudes toward reading and writing in a more involving and vibrant classroom. After the project ended, the high school teachers continued with the practices and offered workshops on the student-centered classroom to other teachers.

The spring semester's work was strongly informed for all the participants in the project by the work of the fall semester. Ron and Jan returned to their college classrooms to see their students through different eyes after experiencing the stress, excitement, and demands of high school. They knew firsthand what their first-year students had experienced before coming to university. They also knew how much these students did not know. Debates about teaching grammar or revision or group projects became livelier after Jan and Ron experienced these issues at work in the high school classroom. They also realized the difference between teaching writing in circumstances in which most of the students have been in the same classes for as long as three and a half years, and teaching a first-year writing course, in which students barely know one another, especially in the fall semester.

In addition, Ron and Jan brought their experiences to the writing instructors at the university, stressing a need to understand the developmental levels of students in college writing classes. Ron has gone on to chair the English department, but not before spending three years working with a new general education plan for the university, a plan informed by his experiences with the developmental processes of students across grade levels. Jan directs the writing programs at the university and has applied the experiences of the exchange to the improvement of writing instruction.

For their part, local high school students approached college with far more knowledge of revision practices than any other students attending college in those days. And the four teachers in the exchange, as well as the other teachers in their schools, benefited from the exchange because the teachers were committed as part of the project to work with others in their schools to give them a picture of the exchange experience.

This exchange experience led to a deep understanding of the practice and theory at work at each level of teaching writing and literature. The MLA essay notes that "each pair of teachers had to determine the level and thinking and writing development characteristic of their students and to find ways of cultivating students' writing abilities so that the students' thinking and writing would mutually enhance one another" (Fortune and Neuleib 116). The group met regularly to understand the kinds of intellectual development they were seeing in the students in all these classes and levels. These meetings helped teachers to "articulate the common set of curricular principles they had agreed on in earlier phases of the project." In the summer of 1984, the group of teachers met to further refine the curricular principles they had developed in this long and intense co-teaching project.

Several positive changes resulted from this first NEH project in central Illinois; teachers learned to modify their teaching in a variety of ways (Fortune and Neuleib 117):

- using problem-solving assignments to engage students
- using rhetorical contexts to enliven writing assignments
- teaching discovery and revision in writing activities
- emphasizing rhetorical choices at all stages of composing

These changes may seem self-evident in light of current composition theory, but for the teachers in 1984, many of these strategies were new and challenging, especially as represented at various grade levels. These teachers began to emphasize the teaching of revision in high school long before anyone asked questions about how to keep peer groups on task or how to help students understand major revisions in thought and structure. The long-term results of this project have been many—for example, Linda, who taught the senior class in this early NEH project, recently presented at the Illinois State Writing Project with one of her students who had just published his own book, developed in one of her high school writing classes. This project has also led to many others for the ISU English department.

Expansion of Articulation

Linda and her student writer and co-presenter represent just one of the effects of that early exchange. Ron and Jan used their experiences in the teacher exchange to plan and implement a three-year NEH grant that asked teachers to teach literature and writing by using manuscripts and various editions and versions of published texts. Beginning in 1987, ISU brought forty Illinois high school teachers to campus each summer for three years to develop new ways of teaching. The intriguing follow-up on this summer activity was a series of workshops presented in the teachers' schools in which the project supervisors (Ron and Jan) participated. These schools varied from tiny outposts in the far western side of Illinois, such as Hamilton Junior High School in Hamilton, population around eight thousand, to schools in Chicago such as Percy Julian on the near West Side, an overcrowded and struggling inner-city school.

Several publications evolved from these institutes. A series titled *Literature and Writing,* cosponsored by NEH and ISU and edited by Ron, included papers and lesson plans developed by the teachers. In 1992 Jan edited a special number of the *Illinois English Bulletin* that described the series of institutes and presented eleven essays by participating teachers. These included such titles as "Reconstructing the Writer's Process Narrative Revision in H. G. Wells' *Fin De Siecle* Vision: *The Time Machine*" by teacher Mary Peters and institute researcher Ruth Fennick; "Studying the Effect of Change: Student Interaction with Alternate Versions of Jack London's 'To Build a Fire'" by Elaine Dion, junior high teacher from Hamilton, Illinois; and "Using the Manuscripts of Poe's 'The Raven'" by high school teacher Lucy Loper.

Ruth, Elaine, and Jan went on to write three junior high textbooks using the manuscript materials. Elaine also wrote her doctoral dissertation, "Integrating the Creative Processes of Published Writers into the Classroom," as a study of her students' work with the manuscripts in their junior high classroom, demonstrating how very young writers can learn about the complexities of total revision by comparing completely different versions of a story (London published a 1908 version of "To Build a Fire" that has a happy ending!).

The Illinois State Writing Project

The NEH institute on literature and writing was evaluated by Jim Gray, founder and director of the National Writing Project, who not only praised ISU's articulation activities but also insisted that the English department needed to establish a central Illinois site for the National Writing Project. In the summer of 1992, Jan and Ruth began the Illinois State Writing Project, now in its tenth year. Many of the teacher-leaders in the Writing Project are familiar faces from the teacher exchange and the NEH institute. Jean Wallace and Linda Lienhart from the first NEH summer group became first-summer members of the Writing Project.

Both have gone on to be leaders in their schools and in the state. Jean is currently president of the Illinois Association of Teachers of English, and both participated in the Spielberg-sponsored *Shoah* project for teaching the Holocaust held at Universal Studios.

In 1996 Claire Lamonica, a former Writing Project fellow and doctoral candidate who was teaching in ISU's Laboratory Schools, joined ISU's writing programs staff as co-director. With one foot in the schools and one foot in the university, Claire was able to intensify recruitment efforts and identify additional ways in which the Writing Project could serve the area. One way was to sponsor a Young Writers Workshop for middle school students.

The first of these workshops, Subscribe to Writing, was developed by five Writing Project fellows in the summer of 1999 and offered for the first time in the winter of 2000. The workshop attracted two dozen fifth, sixth, and seventh graders who worked with the staff (the teachers who had developed the program) to publish their own magazines in the ISU English department's state-of-the-art desktop publishing labs. The Subscribe to Writing workshop was offered again in the summer of 2000 and the winter of 2001, and each workshop ended with the students asking for more. As a result, the workshop leaders developed a second workshop, Page to Stage, offered for the first time in the summer of 2001.

Young writers blossom in the nurturing workshop atmosphere, and the Writing Project teachers are refreshed by the experience of working with young writers who love what they are doing.

NEH Revisited

The NEH workshops came full circle in the summer of 1998 when the state NEH institute became a national institute and ISU hosted forty teachers from around the United States. Teachers once again produced curricula and papers using manuscripts, but this time they also worked with hypertext and Web pages. The workshops included experts on literature and on Web-based literature projects. Teachers investigated writers such as Dickens, and the Web site for the Dickens Project, http://humwww.ucsc.edu/dickens, provided many opportunities to study manuscripts, editions, and critical perspectives. The teachers produced their own plays on computer from short stories by Fitzgerald, wrote lesson plans on feminist fiction, and worked with multiple versions of short stories by writers such as Eudora Welty and Dorothy Parker. The entire institute was funded once again for the summer of 2001 with

Rodger Tarr and Ron as co-directors and Jan as teacher facilitator for the four-week institute.

Where Articulation Begins and Ends

This story began with a teacher exchange and moved on to more elaborate interactions, but the core activity was that first exchange among six people who were willing to commit a year to working intensely together. Many of us have continued to work together over the years. Kay is currently involved as district leader for the Illinois Association of Teachers of English, the NCTE affiliate for the state of Illinois, now housed at ISU. Edwina has been an active participant in the Illinois State Writing Project and has continued as a teacher teaching teachers. Linda has been a strong teacher-leader in the Illinois State Writing Project and is currently a part of an even larger activity on the *Shoah* project with teachers from Illinois and California.

The implication of these experiences is that teachers, universities, and colleges that want to work together should look for grants and other kinds of support that will encourage exchanges of all kinds. The first step will lead to more, and more kinds of, exchanges. Perhaps the best advice is to dream big but begin small. The day-to-day classroom experience is vital to an understanding of what other teachers experience. Armed with that knowledge, all teachers will be far more effective at understanding one another and at understanding their students' development as readers and writers.

Works Cited

The Dickens Project. Ed. Jon Michael Varese. 1981. U of California, Santa Cruz. 27 Mar. 2002 <http://humwww.ucsc.edu/dickens>.

Dion, Elaine. "Integrating the Creative Processes of Published Writers into the Classroom." Diss. Illinois State U., 1992.

Fortune, Ron, ed. *Literature and Writing: A Journal of the NEH/ISU Collaborative Teaching Project* 1–3, 1987–1989.

Fortune, Ron, and Janice Neuleib. "Illinois State University: The Cooperative Teaching Program." Ed. Ron Fortune. *School-College Collaborative Programs in English.* New York: MLA, 1986.

Neuleib, Janice, ed. *Illinois English Bulletin* 71 (1983): 1–52.

———, ed. *Illinois English Bulletin* 79 (1992): 1–101.

II Modeling Collaboration for Preservice Teachers

If we want to encourage teachers to collaborate across grade levels, where better to model such collaborations than in teacher education courses? The following chapters all describe situations in which high school and college teachers work together across grade levels in the presence of preservice teachers. Thus these projects have the dual benefit of sharing ideas among colleagues at different grade levels and modeling cross-grade collaboration for future teachers.

In Chapter 3, Marguerite Quintelli-Neary describes the semester that she shared teaching responsibilities for a teacher education class with a high school teacher. This collaboration gave both Marguerite and her students a genuine look at what was happening in high school classrooms.

Chapter 4 catalogs Nancy Tucker and Leah Zuidema's experience of having Nancy's college seniors—all preservice teachers—respond to papers written by Leah's high school students. Besides creating a real audience (other than the teacher) for Leah's students, this exchange let Nancy's students put their newly acquired theory into practice as they wrote what they hoped would be helpful comments on "real" student papers.

Chapter 5 also describes a project with multiple purposes. Students in Betsy Wilson's Teacher Cadet class—students considering majoring in education or a related field when they go to college—wrote a research-based paper on a topic in education, not for Betsy but for Tom Thompson, a college professor. Hence, in addition to researching and discussing topics in education, they also discussed college-level writing. To add a student perspective on a cross-grade collaboration, this chapter consists of journal entries of both students and teachers.

3 It Takes More Than a Consortium

Marguerite Quintelli-Neary
Winthrop University

*When Marguerite (a university professor) invited Debbie (a high school
teacher) to join her in team-teaching an English methods course, they
discovered yet another forum in which having both high school and college
perspectives could be valuable. The following essay describes and reflects on
the various stages of their course—one in which they modeled cross-grade
collaboration for preservice teachers.*

The Background: I'm Just a Girl Who Can't Say "No"

As a member of the university Teacher Education Committee and a liaison between the College of Arts and Sciences and the College of Education at Winthrop University in Rock Hill, South Carolina, I am often
asked to serve on subcommittees, to involve my department in projects
that link the two domains, or to try out something new in my own classroom. Generally, this happens right after a meeting session has ended
and everyone else has left the room, and mainly because I am usually
scrambling to put my notebooks together after patiently hearing out
somebody else's newest research project or most tedious complaint.
That's how I ended up on the Curriculum Committee; it's how I was
persuaded to sweet-talk members of my department into joining the
Technology Learning Community; and (three is the magic number here)
it's how I ended up taking on a collaboration that I will always be thankful for. After a late spring 2000 meeting, one from which I was hurrying
away, the new dean of education turned around to ask me if I would
consider inviting a practitioner from the language arts field into my
English methods class, Principles of Teaching English in Middle and
Secondary Schools. I groaned inwardly. Not me . . . not again. . . . I can't
take on one more commitment. So I said "yes," of course. I said I would
think about it.

Once you've agreed to consider a proposal, you're as good as committed, and sure enough, the next time we met, the dean asked if I would
still carry out the plan, adding that a math education supervisor was
also amenable to the idea (nothing like referring to a willing and cooperative colleague to cement the deal). I figured I had no choice at this

point, so I began to ask questions about how much control I would retain over the course, what portion of class time would be allotted to the newcomer to the classroom, and how we would work out the logistics of meeting time and place. In the back of my mind, I already knew who would be the best candidate for this cooperative exercise: she was a teacher at Northwestern High School in Rock Hill, one who had recently been named Teacher of the Year and who had just done an exceptional job of mentoring one of my interns, a young woman named Erin who dazzled students and administrators alike and is now wowing her colleagues in Benin, West Africa, as a member of the Peace Corps. I also reminded myself that the teacher had collaborated with this particular intern on an "Elements of Literature" study guide for her college prep students, an accomplishment that attested to her own cooperative spirit and willingness to incorporate the ideas of a fledgling teacher into an outline she would retain for future classes. She had a natural, relaxed manner with her own students, while at the same time expecting nothing but the best they could produce. Now all I had to do was ask her, hope that she was interested and that her principal would agree to let her participate in the partnership, and negotiate a respectable honorarium for her efforts. I was also banking on the fact that our friendship, which I considered to be collegial, would facilitate the collaboration. I had been her instructor in a graduate course on Communications in the Workplace a few years back, prior to working with her as a mentor teacher in my program. I knew we could work well together and that we shared many educational philosophies, but that during the course we would probably discover points at which we held differing views on pedagogy. But my hasty "yes" compelled me to invite her into what had hitherto been my world.

Working Out the Details: I Get By with a Little Help from My Friends

Debbie Koon, a master teacher, agreed to the team-teaching idea even before I got the whole request out of my mouth. It would be several months before I officially learned under what auspices we would sponsor her: a grant titled "Partners for the Enhancement of Clinical Experiences." She was going up for National Board Certification in 2001; the timing was perfect. She wanted to know where student teachers came from and what we were doing at the university. I was in deep, but I quickly moved to negotiate a workable schedule for both of us: the class met once a week, on Tuesday, from 12:30 to 3:15, and Debbie was to request that her planning period occupy fourth block (from 2:00 to 3:30), with a late lunch period, so that she would have travel time and could reach our campus (five miles away), park (about another five miles of driving, mainly circling, at peak time in the afternoon), and work with us for the last portion of the seminar before heading back to her own high school campus. Unfortunately, Tuesdays were also her faculty meeting days, but her principal understood that she would occasionally be late because she had to stay after class at Winthrop now and then to deal with a student. The director of the Center for Pedagogy at Winthrop assisted with assigning Debbie's honorarium, ordering her copies of the textbooks (we use Christenbury's *Making the Journey*, Maxwell and Meiser's *Teaching English in Middle and Secondary Schools*, and Wagner and Larson's *Situations*), and securing her a parking decal; my department chair, who supported the project enthusiastically, met her; and, finally, over the summer Debbie and I sat down to draft a schedule and syllabus. I watched as she jotted notes on a syllabus from the previous year and wondered how I had allowed myself to be put in a situation in which another professional would scrutinize my every proposal. I had to face a loss of control—an ironic touch, since I had always told my preservice teachers that teaching was *not* about control; it was about facilitating and letting the class take on a life of its own. With collaboration there would be no place to hide; the class would be exposed for what it was, good or bad. But while there was no room left for ego, there was lots of space for trust in the notion that two heads could be better than one. Research shows that "alliances in school partnerships are less about 'highly structured working relationships, rules and mandates' than they are about 'informal cooperation, shared values, and personal relationships'" (Poetter and Badiali 161). I had to trust in my intuition that we could both be flexible, that we shared many values, and that we would work well together, the way we sometimes click with committee members with whom we serve.

We surveyed the composite results of the new syllabus we had crafted. The final draft of the document was incredible: with amazing diplomacy in the fusing of theory and practice, Debbie had tucked in some reality checkpoints and added a few assignments, as I clung to some ideas or projects that I could not (microlessons) or would not (collaborative documents for interns in the field experience, a co-requisite for this course) let go, both of which she agreed belonged in the master plan. Finally, we agreed to get together once a week during the beginning of the semester to plan the following week's class, with the understanding that we could manage it by telephone or e-mail as we became more comfortable with the arrangement.

What complemented the collaboration (although I am afraid, to this day, to ask the intern how she honestly felt about it) was Debbie's agreement to take on another English intern while team-teaching the class with me. This student would get to see her mentor on two different levels: as her mentor for the two-morning-a-week field experience, and as her professor on Tuesday afternoons. I deliberately selected an exceptionally strong student, Caroline, who appeared confident in both her content area and pedagogy, and Debbie and I noted that we would have to take care not to single her out in the methods course in any way when Debbie joined our class in progress each Tuesday. What served as confirmation that I had not committed an ethical or social transgression was the announcement Caroline often made at the beginning of class that "Ms. Koon did the neatest thing today." The activity generally authenticated some theory we had just discussed, reminded us all that we were privileged to share in the expertise of this teacher, and reassured me that I was not a total moron for having invited this instructor into the class of thirteen preservice teachers (my lucky number).

Tuesday's Plans: Day by Day

I introduced the student interns—a group that included both undergraduate and graduate students—to my new cohort the first day of class, having announced that she would be joining us right after the break (hoping that she wouldn't make a liar out of me). We had gone over instructions for the collaborative document, an elaborate piece of paperwork that I require students to complete with their mentors in the field, in which they set forth discipline plans, project teaching goals, compare pedagogical philosophies, and discuss their expectations of each other. Students also get to talk about very basic needs such as the location of the faculty restroom and telephone protocol. This discussion sets them up as professionals who demand equal respect from the public school students in a slightly skewed experience, allowing the mentor to jump in when signaled and defer to the intern when appropriate. I droned on and on about the clinical experience, what they should tolerate, what they could not legally be asked to do. Finally, I assigned readings in the Maxwell and Meiser text and set up some role-play exercises from *Situations* right before our brief midclass break. Some students followed me right down to my office (refusing to acknowledge the break), and we all returned to find a smiling face awaiting us in the classroom. Debbie had taken a seat at the seminar table and was grinning from ear to ear. She looked happy to be at Winthrop, and the students seemed equally happy to encounter someone who looked less worried than I was looking the day before they were to set out for their teaching assignments. They pelted her with questions about her teaching career, and she answered every one. It was a moment of bonding and acceptance, and I didn't interrupt, except to emphasize the qualities that made Debbie one of the finest teachers in our consortium.

By our second meeting, I realized that I would have to space out class presentations such as the role-plays and forthcoming oral reports, as well as the videotaped microlessons, so that Debbie could always hear or see at least one. The students complied without complaining, which is unusual, since they nearly always want to get performances over with as early in the class period as possible. Debbie corroborated my methodology as we watched them work out situations in which a teacher had to defend a grade, confront a sports star who shirked responsibilities in English class, or deal with a student who had downloaded a research paper from a computer. She reaffirmed the importance of documenting events, eliciting the support of colleagues and administrators (particularly in alerting them before disaster struck), and building in check systems so that students could not plagiarize without putting in more effort than the original assignment required. But it was through her anecdotal approach that they discovered the value of the theories; therefore, we decided to divide class time into exercises that introduced theory (my lecture and discussion), exploration (their projections of what could or should occur), and practice (Debbie's reports of what worked and what failed in the real classroom). There were days when such a format took on a Siskel and Ebert quality: "I agree with Dr. Neary completely," she would nod, or, "That's not exactly what happened in my classroom." Discrepancies, however, did not undercut the value of theory or discussion; they reminded the interns of the open-ended quality of so many pedagogical issues, and that what worked in one scenario will not necessarily work in another.

As I introduced the teaching principles we consider best practice in the twenty-first century, I envisioned Debbie's classroom (which, fortunately, I could authenticate through the intern, Caroline, who was placed there two days a week), one in which the walls were covered with student-painted illustrations of great works of literature (occasionally life-size pictures), in which desks were arranged differently each time you entered the room, and where a small Zen fountain emitted soothing sounds all day long. She spoke of the low-ability student who took charge of keeping the fountain's water supply constant (even if he couldn't write very well); she told the interns why she always requested a challenged group of students each year, even though she taught AP English, and admitted there were days she could barely handle some of the discipline problems (heightened by a student whose Tourette's syndrome was not responding to medication). This revelation enhanced our discussion of ability grouping, tracking, and the current movement toward untracking; further, it proved to everyone that teachers are human beings who suffer from frustrations and learn from their own experiences. Only when teachers refuse to share those experiences does learning not take place. Caroline burst into class one day with the horror story of a female student who "outed" her own sexual abuse in the course of a discussion about a character who endured similar treatment, noting that Ms. Koon "handled it exactly the way we were taught, deflecting attention from the student and bringing the entire class back to the text." I couldn't have been more pleased, even though I grieved for that student.

Finally, it was time for Debbie to present entirely new material to the group, whose trust and respect she had secured in the first few weeks of class. We talked about parent and community involvement, and, because the community newsletter requirement on the syllabus was Debbie's idea and a new component of the course, I asked her to explain the reasoning behind this document, for we were asking the students to create their own original artifact, one that incorporated activities that were going on in their own classrooms. She provided models, spoke about the impact of the newsletters, and explained how the concept created an interactive learning environment. One student was so taken by the assignment that she continued generating a biweekly newsletter for the remainder of the semester. Debbie and I designed a rubric for the assigned newsletter and graded the submitted pieces collaboratively, adding positive comments to especially creative works. The students recognized the difference between mediocre and superior newsletters (although they had all received training in technology, some of them implemented visuals and special formats more than others), and they respected the final evaluation arrived at by *both* of their professors. Students were also reminded that rubrics were not just theoretical devices but real, working measures of the quality of their work. Grades were not determined in an arbitrary manner. And the fact that Debbie fished out rubrics she had used with her applied English and AP students (to show range and adjustments) further persuaded them that we were not dealing with the abstract.

As mentioned earlier, it can be an ego-threatening experience to invite another teacher into your classroom as a collaborator, and I am reminded of the dilemma that so many mentors face when their student interns prepare to leave the school and graduate, when the middle school or high school students must have "the old teacher" back again. It is fun for students to have a fresh, new face in the classroom, the pleasant countenance of someone who is new to an experience and/or does not live at the school every day. Maybe we could all use a dose of that reality now and then; I know that when I guest lecture at local schools, the students are often all ears simply because I am different and new—and "not the regular teacher." But if that part-time status is part of the magic, why not utilize it to maximize interest and participation? And if the knowledge students acquire and lifelong learning are part of the package, then I suggest that a university supervisor give this opportunity serious consideration.

An area of knowledge with which I was admittedly only somewhat familiar was the set of district standards under which high school teachers—and thus the interns—would be operating. While I had always discussed NCTE, IRA, and South Carolina state standards and their application to the material, as well as examined pacing guides to show students where the curricular standards were met, I had shied away from the demands of the district. Our plans had already become riddled with "bullets" that enumerated how goals were reached; lesson plans were beginning to look more like the products of robots and less like the efforts of caring and creative planners. It seemed too much to overwhelm new interns with multiple standards at the same time that we were introducing them to the ADEPT (Assisting, Developing, and Evaluating Professional Teaching) system by which their teaching would be measured. But when Debbie sent me a packet of "essential," "expected," and "extended" skills to which our interns would be held accountable if they taught in the Rock Hill School District, it was time to take a hard look at these goals. When we examined the charts and realized that ninth graders were required to be able to explain the influence of historical context on a poem's form, we knew that a teacher could be held accountable for this skill, and that the broader goals we had located in NCTE and state documents were very generous compared to these expectations. Debbie calmly explained to us that teacher accountability was increasing exponentially, that her principal had informed his faculty that actual teachers' names would appear next to students' standardized test scores in the near future. No one in the Winthrop English methods class could argue that we were not preparing them for reality; it was simply a matter of how much of that reality they could handle before they bailed out.

But because that was neither Debbie's goal nor mine, we used this information to show students how they might create exercises to prepare their future students for high-stakes tests such as the dreaded PACT (Palmetto Achievement Challenge Test), how they could teach vocabulary and grammar contextually without fudging, and finally how they could avail themselves of opportunities to teach students of all learning styles through technological advances, thereby accommodating challenged students. Debbie modeled how she managed to teach *The Crucible* to both her college preparatory and applied English classes, adjusting the amounts of oral reading and the demands of writing assignments to the needs of each group. We looked at the level of skills each activity met according to Bloom's taxonomy and reasoned that curricular objectives could be met differently with students of varying ability levels. Even though I trek into the schools on a daily basis in the spring (biweekly during the fall semester) and am aware of which novels, plays, short stories, and language arts skills are being taught from grades 7 to 12, I could not begin to explain how teachers manage to write out short-term and long-term goals that meet the objectives concisely and clearly, as they are forced to do every day. But having a real practitioner in the classroom who has just refashioned or tailored a lesson on *The Giver* for an inclusion class, one who can explain what worked or did not, adds a new dimension to any teaching methodology course.

These strategies apply to limited English proficient (LEP) and English as a second language (ESL) students as well. Because there has been an influx of Hispanic students in York County, one that can be attributed both to the growing number of agricultural workers who have stayed on and placed their children in the public schools and to the general diversity we are experiencing as part of the greater Charlotte area, we have seen an increased need for bilingual assistance. Debbie, of course, had already experienced this phenomenon firsthand, reminding the students again that the role-play (in this case, on the ESL student) was not about theory, but about a very real issue. Consequently, she suggested that we invite her district coordinator for ESL, Patty Garrison, to Winthrop and graciously offered to arrange having her as a guest speaker. Patty's presentation was not only supportive and encouraging but also heartfelt and downright emotional. By the end of her talk, at least five students were crying (this is not normally one of my goals); I remained dry-eyed out of sheer stubbornness. She ended up leaving the students with a list of pointers about teaching non-native speakers, some district sources, and her personal telephone number. But we were able to benefit from Patty's talk mainly because Debbie enjoyed such a positive working relationship with this incredible woman. Once again, the collaboration proved that shared values were more important than formalities, that networking yielded more sources for preservice teachers than many official leads.

And it is often networking that prompts student interns to work even harder than they ordinarily do; there is a sense of co-conspiracy, that "we are in this together," which they can share with the public school practitioner but not the university supervisor. As we played Christenbury's variables game, in which students predict the outcome of a particular lesson according to class demographics, grade level and ability grouping, and time of year and lesson topic, they searched Debbie's face for approval of their projections. Such reliance surfaced again when one of the students delivered her ten-minute oral report on censorship and teacher accountability. We had talked about character education, teaching ethics, and consistency, but the introduction of the topic that could cost a teacher her or his job—censorship—was the litmus test for the classroom professional. It was Katie who stumbled into this rugged terrain and took the challenge; she would be the one to spearhead the Winthrop NCTE student affiliate's marathon reading of banned, challenged, and censored books. But her short talk about book banning set off a discussion not only of what can happen when you teach a required text that has been challenged at some point (as witnessed in Debbie's tale of her three-hour "trial" in a closed boardroom with at least a dozen scowling faces when she taught *Their Eyes Were Watching God* in AP English), but also of what a teacher can do to prevent a fiasco. Debbie showed the interns how she prepares rationales for parents during Open House Night, how she explains to them why their children are reading literature that has been challenged, and how she points out the significance of the literature she teaches. Once again Debbie demonstrated, through real-life experience, how preparation such as documenting can help a teacher avoid potential problems; unlike some of the old yarns I dredge up from "when I taught high school" (now seemingly a century ago), her anecdotes are more useful than entertaining.

Having a public school teacher co-teach the seminar also assisted with exercises on question framing and assessment. We had always talked about authentic assessment—student-designed tests, artistic renderings of literary interpretations, the portfolio—but here was a practitioner who actively used the portfolio in her classroom and who provided sample rubrics from her AP English portfolios for us to peruse, critique, and adapt. She shared copies of formal essay and objective tests as well and provided feedback to students on their unit plan assessments (the graduate students were responsible for both methods and materials and formal assessment of the thematic unit). Debbie and I collaborated on the grading of the unit plans as a whole, and it was uncanny how often we both were struck by a well-executed idea, as well as by an activity that suffered from overkill or simply did not fit in. Because once again the students knew that four eyes would be reviewing their small-group generated unit plans (I had grouped them according to grade levels they would be working with in the spring, so that, for example, eighth-grade interns could all use parts of a plan that included a study of Anne Frank and the Holocaust), they were more thoughtful than previous groups had been about designing these units. Many of these students have since come back to "borrow" pages from their units so they could implement them in their own classrooms.

The microlessons, at least half of which were viewed by Debbie, were self-reviewed, peer-reviewed, and graded by both Debbie and me, following a rubric that mandated that each intern address one special-needs student in a ten- to fifteen-minute lesson. I held the video camera and watched the performances more closely after class, when I no longer had to worry about telescoping the lens and shooting close-ups; Debbie observed them from the seminar table, taking notes and conferring with me after the lessons were shot. By the time everyone had assessed each lesson, there was scarcely any need to determine its final grade; the strengths and weaknesses jumped out at us.

One of the most creative grading strategies I have been able to build into this course grew out of our collaboration. This is not the sort of class that lends itself to a traditional essay exam, and we knew that the interns would be completing portfolios for their writing pedagogy and education capstone courses (and I can't endorse capstoning them to death). Debbie suggested that we try out an oral exam for which they could prepare in pairs, one that focused on key topics we had covered in the course. She had used this technique successfully in her AP English class and was willing to give it a shot with college students. We decided to have them pick topics randomly from index cards and then prepare to speak for ten minutes (using only small note cards for prompts); we narrowed down the topics to the broad categories of Best Practice, Lesson Planning, Classroom Ethics and Management, Assessment and Accountability, and Tracking and Ability Grouping. It occurred to us that familiarity with these topics and the presentation format would eventually come in handy when the students prepared for job interviews. We had to arrange for Debbie to spend two full hours with us on exam day. Again, her principal was agreeable to the idea and supportive of her participation in this culminating exercise. On our scheduled exam day, the students waited nervously in the hall, filing in as we called their names, to deliver reports that highlighted the main ideas of their topics and explicated them as thoroughly as possible. We took notes and conferred two evenings later in order to arrive at an exam grade, as well as to come up with a final grade for each student in the course. We were within five points with most students, arguing a B up to a B+ or an A down to an A-, but never far apart on any members of the class.

Debbie came to know many of the students quite well, getting involved in their personal teaching situations and following up on the major and minor crises they reported on Tuesday afternoons. Even though she was working full time with Caroline during spring semester, Debbie was still not too busy to ask about another intern's progress. I wish she could have seen them all teach. We both said "yes" rather spontaneously to a scary proposition and found out that some "yeses" are more equal than others.

Follow-up: We've Only Just Begun

From my perspective, the collaboration was a win-win situation, even though I had balked, mentally, at the original suggestion. At the same time, it would be unfair to recommend a venture like this to other educators without warning them about the extra time it entails. Count on several lunch and dinner meetings from start to finish. And there are always attitude challenges. Be prepared for bemused looks from a few colleagues, who likely think you're trying to lighten your own workload, or who may shrink at the sight of a public school teacher in the role of college professor. Experiments like this do occur in the College of Education (where they have teachers-in-residence and laboratory preschool set-ups), but they are rare in the College of Arts and Sciences.

It would also be unwise to invite to collaborate with you a practitioner—even one you respect and admire—with whom you do not have a good rapport or with whom you cannot share a laugh. It is vital that you maintain your sense of humor and prepare yourself for the unexpected. Students quickly pick up on the subtlest discrepancies or differences of opinion. If you lead them to question a particular aspect of the curriculum (e.g., the sometimes artificial or forced link between literature and technology in applied communications classes), only to find that your team teacher couldn't agree more with the prevailing practice and doesn't see why you have a problem with it, your best course of action is probably to acknowledge the clash of ideas, turn the matter over to the students, and allow them to analyze the situation and formulate their own theories. They will eventually be working with colleagues with whom they occasionally disagree but can still maintain collegial relationships, so it is not necessarily a bad thing for them to witness some disagreement. Further, it is impossible to predict how another human being will react to something one of your students does or says; it is best to let go of the notion that these are exclusively your students, for they are now being taught and assessed by two professionals. I caught myself more than once referring to "my" girls (the seminar group was, oddly, 100 percent female during this collaboration), only to quickly correct myself and let go of the proprietary notion.

If ownership is a quality we want to build into the students' sense about material they have mastered, it is certainly not one we wish to appropriate for course design. I thought I had observed far too much territorialism to engage in the obnoxious practice myself; inviting a professional who views the material you teach from a related yet different perspective is a healthy way to avoid turf wars while improving what you have long considered a wonderful creation.

As for my team teacher, I can only try to capture her thoughts on the experience the best I can. She has indicated to me that this trial semester opened up a new teaching world to her and that she is considering entering a doctoral program, a notion that had previously daunted her. The differences between the Winthrop campus and her high school, Northwestern, underscored what she has been preparing her own students for over the past sixteen years. It was not a campus tour Debbie took, but a journey to the center of the college experience, one that made her privy to how we *really* operate once the classroom door is closed. She was amazed to discover that even college seniors and graduate students sometimes invent excuses for not being prepared for class and was gratified to learn that the preservice teachers were genuinely interested in pedagogical issues and in being able to offer their own students authentic learning experiences. Because of her solicited intrusion into the classroom, we both learned more about why these interns had chosen to enter the field of teaching (it wasn't the money) and what frustrated them most (it wasn't the hours). I consider it a major coup that most of them went on to complete the full-time student teaching semester, even after being exposed to the harsh realities of the teaching world. I can only surmise that it was helpful to hit them with the bad news first (e.g., class size issues) and the good news second (how to cope). Only two of the original thirteen remained "out of rotation," and these two picked up student teaching the next fall.

The students reported favorably on the enterprise; the course evaluations (which all faculty fear to some degree; if they say they don't, they're lying) reflected this, as they mentioned Debbie and spoke favorably of the team effort. Two members of the class, Lori and Katie, had agreed to take part in a panel that we proposed for a future NCTE conference. I had been told there was some travel funding built into this grant, and our four-member crew was eager to take the show on the road. The interns wanted to discuss how they profited from the partnership; Debbie and I wanted to promote the concept so that other educators, who might be intimidated by such an offer, could shed some of the anxiety and give it a try.

Almost all of us made it to the 2001 NCTE Annual Convention in Baltimore; by then Katie was teaching at Booker T. Washington Middle School in Newport News, Virginia, so we all met via telephone, e-mail, and snail mail to plan our presentation, which included tapes from the ESL coordinator, who was able to address our class because of the partnership. In the fall of 2001, I was fortunate to once again be able to offer a similar partnership to my interns. My department chair has already mentioned that we should think about building this partnership into our program so that when the grant money runs out the collaboration can continue. I have sent a letter to Debbie's principal, reminding him of the value of the work she has done on our campus, and will continue to support her collaboration with the university.

Of course, I have already given thought to changes I would make in the collaboration the next time around. I need to make a conscious effort to be less controlling, to worry less about returning papers on time and more about the shared grading process. I also would like to build in some sort of office hour for my cohort so that students who may feel more comfortable talking to her have the opportunity to do so. Since I supervise students for the field experience while they are taking this methods course, it is entirely logical that they would want to seek her advice or consult with her on a teaching issue before they approach me. I wish we could alternate class meeting places, but our campus is more central to the schools at which the students intern than the high school. Moreover, I am generally rushing back to Winthrop midday after visiting an intern onsite the morning of the day we meet for class, so it would be difficult for me to relocate once again.

I need to allow more time for reflection in the actual seminar: we hurried from topic to topic, often going beyond our allotted class time (though no one ever complained). Because I have an even larger group slated to take the course next year, I may have to trim presentation times just so that all students have opportunities to express their ideas. I enjoy starting each class with a "story of the day" from one intern, based on a public school experience, or, if no one is in a talkative mood, a prompt to which everyone responds briefly. I hate for my collaborator to miss these moments, yet I am thankful that she can get to campus as soon as she does.

Each group of interns will have its own personality, and there is no guarantee that they will respond as positively to the team-teaching approach as the first group. But I am grateful that I was asked to try out this collaboration and that nobody ever asked me if I really knew what I was doing. Because I would have said "yes."

Debbie's Turn

Following is a transcription of an interview I conducted with this very busy teacher shortly after she submitted materials for her National Board Certification. We recently learned, as our NCTE panel was presenting a report on our venture, that Debbie was one of those honored with the distinction of attaining National Board Certification. It seemed only fair to give her a chance to let us know what was going on from her perspective; I knew I had to take the risk of asking her about what really went on behind the scenes, even if it meant finding out that her assignment was more arduous than I had anticipated.

> *Marg:* Can you describe your initial reactions to the prospect of team-teaching an English methods course with me at Winthrop University?
>
> *Debbie:* While I was excited and honored about being asked, I was also anxious. My first thought was, "Can I do this? Am I competent enough to make a difference with these college students?" My gut reaction, however, said, "Go for it; I have a really positive feeling about collaborating with Marg. This is not an opportunity I can pass up!"
>
> *Marg:* How did you approach your principal about the project?
>
> *Debbie:* After making sure that my fall schedule would allow me to leave school early enough to team-teach the class, I saw my principal at school during the summer. My first words to him were: "I have a great opportunity to make a difference with mentoring interns, so please say 'yes.'" After we both chuckled, I told him about the offer to team-teach a methods class at Winthrop. As I suspected he might, he asked, "Deb, would your schedule here allow for

that?" He smiled; he knew I had already thought of that. He was totally supportive and often asked how the class was going and how I liked working on the college level.

Marg: Did you share what you were doing with your own students? How did they respond?

Debbie: Yes, I did share what I was doing at Winthrop. They, too, were supportive and actually impressed. I remember one student saying, "Wow, Ms. Koon, that's cool that you're teaching teachers." It worked out beautifully because one of the students in the methods class, Caroline, also came to my classroom two times a week for her field experience; therefore, she and I talked openly about our class experience at Winthrop. As I've learned over sixteen years, students take pride in their teachers' accomplishments. Once they know you're teaching college, they think you're smarter, more competent. Okay, so I'll accept that attitude. Ha!

Marg: How about your colleagues? Were they supportive?

Debbie: My colleagues were supportive, but they really had little to say at first. I'm sure there were the usual questions among themselves like "How did she get to do that?" or "How did she get approval to leave school early every Tuesday?" I guess, too, that I was modest in talking about the class because it was all still new to me, and each seminar was a learning experience for me. I didn't want to get too cocky because I was, in a sense, feeling my way with each class. What was really interesting, however, was that later on some of my colleagues approached me about passing some ideas to them about new strategies and methods. They began to ask, "How's that class with interns going?"; "Are you going to do this again?" Some of them said to me, "Deb, you're taking on something else in addition to National Board?"

Marg: How did it feel to join the seminar every Tuesday afternoon?

Debbie: I remember going to my first seminar class. I didn't know what to expect. What silly things went through my mind: Will I look professional enough? What am I going to say first? Will Marg think I'm the right choice after all? And then I walked into the classroom, as you were discussing some pedagogical issue. Okay . . . here goes. What a potpourri of women . . . future teachers . . . so eager . . . and, yes, they all took some thoughtful moments to size me up a bit. As I was reviewing my adventurous and hectic day of teaching, I heard the welcoming laugh that says, "Yeah, we suppose you'll be okay . . . ; now start wowing us, Ms. Koon." Each Tuesday was a risk for me, but I simply followed your lead and worked from a foundation of experience and common sense. Each seminar got better and better and the time flew by so quickly. The best part for me was my actual collaboration with you. I think we made a solid team, and the students knew it. What a relief, what a challenge, what fun!

Marg: What impression do you think you made on the preservice English teachers? How could you tell?

Debbie: I tried to be as honest as possible about the realities of teaching. And while I admired the students' eager and very idealistic attitudes about having their own classrooms, I wanted to establish myself as more than just a cheerleader. I must admit that I experienced some pleasure in reenacting some of the tougher moments in my sixteen years as an educator; I remember seeing some pretty wide eyes when I told them stories about unsupportive parents, confrontations in conference rooms about censorship issues, and disrespectful, aggressive teenagers. They needed to know, right up front, that stepping into a classroom brings many risks and fears, and just as many victories. Of course, what they did learn each class meeting was my commitment to teaching, my love for literature, and the art of communicating with teenagers. After a few classes, I saw more nodding heads and heard more "What do you think about this idea, Ms. Koon?" The best clue, however, came from the students not wanting to leave at 3:15; they stayed after class to talk to us about this idea or that idea. I played my music especially loud on my rides home from that class. What a sense of worth, of accomplishment . . . of relief for having completed yet another seminar class successfully.

Marg: What surprised you most about our class?

Debbie: I was surprised at the level of knowledge these students already had. There was some excellent "real world" stuff going on in their education classes. When I think back to my strategies and methods class, I can remember one thing: P.L. 94-142. These students talked theory and methods, do's and don'ts continually. They were much more prepared than I had expected, so I could act as more of a facilitator and co-learner who just happened to have sixteen years of experience!

Marg: If you could change one thing about your involvement with the English methods partnership, what would it be?

Debbie: This question is an easy one. I really wish I could attend the entire three hours of class. There were days when I came in and knew that I had just missed some productive discussion or activity. I think I could have helped more of the individual students had I spent more time with them.

Marg: What sort of response did you receive from your administrators about your participation in the course?

Debbie: The administration was super. My principal continually asked about the class, and, knowing his high standards, I was thrilled when he said to me, "I knew you would fall right into the flow. Winthrop certainly chose the right person." Patty Garrison, our language arts, foreign language, social studies, and ESL coordinator, was so excited when I asked her to come talk to the students about ESL issues. She still talks about what a good experience it was for her.

Marg: How has this experience impacted your own teaching?

Debbie: I don't know if all of you knew this, but each seminar was a lesson for me, too. Talking about the latest teaching methods influenced me to update and try new approaches. I also polished, adjusted, and reinforced my own attitudes toward the profession by collaborating on a weekly basis with a knowledgeable colleague and fourteen inquisitive, intelligent future teachers. I think more objectively now than I used to about handling touchy issues like censorship, parent conferences, tracking students with exceptionalities, and effective classroom management. After this collaborative experience, I feel much more "in the loop" and updated on the world of teaching English.

Works Cited

Christenbury, Leila. *Making the Journey: Being and Becoming a Teacher of English Language Arts.* Portsmouth, NH: Boynton/Cook, 1994.

Maxwell, Rhoda J., and Mary Jordan Meiser. *Teaching English in Middle and Secondary Schools.* Upper Saddle River, NJ: Prentice-Hall, 2001.

Poetter, Thomas S., and Badiali, Bernard. "Growing Teacher Inquiry: Collaboration in a Partner School." *Peabody Journal of Education* 75.3 (2000): 161–75.

Wagner, Betty Jane, and Mark Larson. *Situations: A Casebook of Virtual Realities for the English Teacher.* Portsmouth, NH: Boynton/Cook, 1995.

4 You've Got Priority Mail: "The Single Most Valuable Activity of Our Semester"

Nancy S. Tucker
University of Michigan–Flint

Leah A. Zuidema
Michigan State University

When Nancy taught teacher preparation classes at Michigan State University and Leah taught English at Byron Center High School, they developed a connected learning experience that they believed would be beneficial to Nancy's preservice teachers and to Leah's high school students. A detailed account of their separate and joint adventures follows.

Nancy: Early in 1999, as I was designing a syllabus to teach a fall class that would prepare preservice English teachers to teach writing to secondary students, an idea began to buzz in my head. I'd been teaching graduate classes in the Critical Studies in the Teaching of English program, in which most of the students were high school teachers or were planning to teach at the community college level. I'd also taught a number of classes to college seniors, English majors and minors who were working on teacher certification. I kept reflecting on the texts we had used as part of our work in both of these programs. There was one constant refrain: authentic texts are tied to real reading and writing experiences.[1]

"Authentic texts," I found myself muttering. "Real learning experiences. We preach to our preservice teachers that *they* should incorporate authentic texts and experiences into the classroom, but as teacher educators we have feet of clay. Why not try to make a change? Why not find real students to whom our preservice teachers might respond?" The more I thought about it, the better I liked the idea. But where was I to find a class with a teacher who would be open to the idea? I recalled a graduate class I had taught the previous semester in which we had rousing discussions about authentic reading experiences, and Leah came to mind. I knew she taught high school, I knew her school had technology that might facilitate my students' access to her students' writing, and from our conversations in class, I knew her to be a dedicated teacher who was always looking for new ways to encourage her students. I thought she might be open to this idea. So I called her.

Leah: Nancy's phone call was the exciting solution to a problem I had been thinking about since the spring. To complete an assignment for Nancy's course, I'd attended the 1999 Spring English Language Arts Conference at Michigan State University (MSU) (sponsored by the Michigan Council of Teachers of English and known colloquially as the Bright Ideas Conference). One session that had particularly interested me was Jill Van Antwerp's presentation, "Providing Audiences during the Writing Process." Since that time, I had been searching for authentic audiences for my student writers—for readers other than their teacher, for people who would take an interest in my students' writing without assigning grades. I wanted the act of communication itself to motivate my students; I wanted them to experience writing thrills that weren't related to grades. Nancy's proposal seemed to meet those needs, and I was eager to get involved. I never had any real doubts; my experience as Nancy's student led me to believe that if she thought this project would be a good idea, she was probably right. As we talked more about it, I gained confidence that we could do this in a way that would be professional, as well as respectful of and helpful to my students. The factor that cemented my decision was the interest I was developing in teacher education; this project seemed like a natural way to connect my work with preservice teachers, so I was all the more eager to get started.

The Procedure

Nancy: Leah and I agreed that her students would write papers that my preservice teachers would then respond to. These papers would be returned to Leah, who would then distribute them to her students. Originally, I had hoped we could do this by means of e-mail or a Web-supported program designed at Michigan State called Interact; however, due to technical difficulties and privacy concerns, we couldn't manage that. Instead, we worked by means of the U.S. Postal Service's Priority Mail system.

When I met with my preservice teachers, they were excited to find out that they would be working with the papers of "real students" who were actually writing in response to a classroom assignment. Often, one of the complaints I had heard was that we were long on theory and short on the practical aspects of teaching writing. Even in simulations, we frequently had to resort to a carefully selected piece of work by a purported student writer but taken out of the context in which it had originally been written. My preservice teachers were particularly energized to realize that their comments might make a difference to some beginning writers.

Leah: My students were wide-eyed when I first introduced the project to them. The room was very quiet, and it was obvious that the students were working hard to process what it might mean to write for an audience other than their peer feedback groups and their teacher. After some silent hesitation, they started to ask questions: "So somebody else really asked to read our papers? How many people will be looking at them? What if there aren't enough people to read all our papers? Are you going to mail just the best ones?" I assured my skeptical students that I wasn't the only one interested in their writing, that I would send every student's writing to Nancy's class, and that each of them would receive feedback from at least one preservice teacher. When the class period came to an end, I could see the pride on my students' faces and sense their unprecedented eagerness to start writing the essay I had assigned that day.

The Byron Center High School (BCHS) students wrote drafts, workshopped in peer groups, and then revised and printed out two copies of their papers. The students were more conscientious than I'd ever seen them about "getting it right," and I observed a significant increase in their efforts to solicit feedback from me and from each other. When the due date arrived, each student gave one copy to me for my written feedback and then wrote a letter to the readers at Michigan State and attached it to the second copy, which was labeled only with the writer's first name and the last name initial as a way to protect their privacy. In their letters, students briefly summarized their essays, recounted the revisions they had already made, and listed questions and concerns they had about their papers. The letters had a twofold purpose: first, they were designed to help give the readers an orientation to the assignment and to each student's thoughts and concerns about his or her paper; and second, they provided my students an opportunity to think about the work they had done, as well as a chance to ask questions of their readers. (I required a similar document whenever students turned in papers to me; the students' reflections helped me to gauge the writers' self-awareness of their texts' strengths and weaknesses and to tailor my responses accordingly.) When we finished the letters, I gathered up all of the revised papers with their letters attached, included a copy of the assignment so that the readers had a context for their responses, and sent them to Nancy and her preservice teachers at MSU. Then we waited for replies.

Nancy: Within a few days, the packet from Leah and her students at BCHS arrived. We had set aside class time for this work because I felt it was important to integrate the actual practice into the theory that we had been reading and discussing. My preservice teachers were excited and also a little nervous about "doing it right." We had been working in class on our own writing and responding to each other's papers, but this added a level of responsibility and seriousness to our responses. We talked about responding as interested readers, in a fashion similar to what they had been doing already in their own peer response groups. I asked them to do three things: (1) respond to the questions the writer had asked; (2) point out one or two strengths of the piece; and (3) make a suggestion or two regarding changes the writer could make—those suggestions could be in the form of questions they had as readers or of ideas for productive changes based on the fact that they had more writing experience than Leah's students. I insisted that they be respectful of the student's work.

To provide a general baseline for response, I picked two papers from the set Leah had sent and put them on transparencies so that we could all look at the same papers together and talk about what we saw in each piece of writing—the strengths, the weaknesses—and to model some responses aloud before we actually worked with writing responses to these papers.

To combat the obvious problem that Leah's class and my class did not have the same number of students, we used two different strategies. The first time Leah sent a batch of papers I handed one out to each person in class, which left several papers without readers. When one of my students finished a paper, I asked him or her to take another so that we were certain that each paper had been read and responded to by at least one of our class members. As others in class finished reading and responding, they traded papers, so that the writers could have more than one reader responding to their work.

The second batch of papers Leah sent was from a smaller class, so we divided into groups of three or four preservice teachers, and I distributed sets of papers to each group. My students had some choice about how to make the groups work effectively, but they had to be certain that each paper received a careful reading and a thoughtful response from at least one person. In practice, most of the preservice teachers responded thoroughly to two student writers, while some had the opportunity to respond to three or four on each round of papers. An advantage of the groups was that my students had other readers to share ideas with, to ask questions of, and to help them consider how to respond when they were unsure. Of course, I was also part of the response team, suggesting approaches and pointing out ideas they hadn't fully considered, trying to nudge them in appropriate directions. When we were finished, we bundled up the papers and mailed them back to Leah and her students.

Leah: While I was waiting to get the papers back, Nancy and I sometimes exchanged e-mails so that I was somewhat prepared for any issues or concerns that might arise when I returned the essays to my students. When the packet arrived, I redistributed the essays. If time permitted, I read the feedback before I turned the essays over to my students, but not always—unless, of course, Nancy had alerted me in advance to a specific issue or one of my students requested that I read the comments. All of my students read with interest the responses they received. We then looked at examples of the feedback and discussed why it might differ from one reader to another—and, in some cases, from the feedback I had given them.

We also talked about and modeled ways to discern which feedback—in any writing situation—is the most useful. This became particularly important in one situation in which a preservice teacher substituted much of her own diction and syntax for that of the student writer. In this essay, my student's phrase "pretty much all she had" now read "the essence of her life," the student's "trying to kill Beowulf" became "avenging Grendel's death," and "she would just look at him" was converted to "she glared at him." With the permission of the original author, I read excerpts from the paper aloud, asking the other students to indicate when they heard a word or phrase that didn't match the author's voice. This example helped my students establish a better understanding of "voice" and its importance, and it was the springboard for a constructive conversation about what kinds of feedback are most helpful in peer response settings.

A different type of feedback that was more common was exemplified by another preservice teacher, Jason, whose gentle, encouraging suggestions contributed to marked improvement in Stacy's next revision. Comments such as "If your reader is unfamiliar with the story of *Beowulf*, he/she may be a little lost in the 2nd paragraph" and advice to include more of the "clear, concise, honest" descriptions already evident in the essay helped Stacy make revisions that made her paper much more engaging and clear for her readers. In response to an inappropriate use of the second-person point of view, Jason wrote, "When this happens to me, I almost always switch to 'one(s).'" His comment, like so many of the comments from the preservice teachers, revealed a sensitivity for the writer's feelings as well as an ability to give useful advice.

My students were a little surprised at the variety of the responses they got, but it led us into a valuable conversation about teaching as a learning process and the ways that individual teaching and reading styles can vary. We also discussed how a variety of responses can be advantageous to students—as well as a source of potential confusion or frustration. We talked about student strategies for minimizing this confusion and frustration, agreeing that our experience illustrated that no teacher or source knows everything. I emphasized that students should be savvy learners, getting the best from all available sources but not relying completely on any one source. It was a leap for some of my students to realize that differing opinions don't necessarily indicate that one side is wrong. Their questions and comments indicated that this exercise drove home the responsibility students have for their own education; some of them were clearly beginning to grasp that the "student opens head, teacher inserts knowledge" model of learning would not suffice.

Looking Back: Leah and the Byron Center High School Writers

Leah: Our interaction with the preservice teachers was a highlight of the fall semester for my students and for me. To my surprise, this activity positively affected each step of my students' writing processes. They really became writers: first, they worked hard to choose topics they believed would engage their readers. Then, instead of sloughing through the formalities of a token rough draft followed by a nearly identical "revised" draft, these young authors presented their best possible drafts to their workshop groups and took the feedback they received there to heart as they worked on revisions. When it came time to mail their work, they had carefully typed their essays and letters and, in many cases, had even remembered to run the spellchecker (a small victory in our war on misspellings). While some students in my classes had always written for personal satisfaction or even for my comments, this was perhaps the first time that all of my students, rather than just a select few, were motivated to write their best for an incentive other than a grade. Every student—without exception—wanted to impress his or her readers; all of them craved the one-on-one attention they and their writing were getting from college seniors. The few students who missed the mass mailing due date even sought my permission to mail their essays individually, attaching handwritten notes begging Dr. Tucker to include their papers in her class's activities and then taking responsibility for mailing their envelopes themselves.

The magic didn't stop when I put the package in the mail, and it didn't end on the day I distributed the contents of the return package Nancy sent. It continued all the way through to the day students finally submitted their papers to me for a grade. The research detailing the ineffectiveness of comments on students' writing didn't apply in our classroom: these writers paid close attention to every squiggle of advice. They noticed—and told me so—when the preservice teachers' comments either supported or contradicted my comments. They asked questions about how to know which advice to follow and which to ignore. They experienced for themselves the recursive nature of the writing process, returning to brainstorm, draft, and revise until they were satisfied with their papers.

As I mentioned earlier, my students also got a new perspective on the roles of teachers and students. Instead of thinking of teachers as adults who had been locked in classrooms their entire lives (with occasional escapes to the grocery story, gas station, or high school basketball game), the BCHS students began to rethink who teachers are, how they get to be teachers, how they are trained, what they know, and what their limitations are. They also began, on a small scale, to rethink their own roles as students. They began to empower themselves as writers, to make their own choices about what to do instead of asking, "What do *you* want me to do on my revision?"

My students weren't the only ones to benefit. I too grew in several ways throughout the instruction process. Knowing that an entire class of teachers-to-be would be reflecting on my assignments with my former professor added an extra level of accountability to my writing process. I was self-conscious about the fact that students' struggles with writing sometimes stem from poorly crafted assignments. I didn't want my shortcomings to be the impetus for a "teachable moment" about the importance of carefully designed writing prompts!

Knowing that my responses wouldn't be the only ones (aside from peer feedback) on students' papers also made me more analytical about the nature of my own comments. My response strategies weren't significantly altered, but I retained them only after deliberately confirming that they met standards I consciously and intentionally set. While I purposely completed my responses to students' drafts before the return package from Nancy arrived because I didn't want to be swayed by others' praise and suggestions, I also wanted to learn from the comments made by the preservice teachers. By reviewing the responses from Nancy's students, I got the chance to read student papers in more than one way and to expand my own response repertoire.

One other benefit for me was that this collaboration provided a window into the world of teacher education. Looking at the college students' feedback and discussing their learning process with Nancy helped me think about my own incomplete learning-to-teach journey and about the work I would be doing for the first time in the spring semester with a teacher intern from Calvin College. In the same way that experienced writers sometimes come to believe that their skills are intuitive, I had forgotten much of the awkward learning that occurs in the early days of a teaching career. I realized how important my role would be, but I was also encouraged to know that I was now well prepared for it. Glimpsing Nancy and her students at work helped me to be better prepared for my role as a cooperating teacher and to have realistic expectations about what my teacher intern might already know and what she could realistically be expected to learn over the course of the semester. And, as I had hoped when I joined Nancy in this project, my participation heightened my interest in teacher education.

Looking Back: Nancy and the Michigan State Preservice Teachers

Nancy: I confess I was a bit nervous as I carried that first packet of papers into my classroom. All the visions about what could go wrong flashed through my mind: comments that were too harsh, too laudatory, or just not helpful; too much attention paid to mechanics and spelling. I also had some vague concerns about whether my students would find this a useful activity. Then I saw them plunge into the reading of papers, and my doubts about whether we were doing the right thing vanished. I described our general approach to the reading of student papers earlier. What I didn't describe was the combination of excitement, enthusiasm, concern, and plain open-mouthed awe that I saw in my preservice teachers. The excitement and enthusiasm came because they were finally getting a chance to read real papers from real students. The concern came from wanting so much to do the right thing and feeling that their own experience was inadequate. The awe, I think, came from the fact that Leah's students were willing to share their writing with strangers and even wrote notes about the work. The juxtaposition of themselves and real student work seemed to create that awe.

While my doubts about whether I was doing the right thing vanished, I retained some concerns about *how* we were going to accomplish the right thing. My students knew how to write; writing was something that simply came naturally (after years of experience) to them. But they weren't sure they knew how to express that knowledge in response to student writers. They didn't know how to tell other people how to write. They weren't certain what kinds of responses would be helpful and what would be off-putting. Most of them had experienced the red pencil of the English teacher correcting usage errors and spelling mistakes; in fact, that model was almost universal among them. Despite the fact that our class had used an alternative approach for our own writing work, a workshop approach in which we did not focus on red-pencil error correction but on responding to the work with comments on the strengths and suggestions for improvements, they didn't have a firm grasp on how to use our model for responding to high school papers. In fact, as we discussed responses, I realized that while in theory they liked and wanted to use a more open approach, they weren't all sure that an English teacher's job at the high school level *wasn't* error correction.

These concerns became clear as we looked at the models and as we began to read the students' papers. My preservice teachers raised a number of questions about effective response, such as:

- Should I correct grammar, spelling, and punctuation?
- What do I say when it's really good?
- Where do I begin when it needs a lot of work?
- What if it's a good paper, but not on the topic assigned?
- Should I correct grammar, spelling, and punctuation if they *specifically* asked me to?
- How do I respond to a narrative when the assignment asked for an analysis?
- Do all ninth graders (or eleventh or twelfth graders) write this well (or have this many problems)?

- But I can't just ignore the grammar/spelling/ punctuation when it's bad, can I?

Behind all of these questions lurked larger questions: "Who am I supposed to be in relation to this student/writer? And how should that show up in my response, both now and when I have my own classroom?" These questions in turn pointed to the central, most important question: "What is the role of the English teacher?" In answering the small questions, we forged responses to the larger ones, questions involving philosophy and pedagogical approach.

We dealt with all these questions and others as they came up on the model papers and also on the student papers. After much discussion of effective and appropriate responses, the readers wrote to their student correspondents. The responses varied from one preservice teacher who took a minimalist approach—three lines, somewhat cryptic—to another who rewrote much of the student's paper in the margins and on the back. Most of them, however, were able to answer students' questions, provide comments on what they found particularly strong, and then make one or two suggestions to the student writers.

In the process of reading, thinking about, and responding to student writing, my preservice teachers learned a number of things that I think they could have learned no other way. This learning involved methods, but also impinged on their philosophies of teaching and learning.

First, they learned that grammar, spelling, and punctuation, issues that preoccupied them as evidenced by the questions they asked, are not the first things to pay attention to *even if that's what the student asked for*. (While Leah's students had been trained in the differences between revision and editing and had been instructed to ask for revision rather than editing/proofreading help, some still asked for help with grammar and punctuation. I know this surprised her.) The preservice teachers learned that grammar and punctuation should be dealt with as local problems, relatively small and contained, and that the global issues of meaning and point should be dealt with first. They learned that if a student asked for specific help it was a good strategy to point out one or two places the student could make a change. If a mechanical problem got in the way of understanding, they suggested a way for the student to look at that issue in order to make the work clearer.

They learned how to pay attention to writing from the inside, from what the student was trying to say, and to attend to both style and content as a function of the student's purpose. In doing this, they learned how to pick out the strengths of a paper and how to support and encourage these strengths, and also how to ask questions and make suggestions that could lead a writer to think again about what he or she had written. Asking questions and giving real reactions also helped them avoid the vapid, "I liked this, it was good," and instead provide useful suggestions.

My preservice teachers were surprised at the excellence of the best of the student writers and dismayed at the difficulties of the most challenged. They also had to figure out how to respond to each of these groups. How could they support the strong writer while encouraging him or her to take a risk? As one of my students said, "He [Leah's student] writes better than I do. What can I possibly tell him?" We talked about pointing out specific passages that seemed strong and about reacting as a reader to the strengths. We also talked about making suggestions that truly are suggestions so that the writer who is already skilled can stretch him- or herself to try something new.

At the other end of the spectrum, they asked how they could help the novice writer without discouraging him or her too much. We talked about praising what worked in any piece of writing, about restating for the student writer what seemed to be a direction he or she was heading in the work, and focusing on one or two difficulties at a time. I tried to explain that they couldn't do everything with one reading, nor could the writer do everything with one revision, and that sometimes it was best to be up-front about that and position their comments as the first things to work on rather than as the final answer.

They learned that they did know something about writing but also that they didn't know everything. Thus they learned to ask each other questions and to draw on the knowledge of their peers (and their professor); they learned that two responses are probably better than one. My preservice teachers came to understand what Leah's students saw later: that two readers can differ in their responses and yet those two responses can each be valuable for a writer.

They learned how to be respectful in responding. I emphasized the importance of attempting to ascertain what the writer was trying to accomplish in his or her work and to support that endeavor, or, if necessary, nudge the writer in a direction that would be more appropriate for the assignment and the context in which it was given.

One interesting result of our collaboration that I had not foreseen was the conversation generated by having copies of the assignment sheets that Leah had written out for her students. My preservice teachers had a wonderful opportunity to see a writing assignment with their newly acquired teacher eyes and also to see how the students had interpreted (or misinterpreted) the assignment. They asked many questions about why Leah had written the assignment a particular way and speculated about what kinds of information one needed to include in a writing assignment. It also gave them the opportunity to see if and how the BCHS students had met the terms of the assignment. The assignment they were most fascinated with was a prompt to write a descriptive essay that captured one of the *Beowulf* characters in a specific setting from the epic. Students were to select sensory details from the text, invent appropriate details to fill in the descriptive gaps, and organize their descriptions in a way that made a point about their subject. The assignment itself sent the preservice teachers scrambling for their literature books and generated discussion as to which character played which role in *Beowulf*. They agreed that the assignment generated lively and interesting writing. One of them commented, "I never would have thought of doing it this way. It really works."

Above all, they liked reading and responding to student writers. Again and again, even after we were no longer corresponding with and responding to Leah's students, they would bring it up in class. Many of them talked about their responses and wondered if they should have said things differently. One of them stopped me on the last day of class to say she thought responding to student writers was the single most valuable activity of our semester.

None of these skills or insights was achieved without struggle. One particular struggle was a situation that Leah mentioned earlier. Several of our preservice teachers had gotten used to helping their friends revise papers. One approach some of them used was to physically rewrite the student's paper by adding their own words and rearranging the writer's sentences. We had discussed the importance of respecting the writer's work and making suggestions, but several people apparently felt that writing a better sentence was a way of making a suggestion. As sympathetic as I am to that view (having on occasion used it myself in limited ways), it requires a light touch. Several of my preservice teachers became overly zealous, to the extent that one in particular wrote in all the margins of a student's paper, changing wording and word order in every sentence. When I realized what she was doing, we had a serious and lengthy talk about what her approach says to students about their writing and what her role as a teacher would be for her students. She, and the other students I talked with, came to realize that extreme rewriting obliterated the student's voice and did not help him or her learn. I sent this paper along with the others, with an advance e-mail alert as well as an accompanying handwritten note to Leah, explaining the situation. She and her students handled it well, turning it into an opportunity to talk and learn, as we had done.

This situation was a learning experience not only for my students but also for their teacher. It pointed out several things to me: (1) how much my students' previous experiences influence their current behaviors; (2) how important it is to go over expectations very carefully (I thought I had, and my students thought they understood); and (3) how important it is to practice before writing on student's papers. From this, we instituted a change in procedure. We switched to using pluses for positive comments and question marks for areas of concern, jotted in the margins of student papers, coupled with end comments on a separate sheet of paper. This was a system I myself have used for a number of years, but I became much more specific about the need to use either this system or something similar. Some of my preservice teachers also began using sticky notes to respond to particular sections of papers, a trick they had picked up from another high school teacher who had visited our class. Sticky notes allowed them to attach a note but also to change it later if they wanted to; it also seemed less intrusive than actually writing on a student's paper. I'm not certain which methods they will eventually use with their own students, but through this experience they identified some of what they needed to know and some approaches that seemed to be effective. I saw significant growth that could have been accomplished no other way.

I learned other things as well. Through the writing of Leah's students, I refreshed my memory about the spectrum of students that my preservice teachers would encounter in their own careers. I also learned a great deal about my own students and their understanding of the role of an English teacher in responding to student writing. I learned that their metacognitive understanding of writing needed time to develop, but that we could work on it together so that their understanding could grow. I learned that talking about writing is a useful experience for a group of teacher wannabes (and probably for practicing teachers as well), but that talking about responding to writing *as* they are responding to writing is even better.

Finally, I learned to be careful of my assumptions. I came to appreciate the hold that earlier learning has on preservice teachers, finally understanding something I had been in the process of realizing for a long time: students, even preservice teachers, come to us with already extant philosophies of what it means to teach and to learn. These philosophies are most likely unarticulated. Students need time, a place, and a reason to explore both the questions they generate and the answers they may find, which will in turn allow them to articulate a philosophy and pedagogy they can actually use. Practice and theory must come together in teacher education classrooms in such a way that both preservice teachers and their teachers can reflect on the practice that informs their theory and the theory that informs their practice.

Looking Ahead: Adjustments and Adaptations

Leah: This is a project I envision repeating, possibly even from the college side of the fence at some point. The changes I'd make to the high school part of the equation are small but would be likely to have a positive outcome for all parties involved. Before the project got underway, I would set up a mailing schedule with Nancy so that she would know when to expect drafts and I'd know when I could plan on getting them back. A set schedule would make semester planning easier for both instructors and would testify to students about the importance of this project. It would be clear to my students that responses from an authentic audience are a priority, not an afterthought.

If we again rely on the U.S. Postal Service, another change I'd make would be to have my students send two copies of each paper. Printing out two copies of their papers would be a minor inconvenience for my students, but doing so would allow the preservice teachers to practice their feedback on copies that Nancy alone would see and respond to. Her students could then make revised comments (based on Nancy's feedback) on the second copy to be mailed back.

One final change I would make would be to have my students provide feedback to the college students. Possible methods for communicating their responses could include live distance learning conferences, videotaped focus groups, my notes on our class and one-on-one discussions, individual or group letters, or surveys. One dynamic of teaching that Nancy's students missed in this setting was observing and responding firsthand to the range of reactions students have to teachers' comments. As we conducted it this first time, our collaboration prevented them from witnessing the strange mixture of disappointment, satisfaction, frustration, giddiness, and even anger or triumph that can fill a classroom on the day students' papers are returned.

Nancy: I agree with Leah's suggestions for changes, particularly with providing two copies, one for my preservice teachers to practice on and one to be mailed back. Another way we might accomplish the same ends is to provide end comments only, on a separate sheet of paper, as we were beginning to do at the end of the semester. Sticky notes, a choice my students really liked, is another alternative. I also think it would be of great benefit to have Leah's students provide feedback to my preservice teachers; in fact, my preservice teachers asked for some feedback from students which, unfortunately, we did not have time to provide. Leah's suggestions regarding methods to accomplish this are all excellent.

I also think we could do more to take advantage of current technology, particularly the Web. In the short time since this project took place, a number of significant advances in technology have been made that would allow quicker and easier communication between a university and a high school while maintaining the privacy of participants at both institutions. Software such as WebBoard, WebCT, and Blackboard are available at minimal cost or in some cases free of charge. Certain universities, such as Michigan State, have inhouse software that provides similar connections.

Leah: I agree; several technological improvements could make an electronic paper exchange more feasible than it was for us in 1999, although limited computer access at many elementary and secondary schools could make snail mail the most practical means for those populations for some time. Relying on an electronic exchange at least once during the semester, however, would provide a valuable occasion for preservice teachers to discuss the contrasting features and merits of handwritten versus computerized feedback from instructors.

One obvious adaptation of our method would be to substitute groups for the cross-age response. Undergraduate preservice teachers could instead provide feedback to elementary or middle school students. Graduate students in composition theory courses could provide responses to any of the aforementioned groups as well as to undergraduate students in basic writing courses. Middle or high school students could even participate in a modified version of our project by responding to elementary students' writing. In this case, the younger students could benefit from writing for an authentic audience and from identifying positive academic role models. The older students could benefit by improving their ability to analyze writing (others *and* their own); by realizing their own abilities as readers, writers, and responders; by learning how to make compliments and suggestions in a way that could be transferred to peer feedback groups; and by assuming the responsibilities of acting as academic role models for the younger students.

Beware the Jabberwock!

Leah: For secondary school teachers, getting advance permission from administrators and parents and informing them about intended procedures should alleviate worries about cost, time, and curricular appropriateness. I highly recommend ensuring privacy for students by using first names only.

Secondary teachers should also be prepared to handle comments from preservice teachers that conflict with their own suggestions. Differing opinions aren't necessarily a problem. They do, of course, highlight the subjectivity involved in evaluating students' writing, but most students are already aware of this aspect of teacher response. The teacher can capitalize on such opportunities to push the writer's ultimate responsibility for and ownership of his or her writing and also to demonstrate opposing readings of a single text.

Nancy: Preservice teachers need a great deal of preparation for this type of response. Even the best of writers don't always have that metacognitive sense of what it is they do when they write. It would be most useful to include several sessions in which they look at each other's papers as a group and talk about what they see, the strengths and the weaknesses of the draft, and the kinds of suggestions they might make. They also need opportunities to practice responding to student papers, first in whole-group settings where we can shape ways of responding and then in smaller groups. They need to follow this with reflections on their ways of responding and their concerns.

Guard against both the minimalist respondent and the teacher-as-rewriter. Neither is helpful to the student writer, and neither seems to realize that he or she is not doing what needs to be done. The minimalists are not too difficult to deal with—encourage them to get specific about strengths and weaknesses of the writing. As they gain confidence, longer and more substantive responses will be forthcoming. Rewriters are a more difficult challenge. Just knowing that this behavior exists is useful to the teacher educator. The behavior is born of a genuine concern for the student's writing development and a real wish to be of service to that student. It's important to discuss this ahead of time with the class as a whole and then give them practice time, both orally and in writing, to try out their best comments and suggestions.

And So?

Our complementary desires to provide authentic learning experiences for our respective students led us to this joint adventure. And despite some of the challenges we faced, it truly was a positive adventure. All of us, teachers and students alike, came to a new appreciation of teachers, of students, and of the process of learning. Our students learned things that neither of us could have taught them without the cooperation of the other teacher and the other group of students. In addition, we each reinforced some of our own existing knowledge and learned some new things that would not have been possible outside of this collaboration. For us, the most important insight may have been the realization that our goals are not just about changing behaviors, but also about opening minds—including our own—to new approaches and new ways of thinking. While this takes time, energy, and commitment, both from us and from those with whom we work, it is a worthwhile goal, one that we believe will enrich our practice.

Note

1. By authentic texts, I'm referring to actual literature—novels, short stories, biographies, even newspapers and magazines—as opposed to limited anthologies or basal readers with controlled vocabularies. In terms of writing, authentic work would be writing for real purposes to real audiences.

Work Cited

Van Antwerp, Jill. "Providing Audiences during the Writing Process." Workshop presentation. MSU/MCTE Spring Conference on the English Language Arts. Michigan State University, East Lansing. 20 Mar. 1999.

5 High School Students Meet "College Standards"

Thomas C. Thompson
The Citadel

Betsy Wilson
Wando High School

Students in Education 101

Tom teaches first-year students at The Citadel; Betsy teaches seniors at Wando High School, where her course load also includes one Teacher Cadet class each semester. Betsy asked Tom to "teach" one of the assignments in her Teacher Cadet class one year, and they have continued the project ever since.

S outh Carolina's Teacher Cadet program, designed to attract students into the field of education and give them a taste of a career in teaching, offers students the chance to earn three hours of college credit in Education 101, Introduction to Education. Assignments in the course include creating a children's book, writing and performing a play for elementary school students, working as a teacher's aide, creating a hypothetical day-care center, and writing a research-based essay on a topic in education—the project described here. Students also keep a journal about the various class activities.

The project described here began when Betsy asked Tom to teach the research-based assignment (the "position paper") and grade the final drafts. Part of her motivation was simply to have an English teacher handle the lesson (since she teaches business and accounting, not English); her other agenda was to have a college professor discuss and apply college standards, since students would be getting college credit. Both teachers enjoyed the collaboration—especially the after-class talks in which Betsy told Tom what really went on in high school and Tom told Betsy what her students were likely to encounter in college—so the project has continued for several years.

Following are excerpts from student journals, as well as from Tom's and Betsy's journals, which offer several views of this project as it unfolded one spring semester.

Jan. 4—Handing Out the Assignment

Betsy: My Teacher Cadets got their assignment from Tom today. They seemed to have that look in their eyes: "another paper." Still, they all took notes as Tom drew pictures on the board and showed examples on the overhead. They paid attention as he spoke and frequently stopped him to ask questions. Some were anxious and some were dismayed. They were apprehensive about having a college professor grade their essays; most said they didn't know if their work would stand up to "college standards."

Tom: I was a little surprised that the students were so unaccustomed to being given a scoring guide at the beginning of an assignment. The idea of using the guide to self-score their drafts before turning them in seemed foreign to them. Maybe when I respond to the initial drafts they'll catch on and use the guides when they revise.

Nathan: Today was the second day of class and we already had a guest speaker. He gave us some handouts about the requirements for the assignment, then explained that we will have to write a paper on one of the thirty or so topics he handed out. That means finding out about a topic and researching it. I was in a state of shock, not realizing that I had to write another paper. I thought I'd finished that last semester with English, but this is going to be even harder.[1] Dr. Thompson explained that college is different from high school in many ways—especially the "five-paragraph theme." In college, he said, most papers are longer and fit the format to the information. I think this paper might be easier because I won't have to cram all of my information into five paragraphs.

Crystal: Dr. Thompson came to our Teacher Cadet class today. He told us about the position paper and its requirements. Beforehand, we had heard terrible things about it from the first semester students. When Dr. Thompson started to talk about the paper it didn't seem too bad because we get to choose a topic that interests us. As he started to list the requirements, however, I realized that there would be a tremendous amount of work involved.

Janaé: I'm a little nervous. I've heard that this paper is tedious and the professor is critical. In high school, my writing usually receives praise, but I am unsure of how my work stands up to college standards. I hope to do really well on it, but more importantly, I hope to learn a lot in the process.

Collin: Dr. Thompson told us to choose an educational topic and write a three- to five-page position paper on it. Although I believe this assignment will improve my high school writing skills, I'm a little hesitant about having a college professor criticize my work.

Kirsten: I have heard that this assignment is very hard. There will be a lot of work and some late nights. Then again, I think every college student faces that workload from time to time.

Graham: I haven't heard a thing about this paper from anyone. If I take my time and put forth a good amount of effort, I will do all right. If I get some criticism on my paper, I would be willing to share it with the class.

Whitney: I thought that class today was productive. Dr. Thompson was very informative about the position paper. I felt a little intimidated by his speech about the pass/fail rate, but all in all I feel pretty good about the assignment. This is the first time I've ever had an English teacher actually tell me exactly what they wanted to see in my writing. The specific examples were really helpful. The handouts will also serve as a good guideline when I write my paper.

Kristen: At this point, I do not think I am as confident as I should be about my writing. I do not feel fully prepared to write for a professor yet. Still, I think the fear of having a paper graded by a college professor and read by fellow students will make me want to write "the best of my best."

Jan. 31—Students Turn in Their Rough Drafts

Betsy: Today the students brought their rough drafts to class. They evaluated them all, selecting the top three to send to Tom for detailed feedback. As much as they didn't want to do this paper, they all wanted their drafts to be picked for feedback. They all had their own comments about each other's papers, but they all had the same comment at the end: "Why did so-and-so's paper get picked when mine was much better? She or he didn't work as hard as I did; this is not fair! Her paper got picked because they like her more!" I felt like I was in elementary school instead of high school, but it was nice to see the students take some pride in their work. They were supposed to pick three papers, but ended up selecting four instead.

Nathan: I was nervous, wondering what other people would think of my writing. As a class, though, we agreed that having a draft selected or not was not a reflection of the person but only of their writing.

Crystal: Reading my classmates' drafts was pretty interesting. I liked the fact that peers were evaluating them, but I admit that, after reading about three papers, I started to lose interest.

Collin: Mrs. Wilson divided the class into groups of three and gave each group three papers. As each group finished reading a set, we talked about the content, format, and such; this helped us decide which papers were the best. Every person in the class read everyone else's work. I think reading everyone's paper is a good idea to use in other classes, too, because we were able to see different writing styles.

Whitney: In my opinion the three papers selected were not the best. I think that each group of people had completely different ideas of what a "good" paper is.

Colby: When we read all the papers and picked three, I felt that the people who got picked had a huge advantage over the other students. I know we're supposed to learn from their mistakes, but it's not the same as getting your paper graded by the person who will be grading the final draft.

Kristen: We gathered in groups of three to read each other's papers. I think this was a good way of finding out others' opinions about each paper; we could learn what needed work and what was good.

February 5

Tom: I've finally finished responding to the first set of drafts. They were supposed to give me the best three, but Betsy said that two papers tied for third and the class couldn't break the tie, so they gave me both papers. It's just as well, though, because each paper let me talk about a different issue. I wrote comments on each paper and then used the scoring guide to grade it as if it were a final draft. As typically happens with these drafts, most students had failed to meet one or more of the "C" criteria—especially the requirement that they cite their sources using MLA format—so the grades were low: the highest was a C-. I hope the low grades get their attention, but I also hope that my comments help guide their revision strategies.

Although in previous semesters I commented on everybody's paper, Betsy and I thought that the students were leaning on me too much to do their work for them, so we decided that I would respond to only the top three papers. I would write extensive comments, discuss them in class, and leave copies for everyone to use as guides to help revise their own papers. That way, we hoped, students would pick up some principles rather than simply try to "fix" their own errors. We also decided that I would give "shadow" grades—as if the papers were final drafts—to help students apply the scoring guide accurately.

Nathan's draft showed that he had done his homework—he cited appropriate research, even including an interview with his mother about the effects of medication on his ADD brother—but his writing style was dull and he didn't use his evidence well. The opening paragraph included a couple of "there are" constructions (where action verbs would have been easy to use and much more interesting to read) and several more "to be" verbs. Subsequent paragraphs weren't much better, with boring verbs and convoluted constructions that made me reread several sentences. His argument—that people who discount ADD as nothing more than typical adolescent behavior are wrong, because ADD responds to appropriate treatment—turned into a strident declaration that "the notion that the disorder does not exist is outrageous because it does and has been proven." I tried to let my comments show the class specific ways in which weak expression could damage an otherwise reasonable argument.

Crystal wrote a defense for allowing HIV-positive children in the classroom. I thought it was weak stylistically, but in this case the argument was equally weak. I think I found five sound sentences—one early, two in the middle, and two more near the end—that could have served as the foundation for a good argument, but those sentences showed no relation to each other, so I couldn't see them as constituting an argument. Several of the claims (such as "AIDS fears people" rather than "people fear AIDS") made me wonder whether the root problem was the writing or a simple lack of understanding of the issues. I tried to use my comments to discuss ways to construct a coherent argument.

Janaé wrote a classic five-paragraph theme defending school uniforms. It had all the problems inherent in the effort to force the material into such a format: the tripartite thesis included three elements unrelated to each other, there were no logical transitions between paragraphs (except the word *next*), and the content suggested that she had simply gone to three sources and dumped something from each source into the paper. On this draft, I discussed fitting the form to the material rather than forcing the material into a predetermined form.

Finally, Collin's piece—an argument for mainstreaming—had the least "wrong" with it, but the argument lacked explanation and illustration. I tried to identify specific places that needed explication and then talked about the importance of including adequate and appropriate examples.

As a group, these drafts let me make some observations that I hope will be useful to other members of the class. I wrote far more on each paper than I normally would have since I was trying to identify lots of specific examples of writing problems and to offer specific suggestions for addressing those problems—though I suspect I wrote too much. My individual comments were longer than usual since I wrote them to the class as a whole rather than to the individual writers. I guess I'll find out soon enough the degree to which my comments helped.

Feb. 6—Tom Returns Sample First Drafts

Tom: Today I returned the papers. With overhead transparencies of two complete drafts and excerpts of the other two, I tried to point to a variety of examples of "strong" and "weak" writing: specific and vague thesis statements and supporting claims, credible and flimsy evidence, clear and muddy writing, engaging and dull style. Nathan quietly accepted what I said about his paper, Crystal wanted to argue about my comments on hers, Janaé seemed to have trouble accepting my comments about the five-paragraph format, and Collin was absent. After class, I left copies of all four drafts so everyone in the class could read them more closely if they wanted to.

Just as I suspect I wrote too much, I think I talked too much about minor issues. I spent so much time talking about stylistic issues in Nathan's and Crystal's drafts that by the time we got to Janaé's five-paragraph theme, we were almost out of time. We did, however, do some good work in the time we had left: we went round and round about the five-paragraph theme format, with the students arguing that since all three points focused on benefits of school uniforms, they all "fit" in the paper. I responded by identifying what I thought to be Janaé's "real" thesis—that uniforms "help schools assert their authority" (rather than the thesis that "school uniforms are a good idea because they reduce violence, create a better learning environment and save money"). I then tried to show that "saving money" has nothing to do with "asserting authority" and that it certainly bears no relationship to reducing violence or creating a better learning environment. Did I get through to anyone? I'm not sure; maybe I'll find out when I read the final drafts.

Nathan: We received our graded drafts today. I wasn't afraid of my paper being mutilated because everyone in the class had already seen what it was about. I got a D+, which satisfies me for now. I have plenty to improve on. I made some stupid mistakes, but that's why I'm doing this paper.

Crystal: To be honest, I really put little effort into this paper. I was already discouraged by the fact that just about every paper in the past had failed, so I decided I shouldn't bother putting a lot of effort into a paper that was going to fail anyway. I wrote it, typed it, and edited it all in one night.

Janaé: Today, I went through a roller coaster of emotions. I was content, because I knew that along with the pitiful papers Dr. Thompson would bring his sense of humor. I was also a little tense, though, because one of those pitiful papers was mine. I was a little puzzled and frustrated by my experience: only months earlier my writing was winning praise; now a college professor is saying that the writing isn't quite "there" yet, that it is "lacking something."

Though Dr. Thompson was dissatisfied with the quality of the papers, he was very open and helpful. He answered all my questions and gave me helpful hints to improve this paper and papers to come. My format of the actual paper is pretty good, but I need to develop my ideas more and rid myself of the five-paragraph format. Though the assignment is a little tedious, I really like having my work evaluated by a college professor so I know where I stand regarding college English standards.

Kirsten: I almost cried for the students whose papers were already graded; I am scared about what grade my paper will get. I know I made the same mistakes as the other students. The way Dr. Thompson corrected the other papers has given me an idea about what college classes are really going to be like.

Whitney: I think today's lesson was beneficial for many reasons. I was able to get a feel for the way Dr. Thompson grades, and I understand now what he wants and doesn't want in our papers. The one thing I disagree with is that he graded only four rough drafts. Those four people have an advantage over the rest of us. My paper was not chosen as one of the top four, so I have no clue what Dr. Thompson thinks about it. I'm a little nervous about turning in my final draft, but I'm eager to hear what he thinks about it.

Jennifer: At this point, I'm glad that my paper didn't get chosen to be picked apart. Seeing the papers he graded shows me that I cannot get away with some things in college that are overlooked in high school.

Colby: I'll be glad when this assignment is over. It's a lot to handle with everything else going on, but I know it will be the same way when I go to college.

February 7

Betsy: All eyes were on Tom yesterday when he arrived. The students were attentive and took even more notes than the first time he visited. They didn't seem to mind that they got low grades and that everyone read the comments on their papers. They were disappointed with their performance, and it showed on their faces. They were very quiet when Tom left. I made extra copies of each graded paper and asked if anyone wanted to take an example home to look over. No one accepted the offer. Today after class, however, one student asked if she could take one of each paper home. Within minutes, seven of the ten students requested copies for themselves.

Feb. 21—Students Turn in Their Final Drafts

Nathan: What a relief! Now I can rest easy until the grade comes back. It was a lot of work, but I learned a lot about attention deficit disorder that I didn't know before.

Crystal: I am so glad this assignment is over. Still, I appreciate the experience. It will help me when I get into college.

Janaé: Well, the long-awaited day is here—I turn in my final draft. I revised it three times. I am a little nervous, but I know I tried my hardest.

Collin: Actually, the assignment wasn't as stressful as I thought it would be—probably because I didn't put as much effort into it as I should have. The night before it was due, I was contemplating whether to change anything in it.

Whitney: I am very nervous about getting my paper back. I honestly didn't change much since my rough draft because I was upset about the whole rough draft process. Maybe my paper wasn't one of the best, but I still think Dr. Thompson should have looked it over.

Colby: I'm so glad that this paper is over! The main problem I had was I would put it off, then I would worry about getting it done. I was looking up information on the Internet the night before the final draft was to be turned in. Doing this paper shows me how writing a paper in college is so different from writing one in high school!

Kristen: Turning in the final draft was not stressful for me at all. I made a few corrections in my rough draft, proofread, and allowed others to proofread, too.

February 28

Tom: Only nine of the ten students actually turned in drafts:

- Nathan still stomped his foot in his piece about ADD ("This disorder is there"), but his writing cleared up considerably. This time he followed up his claims with explanations and evidence, and he used his various sources well.

- Crystal showed a little improvement, but I still had trouble following her argument; in fact, I think her claim that "[t]he best way to stop the spread of [HIV] has to be through education" could have been a pillar of her argument, but she buried it near the end of the paper. With another draft or two, she might have a good paper.

- Janaé, the only student who actually contacted me for extra help with her paper, really seemed to take my comments to heart. Her point about school uniforms being a good idea because they save money disappeared; instead, she argued that "uniforms should be required [because they] would lead to less violence and ultimately a better learning environment." She made several claims in support of her position and she acknowledged some opposing viewpoints (though she forgot to answer the opposition). Contrasting her first draft with her final draft should offer a good example of how to revise a paper.

- Collin's final draft was actually worse than the first one. When she tried to use her sources to add substance to her position, she used them poorly, she failed to refute opposing views, and I thought her argument just fell apart. It was obvious that she missed my earlier talk—she was the only one to get the format of the first page wrong.

- Kirsten failed to take a stand. She seemed to want to argue that alternative schools are a good idea and deserve support, but all she did was list and describe various kinds of alternative schools.

- Graham didn't turn in a paper.

- Whitney probably would have done much better if I had commented on her first draft: she had some good arguments in her defense of block scheduling, but she didn't organize the material well and she relied way too much on one of her sources. I wish I had been able to use her paper as a model when I discussed the early drafts.

- Colby's discussion of Title IX failed to stake out a position and failed to use MLA format. Like Whitney's, this draft would have been a good model to show how a couple of easy-to-correct problems can have a major effect on the grade.

- Kristen fell into the trap of using too many Web sources—and using them poorly—in her case against school prayer. I printed one of the sources and highlighted the various portions she had used to show where she had made mistakes and how to avoid such problems.

- Jennifer did a good job arguing that we should educate homeless children; her paper demonstrated how to set up an argument and how to use a variety of sources.

Betsy: Senioritis must have been rampant. When the students turned in their papers, only four of them had actually done any revision—the four whose papers Tom had marked. When I asked why they hadn't revised, they really had no answer; they were just glad the assignment was over. Last semester's students didn't have that problem; they seemed more focused and put more effort into their papers. I guess that by spring they've already been accepted to college so they aren't as concerned about their performance. The four-by-four schedule may have contributed, too: I asked if they had given up in their English class, too, and they said that they weren't taking English this semester because they had all taken it in the fall. I think Nathan's attitude ("I thought I was finished last semester with English") was typical.

Mar. 7—Returning the Graded Drafts

Nathan: When I got my paper and saw all the comments Dr. Thompson had written, I thought, "Oh no, what's going on here?" Then I looked at the grade sheet and saw I had gotten a "B." I read through the comments and noticed that they weren't all bad. The assignment was stressful and time consuming, but it was all worth it to have an idea of what professors would look for in college writing.

Crystal: Getting my grade was not a big shock. I know you only get out of it what you put in. This was a learning experience for me.

Collin: When I got my grade back, I was pretty upset. I admit that I didn't spend a whole lot of time on this assignment, but I never imagined that my grade would drop by adding more to the paper. I would have been better off turning in my rough draft as my final draft than making changes to it. I think this assignment is a waste of class time; no one took it very seriously.

Kirsten: When I actually got the paper back it was a load of worries. What if I can't write at a college level? I know I didn't try to the best of my ability on this paper—I will admit that. I am glad in the end that we did this assignment.

Whitney: I could have played "name that grade" and won. Everyone got the grade they deserved. Overall I am just glad to have the whole assignment in my past. I have learned a lot from this assignment and I know I will be able to use this information in college.

Colby: Doing the paper was a great experience, and I will save the paper when I go to college and use it as a reference. I'm sure that when I write a paper, I will make the same mistakes then as I just did, and now I know how to correct most of them.

Kristen: I was sure Dr. Thompson would find mistakes in my paper, and he did. It did not bother me though. I was relaxed, like the rest of the class, and actually pleased with the work I had done. I am glad I got the opportunity to research a subject I was interested in.

Jennifer: I am glad we had this assignment. I can't say it was fun, but it helps to see how my works stands on a college level. I know now a lot of things that need to be improved in my writing. I can begin to fix them now instead of after I get my first college paper back.

Betsy: Surprisingly, the students all seemed to agree with their grades. In past years, they have wanted to argue for higher scores, but this time they were more accepting of what they got. Maybe they knew that, since they put out less than their best effort, they should expect less than great grades. Or maybe I simply set up the assignment better, telling them in advance about the process and checking up regularly on their progress. A couple of them even said that they planned to take their papers with them to college. In fact, one said that she would take *all four* papers—

the drafts with comments—to college. I think they realize that college-level writing will be significantly different from what they've been used to in high school.

Betsy and Tom Discuss the Project

Betsy: Despite the students' complaints about not having every rough draft commented on, my favorite part of the project is having the students read each other's drafts. Unless they knew they had to select the top few, they wouldn't actually read each other's papers closely. Part of my goal, of course, is to get them to discuss the various topics they write about (in addition to working on the writing itself), and when they read the entire set of papers, I hear comments such as "Is that really true?" "Where did you get that information?" and "Wow!" from around the room. They're actually interested in the educational topics—and my experience has been that it's hard to get high school seniors genuinely interested in much of anything beyond their own worlds. Best of all, I don't have to do a thing—I just sit back and let them read and talk.

Tom: That's good to hear. The reality is that I *could* have responded to all the early drafts—as, in fact, I did the first few times we collaborated on this project—but I didn't want the students to focus on specific comments (in an effort to "fix" their papers) as much as I wanted to illustrate some general principles about what "counts" for research, or how to take the reader's knowledge and experience into account. I guess our plan didn't work as well as we had hoped in terms of teaching them about writing, but it seems to have worked unexpectedly well in terms of getting them to talk about the course content.

Betsy: Definitely. And I wouldn't say that the writing principles were completely lost on them either. As they read each other's papers, they asked questions when they didn't understand something—they served as real audiences. And they got pretty good at teaching each other how to cite sources, too. Further, they paid attention during the initial presentation about the writing; they took thorough notes and seemed really interested in absorbing everything you said.

Tom: One aspect I don't get to see is the long-term effects. You've mentioned occasionally that students have visited you after their first year of college and talked about the assignment.

Betsy: The very first time we did this project one of the students was so upset by her grade that we had to have a parent-teacher conference with the guidance counselor present. The student and parent both complained that since the students weren't in college yet, they shouldn't be graded based on college standards. The conference ended quickly, for once the guidance counselor learned that the students were getting college credit, she agreed that it was completely appropriate to use college standards; but the parent still disagreed, telling me that the situation just wasn't fair. The next year, however, that student came back and actually *thanked* me for letting her go through the experience of having a college professor grade her paper. She said it had helped her do better on her initial college paper—that she got one of the highest grades in her class, and she attributed her success to the preparation (or the reality check) she got in Teacher Cadet.

Then there was another student who visited me earlier this semester. When I asked him whether the assignment in Teacher Cadet had helped him at college, he said yes, that it had helped him be more prepared, to know what to expect. That's pretty typical of what I hear from students who come back—that even though they didn't like the assignment at the time, they're glad they did it.

Tom: I'm glad they eventually decide it's a useful exercise. Even though you originally asked me to give them a "wake up call" with respect to college standards for their writing, I hope they take more from the experience than the realization that college professors might actually check their sources or that grammar and mechanics really do count. I also hope they don't equate the standards we set for this assignment—or the comments I wrote on any particular paper—with a universal standard for all college writing. If they do, they're likely to think that my point was that style is more important that substance (since the first issue I addressed in Nathan's paper was style) or that all college professors despise the five-paragraph theme (since I spent so much time talking with Janaé about moving beyond that format), even though I tried to talk about learning the conventions of the genre and the discipline, and for this particular assignment I tried to stress the importance of building a coherent argument based on claims supported by evidence. Some of their journal comments suggest they were so overwhelmed that they simply didn't put much effort into the project—but then again, maybe they just used the "I didn't really try" excuse to save face in anticipation of or after getting low grades. At least they seemed genuinely engaged when we talked about effective writing, and the discussion forced me to be specific about what I value in student writing. I also enjoy seeing what high school seniors are really capable of producing—despite their claims about not trying—so I have a better feel for what's going on the year before they show up in my classes.

Note

1. Wando High School uses block scheduling for most classes, so rather than taking eight forty-five-minute classes over the course of a school year, students take four ninety-minute classes each semester. Since Nathan took his English class in the fall semester, he had no English classes for the spring semester when he took Teacher Cadet.

III What *Is* "College Writing," Anyway?

Since the previous section raised the issue of "college writing," this section offers some cross-grade discussions on that topic. In Chapter 6, two high school teachers and two college professors discuss the challenges of preparing high school students for college writing when "college writing" means different things at different colleges. One possible solution they offer is to change the question from "How do we make high school writing prepare students for college writing?" to "What does literacy look like, and how can we develop a curriculum that fosters lifelong literacy?"

Chapter 7 also offers voices from both sides of the divide, this time from five teachers at different grade levels. Acknowledging that "those involved in teaching writing [agree] little on how writing should be taught," but also agreeing that "discussion between the various factions of the writing instruction community needs now more than ever to begin" (p. 95), these teachers and their colleagues formed an alliance from a variety of constituencies with the goal of beginning that discussion.

Together, these chapters offer both a model for generating cross-grade discussions at the state level and some ideas with which to begin those discussions.

6 What We Talk about When We Talk about College Writing

Herb Budden
Hamilton Southeastern High School

Mary B. Nicolini
Penn High School

Stephen L. Fox
Indiana University–Purdue University Indianapolis

Stuart Greene
University of Notre Dame

Herb and Mary teach high school; Steve and Stuart teach college. They talk about writing—and they write—with their students; they also talk—and write—with each other. Through those conversations, they begin to understand what kind of writing they expect of their students in high school, in college, and beyond.

Stuart was talking. Stuart Greene is a writing program director, and sometimes that gives him the right. The four of us were sitting around the breakfast table drinking coffee. Sunlight filled the restaurant from the big window behind the cash register. Mary was there with Stuart and his former colleague at Madison, Stephen Fox—Steve, we call him—and one of Stuart's former students, Emily Tymus. We were in Milwaukee at the 2000 NCTE Annual Convention, except Herb, who couldn't come. But we were all from somewhere else: Stuart, Notre Dame; Steve, IUPUI; Emily, Nicolet High School in Glendale, Wisconsin; and Mary, Penn High School in Mishawaka, Indiana. The absent Herb is from Hamilton Southeastern High School, in Fishers, Indiana.

There was a coffee pot on the table. The coffee and cream kept going around, and we somehow got onto the subject of writing.

Emily said that the people with whom she used to teach focus on the five-paragraph essay.

"My God, don't be silly. That's not writing, and you know it," said Steve. . . .

Only ten weeks separate a twelfth grader from a "thirteenth" grader. These two and a half months are metamorphic ones, but, essentially, the eighteen-year-old who graduated from high school in June is the same young adult navigating the maze of first-year college orientation in August. Are the strategies required for successful instruction in writing that much different in senior English and first-year composition?

It depends on whom you ask.

What separates first-year college composition faculty from high school senior English teachers? Is it mostly a gap in communication and perception? Again, it depends on whom you ask.

If you ask the authors of this essay—high school and college writing teachers who have worked closely together—we will answer, "Yes and no. All of the above." Because we believe that literacy, and thus literacy instruction, is local and individual, we do not insist that twelfth-grade English should look like first-year college composition. Because we believe that literacy is also social and socially constructed, and because we do care about the individual students in our courses, we have looked for ways to communicate, to change perceptions, and to bridge curricula.

The two of us who are high school teachers—Budden and Nicolini—work to help seniors develop habits of mind or dispositions about the writing process that they can adapt and transfer to college-level assignments. Rather than focus on artificial, vague writing tasks that are deemed pseudo first-year comp tasks, we focus on writing for authentic purposes and audiences, emphasizing the importance of style and voice. Our students' level of engagement in and responsibility for their work is more important than creating a false sense of collegiate "rigor." While our classes are challenging, with sophisticated writing tasks requiring critical thinking on the part of the writer, they do not conform to some abstract notion of what college writing is. Rather, through our collaborations with higher education faculty, the high school teachers have a firm sense of how best to prepare students for college-level writing.

Unfortunately, our methods are not always embraced by others in the schools. In fact, quite the opposite is true; we are often looked upon as *not* preparing students for "the rigor of college writing." We hope this essay dispels some of the myths surrounding the notion of what it means to prepare student writers in a college prep course.

The two of us who are university professors—Fox and Greene—recognize the messy process of composing with adolescents and understand the vast differences between the cultures of the secondary school and the university. Both of us have volunteered extensively in various public school settings, and we have worked, as have the high school teachers, with at-risk and reluctant writers as well as the eloquent and eager. Never have we implied that our jobs would be easier if high school teachers did their jobs better.

Unfortunately, ours is an opinion too seldom voiced. Too many college composition faculty berate secondary school teachers, blaming them for college students' inability to punctuate, to cite, to synthesize. We find such criticism misguided and unhelpful, though all of us writing this essay work to improve the teaching of writing in the schools as well as in college classrooms. Rather than criticize from the balcony, we want to focus on the power of collaboration between teachers at both levels and on the positive results that can occur.

Mary Nicolini

What is the purpose of twelfth-grade English? For some, dual credit options—whereby high school students earn both high school and college credit—are a good deal. The two-for-one approach appeals to economic-minded students and parents; it saves time and money—the grade students earn their last year of high school is the first on their college transcript. For the serious student, the rigor of this approach appeals; however, it also sends a subtle message that the "regular" high school curriculum is too trivial to bother with. Advanced placement (AP) courses are more of a crapshoot—students don't know if they have earned credit until after graduation—yet AP too offers the option of earning college credit while still in high school. The $72 test fee is a bargain compared to university tuition. But can thirty-six weeks of learning be captured in a three-hour exam? Is my main purpose as an AP teacher to prepare students for the AP test?

Teaching senior English is about more than that. What I try to do in my twelfth-grade classroom is get my students to think about ideas—to generate original theses about topics of interest that they will defend and support using specific details and concrete examples. I want them to grapple with essential questions such as "How shall we live?" and "What does it mean to live well?" These issues have interested other writers and thinkers, from Socrates and Thoreau to Annie Dillard and Scott Russell Sanders. Focusing on these questions will serve my students better than analyzing the rhetorical structure of a passage of eighteenth-century fiction.

What I try to do in my public school classroom is the same thing I emphasize in the college courses I have taught: I want my students to think about ideas, to generate original theses about topics of interest that they will defend and support with specific details and concrete examples. At Indiana University–Purdue University Indianapolis (IUPUI), my clients were returning adult students in a noncredit basic composition course; at the University of Notre Dame, my students had essentially "flunked in" to first-year composition—their scores on their AP English tests were not high enough to test out. (Even graduating as valedictorian and being accepted to a prestigious institution such as Notre Dame pales when compared to getting a 4 or 5 on the AP English test.) Each group has attitudes and concerns unique to their status.

A phenomenon unique to—verily, endemic of—education is the "get 'em ready" syndrome. Preschool teachers feel compelled to "get 'em ready" for kindergarten; primary teachers for upper elementary; fifth-grade teachers for middle school; middle school teachers for high school; and high school teachers for college. Rarely do we take the luxury to Be Here Now: rather than getting 'em ready, we need to let 'em be.

Even if I saw my primary responsibility as a high school teacher to be to "get 'em ready" for college, I don't know exactly how I could do this. How do I get Jim ready for Stanford while getting Maria ready for MIT and Agnes ready for Ball State and Vince ready for Purdue? My students go on to be engineers, pharmacists, doctors, and architects— how can I best anticipate the requirements they will be asked to meet in their college careers and beyond?

Further, the range of first-year composition programs varies greatly from school to school; I can't purport to have the magic plan to get 'em ready for all of them. The best way to meet students' diverse needs is to have them think about ideas and generate original theses about topics of interest that they then defend and support with specific details and concrete examples—skills that will be essential no matter where they attend college.

My focus on portfolios dovetails with the goals of composition at Miami of Ohio, but, as Brian was told on his first day of first-year composition at a large state university, "Mary Nicolini and I have very different views on the teaching of writing." Brian's new teacher was right; we do have very different views on the teaching of composition. I value voice and style in writing, and she rewards low-level recapitulation of facts. I know that in doing so she feels she is more "rigorous" than I, who allow my students to write in the first-person singular. My interest in and attention to the personal essay cause some of my high school colleagues also to question my rigor; according to them, narrative is kids' stuff, just telling stories. Yet I agree with Sanders, who writes:

> I began asking my students to write in the first-person singular.
> Instead of "One might deduce from the foregoing examples," I
> would suggest: How about "I think"? Instead of "The white whale
> inspires dread in the reader," try "The white whale scares me."
> . . . [S]ome students balked at this advice, and some still do. . . .
> After receiving A's for fancy phrases, they don't like receiving
> C's because I find the phrases empty. ("Who Speaks" 114–15)

(Nine years earlier, in his *Secrets of the Universe,* Sanders wrote of writing instruction that prohibited the use of "I": "even in emergencies we could not speak in the first person singular" [193].)

"Rigor" is another area in which twelfth-grade teachers do a disservice to the college-bound senior. "I must get them reading for the rigor of college writing!" is their rallying cry, yet I wonder how they define this word. Too often it is a false rigor: doing more faster, not necessarily in more depth. Assignments and audiences are artificial. (Interesting that we frequently use the word *rigor* as a good thing for which to strive, when in fact its true denotation is "harshness," "severity," "inflexibility"—not the stuff I place at the center of my classroom.)

Curiously, many adjuncts and associate faculty members with whom I teach have never taken first-year composition themselves. Through AP coursework or other options, they tested out of the course at the start of their postsecondary career, yet four or five years later, as they work on their graduate degrees, they find themselves slaving in the adjunct ghetto. What model do they draw from to structure their teaching? While many colleges offer workshops and require course work to prepare adjuncts, often these teachers draw from their memories of their higher-level writing classes or their own high school experiences. The paradox of someone who tested out of first-year composition teaching a room full of students who flunked into the course is subtle, yet significant.

Occasionally, the sophomore or junior who wasn't required to take first-year composition actually regrets the omission; the benefits of what then seemed a great financial boon are lost while embroiled in higher-level course work. What happened to the "extra" three hours they gained by testing out? It's kind of like setting your clocks back for daylight savings time; that hour gets absorbed in the day-to-day minutiae of living.

The culture of first-year composition is one of shared experience; testing out robs matriculating first-year students of this opportunity. Most first-year composition programs work hard to expose students to writing strategies that will serve them regardless of their degree program. While I have been accosted by the philosophy professor and the political science professor who complained that I didn't get their students ready in first-year composition to write about the ideology specific to their subject, many of my students are able to apply the techniques across curriculum and content area.

In both my experiences teaching first-year composition (to returning adult students in noncredit English at IUPUI and eighteen-year-olds at Notre Dame), neither writing program director implied that his job would be easier if I'd done my day job better. Alas, those two directors (one of them coauthor Stuart Greene) are more enlightened, perhaps, than many postsecondary instructors. When I attend state and national conferences on English language arts, it is not unusual for complete strangers to attack the rigor with which I conduct my classroom, remarking that my failure to prepare my students made their job harder. This is curious to me; does the college football coach blame the high school coach for the faults of his recruit?

So what do teachers of English language arts talk about when we talk about college writing? First, we don't talk enough about it, or at least we don't talk across levels enough. If high school teachers really want to prepare students for college (while at the same time meeting national, state, and local standards), they need to talk to college composition professors to find out what would be useful. For students, doing a specific writing assignment is less important than knowing how to make meaning with words. Often teachers declare that they must teach a certain genre because students will "need it in college." I disagree. Most important to me when teaching a genre or writing strategy is not *how* I should teach it but *why* I am teaching it. If the only reason I'm teaching a particular writing assignment is because students "need it for college," then it is a waste of instructional time.

"It would be helpful if they knew what a thesis was," college professor Ed Kline told me in 1995. I can prepare students for that.

Steve Fox

When we teach writing at any level, kindergarten through university, we can begin by asking, "What does literacy look like?" Our goal in a writing classroom (a classroom where people are writing, not necessarily an English class) is to foster lifelong literacy. As adults who have been using our literacy for decades, we can take inventory of the literacy acts we have engaged in, especially those that have been meaningful to us. Here is a quick list I drew up for myself:

- writing in my journal (high school, college, teaching in Hong Kong)

- writing poems in high school that were published in our literary magazine
- writing letters to my family when I was at camp, in college, and overseas
- writing my literacy autobiography
- writing an application essay for graduate school
- writing a letter to the editor of our local newspaper
- writing an open letter to fellow students in seminary (I posted the letter on a bulletin board)
- writing a story in second grade that the teacher put on the bulletin board
- writing e-mail messages on various e-mail lists, expressing my views on issues such as the use of part-time faculty or the first-year composition curriculum
- helping to write the first-year composition curriculum at IUPUI
- writing my dissertation
- writing sermons when I was pastor of a struggling inner-city church
- writing the abstract of my dissertation
- writing job application letters
- writing a letter to the school board on behalf of our children's option program
- writing my personal statement for promotion and tenure dossiers

Focusing on the writing dimension of literacy, compose such a list for yourself.

If we were in a room together and could compare our lists, we would find an incredible array of literacy acts. Adapted from the linguistic concept of speech acts, the term "literacy acts" suggests writing and reading that accomplish something in the world. Clearly, letters, reports, dissertations, memos, e-mail messages, curriculum guides, and so on can be seen as transactional writing, writing that allows us to take action in our world. What about poems, stories, or journal entries? Does such expressive or aesthetic writing qualify as a "literacy act"? Certainly when we write such texts with a view to affecting other people, I think they can be seen as means of acting in the world. If I write a text in order to move readers to tears or laughter or indignation, or to open their eyes and ears to the beauty of language and the beauty of life, then I am engaged in a literacy act.

So what about school-sponsored writing: taking notes, writing book reports, writing term papers, writing essay exams, writing for high-stakes tests? Doesn't such writing seek to accomplish something in the world—to earn grades, to please teachers, to gain admission to certain programs and universities, to inform others, to understand and apply knowledge? Yes—sometimes. If a student is fortunate, some of this school-sponsored writing will indeed enable learning, inform and move readers, and open doors to lifelong opportunities. But for many students, and for all students some of the time, school-sponsored writing frustrates learning, informs no one, earns reprimands and censure, reinforces undesirable self-images, and closes doors. And most discouraging of all, for many people school-sponsored writing does not foster lifelong literacy and probably deflects people from such literacy.

Thus, instead of asking how to make high school writing prepare students for college writing, let's ask what literacy looks like, and we will have a better chance of developing a writing curriculum that fosters lifelong literacy. By focusing on literacy, on engaged democratic citizenship, on what my coauthor Mary Nicolini calls "writing in the present tense," we as teachers need not serve anyone's agenda except that of our students as we anticipate their fully adult lives, not their short-term jumping through other people's hoops. Robert Yagelski, in his book *Literacy Matters*, argues that "an understanding of literacy as a local act of self-construction within discourse can illuminate our work with students as writers and readers and help us help them gain access to a literacy that enables them to claim agency for themselves in this complex and difficult world shaped by discourse" (188; see also 89–126 for a full discussion of this concept). Yagelski's thoughtful book draws on his work with high school and college students; he asks himself and those of us who, like him, teach literacy how we can make literacy matter in students' lives. His is no clichéd call for "relevance," but rather an attempt to integrate the personal and the social, subjectivity and contextuality—in short, never to lose sight of the local nature of all literacy.

High school teachers may ask, "All right, that sounds good, especially from your secure position in a university, where they expect you to theorize and pontificate for other academic scholars. But here on the front lines, we have to answer to many people, not just our fellow English teachers. Principals, superintendents, school boards, parents, legislators, the chamber of commerce—all expect us to produce certain results. They expect us to prepare our students to do well on state-required tests, to earn credit for composition courses by doing well on AP exams or college placement tests, and to do well in first-year composition in college. Before our students can move into lifelong adult literacy, they must jump over these many hurdles."

Valid points. College composition teachers face similar expectations of other professors, deans, boards of trustees, employers, and legislators. We don't have high-stakes tests hanging over our heads (unless we teach at universities with "rising junior" or other such exams), and we sometimes have more freedom in the classroom than high school teachers—but not as much as they might imagine. Many first-year composition instructors teach according to a common curriculum developed by a composition director with the input of other instructors; and usually that curriculum must take into account the perceived writing problems of students in other college courses and the expectations of professors in other disciplines. And some college composition teachers work closely with high school teachers and preservice teachers. We empathize with their situation and even work to change the situation.

What we all know, when it comes down to it, and when we have time to talk to alumni and to investigate literacy research, is that highly literate people learn how to adapt their literacy abilities and experiences to meet new situations, including high-stakes tests, college admissions requirements, college writing assignments, and so on. What college composition instructors wish to see in their students is this: a history of reading widely and well, of writing often and in many genres, and of analytical thinking that informs their reading and their writing. In short, we want students who are engaged with language and who eagerly use oral and print literacy to explore the world around and within them. Isn't that what high school English teachers wish to see in their students? Do any of us really care whether our students in twelfth grade or "thirteenth grade" can construct elaborate outlines with Roman numerals, or write five-paragraph "themes" that spit forth a thesis and three topic sentences like a slot machine, or compile dozens of note cards on a broad topic such as "censorship" or "the assassination of Abraham Lincoln" or "Hamlet as a classic tragedy" and transfer the information on those note cards to a ten-page research paper that neither the writer nor the reader will ever read again once the grade is recorded? We throw up our hands in despair over the abominable term papers and the excellent term papers; we fear both the failure and the success of such students—including the success of those who write the abominable papers and the failure of those who write the excellent term papers.

If high school teachers and their students want to know what kinds of writing are required in college, they can certainly find out. They can arrange a visit to a local campus, speak with composition faculty, and even visit a composition class. They can contact alumni of their high school who are attending various colleges and universities. They can search for writing program and writing course Web sites. Elsewhere in this chapter we talk about programs in Indiana that facilitate high school-university communication about English curricula. No matter what high school teachers and students learn from such research and contacts, it helps to remember that not all first-year composition courses are alike, not to mention the range of writing assignments across the disciplines at different universities. But let me offer some observations, based on the writing programs I've worked in.

What we emphasize most in those writing programs is analytical thinking. We ask students to use their own experience and knowledge, along with ideas drawn from books or readings in the course, to identify questions, issues, and problems. Assignments vary:

- Write a literary narrative about a significant experience in your life (sometimes the type of experience is specified, such as an experience with schooling or literacy, or an experience related to "work," broadly defined).

- Write a literacy autobiography.

- Write a thesis-based paper about a significant issue (the issue may emerge from the narrative or autobiographical writing or from class reading and discussion).

- Analyze one or two advertisements, showing how they try to influence readers.

- Interview a person about his or her work experience (or literacy experience, or views of writing in his or her discipline) and write a report based on that interview.

- Respond to a nonfiction trade book (books have included Richard Rodriguez's *Hunger of Memory,* Mike Rose's *Lives on the Boundary,* Juliet Schor's *The Overworked American,* Studs Terkel's *Working,* George Ritzer's *McDonaldization of Society,* and Jon Krakauer's *Into the Wild*).

In these assignments, students are not sent out to do unfocused, undirected "research." They are not asked to "choose" a thesis, write an outline, and flesh it out with information. They are asked to remember, to read, to talk, to explore, to brainstorm, to freewrite, to question. Out of this work, out of much writing, emerge questions and issues. A tentative thesis may emerge, or the students may write their way into a thesis by the end of a rough draft. As the students draft, respond, and revise, their ideas evolve, their focus often narrows, and their theses change, sometimes dramatically. We ask them to analyze, and to analyze is to question, to wonder, to empathize, and to understand.

Besides analytical thinking, two other important features of writing are emphasized: a flexible writing process that includes self-evaluation, and thoughtful, imaginative, appropriate use of language. In every course I teach, from basic writing to a senior seminar, I discuss the writing process with students. To make students aware that writing is a process, to remind other students of this, and to encourage students to incorporate new strategies in their writing process is always a valuable use of time. The temptation to write a "perfect first draft," usually a day or two before the deadline, bedevils all writers. Whatever writing teachers at any level can do to help students use a full range of writing strategies, from heuristics to drafting to revising to editing, will help those students more than any nifty set of formulas or patterns. If high school English teachers (and teachers in other disciplines) have students engage in frequent writing that spans the full range of writing processes, they will have gone far toward preparing those students for college writing and for lifetime writing.

The second feature we emphasize is thoughtful, imaginative, appropriate use of language. We know that the isolated teaching of grammar does not improve writing. We are pressured to do such teaching by people inside and outside the schools and colleges, including some of our own students. But I would encourage all of us to stand firm on this point. If anyone asks, "Do you teach grammar?" either answer with what you do teach about language, or simply reply, "Yes, I do." Because if you help students understand how to use language appropriately for their specific writing situation, how to make editing an integral but not stifling part of their writing process, and how to understand the way language works in our society, then you are teaching "grammar." If you want to stretch someone's thinking, reply, "I teach rhetorical grammar."[1] We do students no favor when we teach isolated, formal grammar lessons to satisfy curricular requirements or public pressures, and we do them no favor when we throw the baby of rhetorical grammar out with that discredited bathwater.

Let me put all of this another way, based on a study of first-year college students who were placed into basic writing at our university, a prerequisite for students who don't place into first-year composition. From this limited sample, I tentatively concluded that basic writers need motives, models, and methods for writing. That makes them like all writers, then, doesn't it? Thus, if we assess any students we teach on this basis and develop curriculum and teaching strategies that help students develop motives, models, and methods for writing, then we can feel confident that we are preparing them for future writing, wherever that will take place.

By motives, I do not mean external motivation (such as grades or assignments), but internalized drives—meaningful reasons for writing.[2] We cannot give people such motives. But when we recognize the most powerful motives, we can help students find such motives for themselves and let motives replace motivation in their writing lives.

The students in our basic writing study described writing poems, stories, and nonfiction regularly and sharing them with readers in various ways. Their motives seemed to include a desire for self-expression, a desire to connect with other people, a desire to create something beautiful, a desire to affect other people's thinking, and a desire for what John Warnock calls "glory."

Besides motives for writing, it helps to have models, people whom one sees as writers and whom one admires. While fifteen of our twenty interviewees reported one or both parents doing some reading, only four of twenty reported their parents doing any writing. One said his mother likes to write, two said their mothers wrote poetry, and one said both parents wrote for work. All four of those students whose parents wrote talked about writing themselves. The two whose mothers write poetry had also written poetry themselves, and the one who said his parents write for work spoke of doing business writing himself.

Other models for writing are published writers. Some of our interviewees clearly had such models, and our question about what "being a writer" means to them often revealed this fact. One woman spoke of her dream of being a novelist and described being a writer as "creating images in other people's minds. . . . [B]eing able to, like, create something no one's ever thought of or heard of." This was one of the most poetic descriptions we heard of being a writer. Many said that being a writer meant being paid for one's writing or receiving recognition for one's writing. Others spoke of writers as those who love to write, those who enjoy writing, or those who have something they must express. They also saw writers as people who could express themselves well. One student, who was in the midst of writing a sociology paper on illiteracy, said being a writer is being able to function in society.

True, not all of those with powerful models for writing were themselves writers or comfortable with writing. It's possible that some models for writing are intimidating; that's why composition instructors often have students read other students' writing as a more accessible model. Another problem might arise from the dissonance between students' perceptions of what a writer is and the writing they are asked to do in school and will be expected to do in their professions or careers. A student faced with the task of writing a letter to the editor, or an argument about a local issue, or a definition of a term, or a problem-solving report might find little help in the models of writing provided by famous or popular novelists. Such models might suggest that writing involves pleasure, that it comes easily, that it requires imagination, or that it requires a highly developed sense of fantasy, story, and character. Students with these models of writing might not realize that there are other models more appropriate to their situation.

An interesting question is whether students who clearly have models of writing and motives for writing do well in high school and college writing assignments. Are models and motives powerful enough to help a writer overcome other writing or academic problems? Would this be a strong argument for self-directed placement in high school or college writing courses?

Most of us would agree that it helps students with motives and models to have effective methods for writing. We don't have protocols or portfolios for the students in our study, so our conclusions are based on the students' self-reported writing processes and methods learned. Many of these students had a difficult time describing their writing or themselves as writers, offered sketchy accounts of previous school writing experiences, and struggled to explain what "learning to write" meant to them. It isn't easy to talk about writing as a process or to explain what one does when one writes; in our writing courses, one valuable thing we give students is the language to explain how they write and how they might write. Many of our students who place directly into first-year composition might also sound inarticulate if asked these questions. But when I think about students I've had in the first-semester course and what they wrote and said early in the semester, I'm inclined to think many of them would be more articulate about writing than most of our basic writing students.

The "methods" that would best serve high school students are not specific strategies for acing college writing assignments or formulaic structures for a thesis-based essay or a term paper. Again, having students learn to use writing processes that take full cognizance of audience and purpose is the best approach. High school and college English teachers can argue about the best assignments or the most appropriate balance of narrative, exposition, and argument, but frankly, those are secondary concerns.

The first-year college composition course I teach at IUPUI is highly structured, giving students guidance in writing particular types of analytical essays, but I would not ask high school English teachers to adopt these assignments. In fact, for high school students I might instead offer my approach to Advanced Expository Writing, a junior-level college course that I model in some ways after the approach of the writing project that Mary, Herb, and I co-direct. In that course, I ask students to propose assignments that they want to do, keeping in mind the course goals and their individual goals. The outcome I expect: a thirty-page portfolio of writing, with an introductory evaluative piece included in the thirty-page total. No two portfolios will look the same, but I expect each one to demonstrate an understanding of writing as a purposeful, local activity. In Herb Budden's section, he describes an approach to high school writing much like this. Such an approach allows high school and college writing teachers (and students) to talk the same language without losing the richness of their own contexts.

Herb Budden

The connections between high school college prep English classes and first-year college composition classes ought to be obvious, yet, as many of us discovered through our involvement in a project meant to explore those connections, there are many gaps in our mutual understanding of the purposes and goals of our respective courses. Project SEAM, funded by Lilly Endowment, allows teachers at the high school and college levels in the Indianapolis metropolitan area to meet on a regular basis.

The intent of the project is to enable teachers at secondary and postsecondary levels to meet and construct ways to narrow the gaps in curriculum, assessment, and instruction that student performance data in area colleges show between the two levels. The teachers have a good deal of freedom to forge their own way toward finding solutions to the problem.

One of the first ways the teachers approached the task was to survey themselves about their conceptions of necessary skills for students and how much emphasis they gave to various areas of content knowledge in their individual courses. The survey items were taken from the Content Knowledge document developed by Mid-continent Research for Education and Learning (www.mcrel.org). The survey results revealed less agreement than one might have expected; one major conclusion we came to was that because of the fundamental differences between the secondary and postsecondary school day, the teachers had very different sets of priorities. For instance, high school teachers ranked third in importance the statement, "Apply reading skills and strategies to a variety of literary texts (e.g., fiction, nonfiction, myths, poems, biographies, autobiographies, science fiction, supernatural tales, satires, parodies, plays, American literature, British literature, world and ancient literature)," but college teachers ranked it forty-eighth. For high school teachers, who have about 180 contact hours with each student each year, such a skill is important. The college teachers' responses might reflect the greater specialization of their classes or the fact that they don't use the term "reading skills and strategies." Again, literacy must be contextualized.

One hope for Project SEAM is that it will be able to foster interactions that grow more substantive simply because teachers will discover that no quick fixes are available, that skills analysis and surveys will probably always point the way to values, philosophy, and institutional constraints rather than to "Aha, that's it!" answers. Put another way, when teachers are ready to move away from skills and begin thinking about conceptions of literacy, genuine solutions to very real problems may begin to emerge. While the work with Project SEAM is ongoing, many of the teachers involved from both levels have expressed the notion that the main value of the project has been the opportunity for people to get together to talk. Informal conversations and new professional relationships that develop out of conversations between teachers are always valuable in and of themselves; Project SEAM is no exception. What is beginning to grow in these conversations is a sense of the need to examine our assumptions about why we teach what we teach. We need to articulate this to ourselves, to each other, and to our students.

Many of us have attempted to translate into our classroom practice ways not only to enable our students to be successful in postsecondary school, but also to allow them not to feel beaten by their schooling, by what Harvey Daniels refers to as "the death march to literacy" that so much secondary curriculum, instruction, and assessment feels like. In my teaching experience, one key to moving toward a classroom based on sound theory is found in Steven Zemelman and Daniels's book *A Community of Writers*. Their explanation of James Britton's concept of the language continuum has allowed many of us to move away from our notions of discrete writing modes and purposes (translation: personal narratives and creative writing are not what being prepared for college is all about—college is all about academic writing, which is mostly exposition and persuasion) and toward a more encompassing view of writing instruction that can indeed include the types of writing that students may actually enjoy doing, the kinds of writing that help move one to lifelong literacy, as well as the kinds of writing that foster the rigor of mind required by college courses that emphasize analytical thinking.

Britton's liberating idea is that language is neither strictly "transactional"—businesslike and filled with bristling intentions to persuade or inform a specific audience—nor strictly "poetic," in which the language itself becomes the object of contemplation. Instead, he suggests that we all have a home base of language—"expressive" language— which is the comfortable language we use in our heads in our own way. The other kinds of language form a continuum emanating from this home base. But they are all nevertheless always connected as an organic whole, like the rings in a tree, because transactional language can be poetic and poetic language can indeed be transactional.

To put this idea into classroom practice in a practical way so that both students and parents understand it, Zemelman and Daniels suggest a matrix of writing activities that includes all of the previously mentioned modes of writing matched up with three major assignment types, depending on course goals. The assignment types are writing-to-learn experiences, teacher-designed assignments (i.e., traditional), and self-selected writing.

The matrix allows teachers to put what they ask students to do in a writing classroom into a context that is easily understood by all and yet is undergirded by a strong theoretical base. The matrix also allows us to examine our mix of writing tasks in order to determine if we have balance (see Table 6.1).

Table 6.1. Zemelman and Daniels's Matrix of Writing Activities

	Poetic	Expressive	Transactional
Write-to-Learn		dual-entry responses to outside reading	reflective writing; goal setting
Teacher-Designed Assignments		quizzes over text	traditional essays
Self-Selected	(open-ended topics —could fall into any mode, depending on student's purpose)		

The tasks intermingle what we know now about the value of writing-to-learn activities, the motivating power of allowing choice in writing topics, and the importance of analytical, academic writing. A twelfth-grade composition class that lasts eighteen weeks might include several dual-entry and/or "says/does" responses to outside readings (writing-to-learn assignments done in expressive language); eight to ten informal papers (self-selected in poetic or transactional language); and four teacher-designed assignments (traditional expository and persuasive papers written in formal transactional language).

These sorts of assignments, used in conjunction with a strong assessment model such as the 6+1 Traits (*Northwest Regional*, www.nwrel.org), enable students to tap into points all along the language continuum. If students keep a working folder of drafts and revisions of all work and then are allowed to revise some of each mode and assignment type together with reflective writing (expressive and/or transactional language), they will have undergone a coherent experience in writing that, in my experience, satisfies on several levels: students feel motivated to write more because of the self-selected topics; they become aware of the value of writing-to-learn; they feel less stress with the traditional assignments in this context; and, finally, they understand the purposes of writing more fully and feel more sense of control over their work. When teachers can articulate such things about writing to their students and colleagues at all levels, the communication gaps will begin to close.

Stuart Greene

As the director of a university writing program, I face the challenge of developing a course that includes instruction in writing that approximates the kinds of writing students will do in their classes across the university. This is a complicated (if not impossible) task, one not unlike the challenge many high school teachers set for themselves: to prepare their students to write in college. Unfortunately, writing varies from discipline to discipline. There is no one thing called "writing."

So what do we teach? We teach argument.[3] Argument is very much a part of what we do every day: we confront a public issue, something that is open to dispute, and we take a stand and support what we think and feel with what we believe are good reasons. Seen in this way, argument is very much like a conversation. By this I mean that making an argument entails providing good reasons to support your viewpoint, as well as counterarguments, recognizing the reasons readers might object to your ideas. The metaphor of conversation emphasizes the social nature of writing. Thus, inquiry, research, and writing arguments are intimately related. If, for example, you are to understand the different ways others have approached your subject, then you will need to do your homework. This is what Doug Brent means when he says that research consists of "the looking-up of facts in the context of other worldviews, other ways of seeing" (78).

It is useful to think about writing as a form of inquiry in which students convey their understanding of the claims people make, the questions they raise, and the conflicts they address. As a form of inquiry, then, writing begins with problems, conflicts, and questions that students identify as important. I encourage students to raise questions that are open to dispute and for which there are not prepackaged answers. After all, readers within an academic setting expect that writers will advance a scholarly conversation and not reproduce others' ideas. Therefore, it is important to find out who else has confronted these problems, conflicts, and questions in order to take a stand within an ongoing scholarly conversation. Students should read with an eye toward the claims writers make, claims they are making on the reader in the sense that writers want readers to think and feel a certain way. Our students need to read others' work critically to see if the reasons writers use to support their arguments are those students would consider good reasons. And, finally, our students should consider the possible counterarguments to the claims writers make and the views that call their own ideas into question.

Like the verbal conversations we have with others, effective arguments never take place in a vacuum; they take into account previous conversations about the subject under discussion. Viewing research as a means for advancing a conversation makes the writing process more *real*, especially if students recognize that they will need to support their claims with evidence in order to persuade readers to agree with them. The concept and practice of inquiry arises out the specific social context of readers' questions and skepticism.

Reading necessarily plays a prominent role in the many forms of writing we do, but not just as a process of gathering information. This is true whether we write personal essays, editorials, or original research based on library research. Instead, as James Crosswhite suggests in *The Rhetoric of Reason*, reading "means making judgments about which of the many voices one encounters can be brought together into productive conversation" (131).

To develop an argument that is akin to a conversation, students should think of writing as a process of understanding conflicts, the claims others make, and the important questions to ask, not simply the ability to tell a story that influences readers' ways of looking at the world or to find good reasons to support an argument. The real work of writing an argument occurs when the writer tries to figure out the answers to the following:

- What topics have people been talking about?
- What is a relevant problem?
- What kinds of evidence might persuade readers?
- What objections might readers have?
- What is at stake in this argument? (What if things change? What if things stay the same?)

In answering these questions, writers need to read with an eye toward identifying an *issue*—the *situation* that calls for some response in writing—and framing a *question.*

More than demonstrating that they have read and understood texts written by others, students need opportunities to make new knowledge. But if we agree that students can and should contribute to scholarly conversations, then we must also give students the tools to do so.

Now you know what some of us in Indiana talk about when we talk about college writing. Most important, we *do* talk. And we talk about writing, not just college writing; about our students' full literacies, not their test scores. We are able to talk together about writing—and to write together—largely because of a unique organization, the Indiana Teachers of Writing (ITW). ITW was founded twenty years ago by a group of Indiana teachers who wanted to support each other in their exciting new approaches to teaching writing at *all* levels, kindergarten through college. They wanted to disseminate, explore, and implement the best practices in writing instruction. ITW has helped create and nurture professional relationships among writing teachers across levels and across geographical and administrative boundaries. Steve, for example, met Herb and Mary through ITW and ended up serving on the ITW board with them, and now the three of them co-direct the ITW Writing Project.

In conferences, workshops, and summer programs sponsored by ITW and the ITW Writing Project, we come together for invigorating cross-talk about the teaching of writing. We also write and share our writing with each other, believing that a writing teacher should be a writer. Perhaps our own struggles with writing account for our shared convictions about what matters in writing classrooms. Staying alert to our own self-construction through literacy, we appreciate and encourage our students' self-construction through literacy. Our rigor has not become rigor mortis; our articulation has not become constriction.

Now that we've told you what we talk about, we need to get back to our students. They have been writing, just as we have. We expect to be surprised by what they show us and to enjoy seeing their portfolios take shape. Perhaps we will share this essay with them. They like to talk about writing, too.

Notes

1. See Martha Kolln, *Rhetorical Grammar: Grammatical Choices, Rhetorical Effects*, and Scott Rice, *Right Words, Right Places*, for helpful discussions and explanations of such an approach to grammar instruction.

2. In a personal conversation, Eli Goldblatt of Temple University told me that a study they did found that whether a student was motivated by internal or external agency was a key factor in how well students do in college.

3. The following is based on Stuart Greene's "Argument as Conversation: The Role of Inquiry in Writing a Researched Argument."

Works Cited

Brent, Doug. "Rogerian Rhetoric: Ethical Growth through Alternative Forms of Argumentation." *Argument Revisited, Argument Redefined: Negotiating Meaning in the Composition Classroom*. Ed. Barbara Emmel, Paula Resch, and Deborah Tenney. Thousand Oaks: Sage, 1996. 73–96.

Crosswhite, James. *The Rhetoric of Reason: Writing and the Attractions of Argument*. Madison: U of Wisconsin P, 1996.

Greene, Stuart. "Argument as Conversation: The Role of Inquiry in Writing a Researched Argument." *The Subject Is Research: Processes and Practices*. Ed. Wendy Bishop and Pavel Zemliansky. Portsmouth, NH: Boynton/ Cook, 2001. 145–64, 240–41.

Kolln, Martha. *Rhetorical Grammar: Grammatical Choices, Rhetorical Effects*. New York: Macmillan, 1991.

Mid-continent Research for Education and Learning. © 2001. 17 May 2001. <www.mcrel.org>.

Northwest Regional Educational Laboratory. 14 Jan. 2002. 17 May 2001. <www.nwrel.org>.

Rice, Scott. *Right Words, Right Places.* Belmont: Wadsworth, 1993.

Sanders, Scott Russell. "The Singular First Person." *Secrets of the Universe: Scenes from the Journey Home.* Boston: Beacon, 1991. 193.

———."Who Speaks on the Page?" *The Force of Spirit.* Boston: Beacon, 2000. 114–15.

Warnock, John. "Glory." *JAC: A Journal of Composition Theory* 18.3 (1998). 509–17.

Yagelski, Robert P. *Literacy Matters: Writing and Reading the Social Self.* New York: Teachers College P, 2000.

Zemelman, Steven, and Harvey Daniels. *A Community of Writers: Teaching Writing in the Junior and Senior High School.* Portsmouth, NH: Heinemann, 1988.

7 Productively Contentious Discussions: Teachers Talk about the Teaching of Writing

Stephen Lafer
University of Nevada, Reno

Launie Gardner
Truckee Meadows Community College High School

Richard Hoadley
University of Nevada, Reno

Terry DeBarger
B. D. Billinghurst Middle School

April Sawyer
Proctor Hug High School

What happens when teachers from different grade levels and different theoretical perspectives come together in a seminar to discuss the methods and goals for teaching writing? Following a description of the genesis of one such enterprise, several participants reflect on what happened in their discussions.

In our part of the world, the northwest of Nevada, there are three major educational institutions: the Washoe County School District (WCSD), Truckee Meadows Community College (TMCC), and the University of Nevada, Reno (UNR). A good number of the students who attend the community college and the university come from the local schools. Many of the students who attend the community college matriculate to the university, and the university is responsible for educating a good number of the teachers who teach in the district's schools and a good number, too, of the instructors who teach at the community college.

One day in 1999, Ana Douglass, an English professor at TMCC and coordinator of developmental writing programs for the college, and

Stephen Lafer, an associate professor in the university's College of Education and the secondary English education specialist for the Department of Curriculum and Instruction, were sitting in a coffeehouse in Reno discussing composition theory. They agreed that they disagreed, in significant ways, on a best approach to the teaching of writing. Lafer advocated an approach shaped by the work of James Moffett. Douglass, on the other hand, favored the Bartholomae/Petrosky approach. The differences led to a series of heated conversations during which Lafer mentioned that the pedagogy he advocated in the English education courses he taught were often seen to contradict approaches used in the region's schools. And Douglass said that the writing program she inherited as developmental director at TMCC was based on principles of instruction with which she disagreed. She also saw her philosophy to be different from those guiding writing programs at the university.

At the time, it was common knowledge in the state that a high number of Nevada high school graduates entering college were being placed in developmental or basic writing courses on entering college. As a result, developmental courses at colleges and universities across the state were growing rapidly, and it was becoming increasingly difficult to find qualified instructors to cover the number of developmental sections needed to meet demand.

With the standards movement in full swing, teachers in the public schools were feeling pressure to move even further away from the student-centered approaches Lafer supported; they were using the tests as reason to support more *pragmatic* basic skills–oriented methodologies. The eight-sentence paragraph had burst back onto the scene, and grammar and mechanics worksheets were as popular as they had been decades before. Lafer's holistic, student-as-thinker-centered, I-to-you-about-it approach was becoming increasingly irrelevant as the testing panic spread. So too were the teachings of the local writing project, its directors in a quandary over how it should proceed in the new climate. Lafer and the project people had been disagreeing productively for many years but now faced together the consequences of teachers' new sense of teachers' needs.

Launie Gardner, the Northern Nevada Writing Project's director, began to meet with Douglass and Lafer, her participation immediately validating the hypothesis that those involved in teaching writing agreed little on how writing should be taught, but also lending more support to the notion that discussion between the various factions of the writing instruction community needs now more than ever to begin, especially since, as Gardner helped make clear, writing teachers at the various levels and in different institutions disagreed not only about methods but also about goals.

The English teacher's primary obligation is to help students become increasingly effective communicators. An essential focus of the work is, or at least should be, development of skills, knowledge, and attitudes that allow individuals to interact through language with others who are not like themselves in thought, belief, attitude, and the like. Willingness to step outside the comfort zone into arenas of discourse in which varied perspectives are aired and allowed to interact, clash, and modify one another is an essential element governing one's ability to participate in productive group decision-making processes so essential to the health of a democratic society. But those responsible for cultivating this willingness, the English language arts teachers, were not engaging in such vital dialectic at a time when just such a discourse was becoming profoundly necessary if students were to be served well by those teaching writing.

The Nevada Writing Alliance was formed to provide a forum for productively contentious, honest discussion about the needs of students and the future of writing instruction in the region. Through this discussion, the alliance would develop a framework for writing instruction in the secondary grades through college that would provide students with the skills they needed to become effective and successful writers. A properly unified approach to writing instruction through the various levels, one that would work toward the ultimate goal of eliminating the need for developmental writing courses of any kind—this would be the alliance's primary objective. In the interim, the alliance program would provide qualified instructors for the developmental courses and at the same time help preservice and inservice secondary teachers understand the college perspective on the goals of writing instruction and the needs of developmental students, students who for some reason leave high school without the skills necessary to succeed as writers at the college level. In turn, college instructors would better understand the realities of the secondary schools and the nature of the work of the secondary school teacher.

The Project

As noted earlier, the primary purpose of the Nevada Writing Alliance is to provide a forum for discussion of issues pertinent to the teaching of writing between individuals involved in the teaching of writing. A basic assumption underlying the alliance model is that these individuals—middle and high school teachers, prospective middle and high school teachers, college writing instructors, Writing Project advocates and directors, and university English education educators—rarely gather to discuss goals and methodologies. For the project to succeed, then, it would have to bring together people who, we had reason to believe, did not gather because they did not want to gather. We searched for incentives and the first we landed on was college credit for participation. Thus, the Nevada Writing Alliance developed the Seminar in the Teaching of Writing, a three-credit graduate course offered through both the English department and the Curriculum and Instruction department at the University of Nevada, Reno. To lure new instructors for the Truckee Meadows Community College developmental writing program, graduate students in the English education program at the university were offered the opportunity to teach while attending the seminar and earning course credit toward their degrees. From this arrangement, TMCC gained a cadre of teachers who would receive training while on the job, new instructors who, unlike the typical adjunct, could be given the guidance needed to serve the program well.

Several graduate students were attracted to the program and almost all performed well in their teaching duties at the community college. Several, in fact, continue to teach in the TMCC program while employed in the school district. These students, who were also enrolled in the English methods course at the university, helped bring a degree of "in-the-trenches" reality to course discussions by acquainting others with the plight of high school graduates not yet able to meet the writing demands of college.

During the first year of the project, the alliance applied for a Dwight D. Eisenhower grant through the University and Community College System of Nevada (UCCSN). Up to this point, the system had never approved funds for the humanities-based disciplines, funding exclusively projects related to mathematics and science instruction. But at the time, the system was becoming interested in collaborative projects involving the universities and colleges and the K–12 system. Ironically, the concern for collaboration arose from legislative demands that the colleges and universities play a role in K–12 schools' "gear-up" to meet instructional demands created by the adoption of the new state academic standards, the same force that had teachers scrambling for basic skills–oriented methodologies. Irony aside, the alliance was awarded $31,000 to be used over a period of two years, in part to pay tuition and stipends for participating secondary teachers.

Whether the project can continue to attract teachers without the tuition money is a question that cannot yet be answered. We also do not know if we will be able to continue placing university graduate students in instructor positions at the college; without such placements, an important dimension of the project will be lost. Even so, we think we would still be able to attract university students since seminar credits can be used to satisfy degree requirements. Our hope is that good things happen in the seminar and that word about those good things will spread and attract new people to the project.

Presently, we do have some preliminary data to suggest that the alliance is on the right track. Following each of the fall for-credit seminar courses, the alliance has offered four spring semester follow-up sessions to which no credit is attached. For both years, attendance has been gratifyingly high. We have also interviewed many of the first year's participants (we will do the same with second-year participants when the year is over), and most have expressed satisfaction with the experience and a desire to participate in subsequent alliance discussions. We have encouraged them to carry their positive feelings into their schools.

Methods and Results

The alliance seminars are rather simple in format. Participants are assigned readings from currently relevant texts and asked to reflect on the readings in response logs. Journal thoughts, then, become the stuff of discussion. The seminar leaders, Launie Gardner, Ana Douglass, and Stephen Lafer, alliance founders, guide discussion in such a way as to encourage participants to use theory to assess in-place strategies and evolve new ones when theory demands. A good part of the discussion of theory is oriented to establishing viable goals for the whole of the writing curriculum. The books used have been extremely effective in moving discussion along in this manner. Participants have read the essays in *Teaching with the Bedford Guide for College Writers* and Joseph Harris's *A Teaching Subject: Composition since 1966*. Though these texts are oriented to issues of college writing, the secondary teachers have found them to be relevant to their work since college writing, for most teachers, represents the logical end of the writing instruction line. The texts, though, do not serve up agreed-upon answers to questions of curricular goals in writing. In fact, they illustrate the elusiveness of goals in the broader context of debates of national and international scope.

Because the actual and real goals of writing instruction remain elusive, there is always a disorganized feel to seminar conversations. It is somehow rough and splintered, with topics taking the stage for spurts and then fading into obscurity, often to be revived on another day when a new phase of conversation has been entered and some of the old stuff can be seen in a new relevance-revealing light. What does seem to weave itself through most of the conversation is inservice teachers' frustration with the constraints placed on them by the institutions in which they work. Teachers often want to agree with the goals to which the theory leads. They want to implement some of the strategies the conversation validates. But they understand the methods to be related to goals that are different from those being codified in the state's academic standards and enforced through accountability schemes relying primarily on standardized tests.

The Writing Alliance has not yet fully realized its goal of creating a true dialogue between college instructors, secondary teachers, and teacher educators. It has, however, uncovered several issues of importance to all and brought about a better understanding by each of the perspectives of others. The profoundly important question of goal—of what writing instruction should attempt to achieve—has already been mentioned. Among the competing goals discussed to date are the following:

- competence that allows one to succeed in the academic world and the world of work
- the ability and desire to engage in writing that leads to self-discovery and personal satisfaction
- the ability to write for the sake of acquiring power—political and otherwise
- the ability to participate fully as a citizen

All of these goals are understood by most to be sensible ones, but the question of which should take precedence continuously arises. So too arise questions concerning a proper sequence of instruction that will get students to where they need to be (wherever that might be). Should, for example, middle school instruction be directly and primarily concerned with the type of writing required by the academy and the workplace? Or is there a progression, a developmental ladder that begins with one type of writing and moves students smoothly toward competency in others, from personal writing, say, to exposition and argumentation? And is the kind of exposition and argumentation sponsored by the academy (if such a thing exists across and between universities) the kind of writing that allows one to write well for purposes other than those of the academy?

These questions, broad in scope as they are, appear to be critical to the development of any kind of understanding of how college and secondary English programs might better work together to get students to where they need to be. The answers to such questions are essential to discovering answers to those that are narrower and more specific: Should instruction focus first and foremost on the thought processes underlying the writing process? Or should form, format, and rules be emphasized? Or is there an integrated approach that somehow simultaneously takes all into consideration at once? Does a focus on correctness inhibit critical thought and creativity? And how long can incorrectness be suffered before it begins to interfere with students learning what is necessary for achieving clarity and desirable effect?

Some who helped bring these questions to the fore have complained at times that the seminar has yet to settle on answers. And it is true that the program has yet to reshape a single curriculum or influence in any meaningful way the operation of any of the institutions that need to be affected. Some claim that they are more confused now than when they joined the seminar. And the truth is that we *are* more confused, probably because we know better the complexity of the issues that concern us.

Can we use any of what we have learned to make things better? Probably, and just by talking. If we don't talk, we blame. And though we do blame when we talk, at least we can talk about the blaming and discover whether it is productive. It may be that laying blame in front of those blamed is not too comfortable a way to carry on discussion. But maybe it is the beginning of a more honest form of blame, one with the potential to become productive if we can discover a way to keep it from destroying our ability to talk.

Nearing the end of year two, we are not certain what we have. We are not certain that what we have is good. But we do have something we didn't have before. And that, at least, makes it possible for us, sometime in the future, to get to the good. Thus it is impossible for us to speak of the Nevada Writing Alliance in a unified voice.

Voices

In the following sections, we present a small sample of the voices of project participants. This is not by any means a representative sample. As with any seminar, each participant walked away with something different. We asked for reflections on each participant's personal experience with the project. Four such reflections follow. One is that of Launie Gardner, a seminar facilitator, alliance co-founder, former director of the Northern Nevada Writing Project, and a teacher of English and social studies in the Washoe County School District. Many years ago Launie was a student in the teacher education program at the University of Nevada, Reno, where she took at least one course from Stephen Lafer. She was also a participant in the Northern Nevada Writing Project when Stephen was a project co-director.

Richard Hoadley is completing work on a teaching certificate and master's degree through the English education program at the university. He was one of the graduate students who took up the offer to teach developmental writing at TMCC and, as his comments show, found the experience to be a valuable one.

Terry DeBarger is a teacher at Billinghurst Middle School in Reno. He works there on a team that includes a science teacher and a social studies teacher who share a long block of instructional time every second day. It is their responsibility to determine how that block can best be used, some days dividing it into equal seventy-minute chunks, other days using the whole block for a field trip or series of presentations by experts in fields related to the themes the group is studying. Terry is not a University of Nevada graduate; he holds an undergraduate degree from Amherst College and is pursuing a UNR degree through the English department's Master in the Teaching of English program.

April Sawyer is a veteran teacher at Hug High School in Reno. As a result of her experience in the alliance project, she is working with Ana Douglass to bring developmental and first-semester college writing courses to her campus. Seniors will be able to take the course as an elective and earn college credit for the second course in the sequence.

Launie Gardner

Oddly enough, until I participated in this grant/articulation project, I had not thought reflectively about how high school and college teachers view or treat students in their English and composition classes differently. Certainly, preparing my students for college was at the forefront of everything I planned for my high school students since my classes were labeled college prep and supposedly 85 percent of my students went on to college. But I think that my assumptions about how to prepare them were based on my own experiences as an undergraduate and the advice of colleagues who frequently let me know what they expect students to do during their senior year (I taught juniors).

As part of a school improvement project, our English department met for fifteen hours to discuss what we expect our students to accomplish at each level of high school so that there will be continuity from the first to the senior year. One thing I knew for sure was that what we expected them to be able to do and what we asked them to do rarely matched. After listening to other participants in the alliance seminar, not only those who teach at the college level but also colleagues from other high schools in the area, I can see now that some of my writing activities were more about preparing my students for their senior-level teachers than for the kind of writing tasks they would be asked to do in college. While I personally do not believe in teaching grammar out of context, for example, I have in the past put undue emphasis on correctness because I knew that the senior-level teachers were sensitive about such errors.

Moreover, I had sold out and taught the Jane Schaeffer method because I knew that the senior-level teachers expected what they called "clear, organized thought" above what tends to be the messiness of true analysis. During the time the seminar met in the fall of 2000, I also taught a basic writing course for the first time at the community college. This helped me see firsthand the difficulties college teachers experience when trying to get their students to think critically about text when these students' writing has become banal because they are so worried about making "mistakes."

And yet I can't say that I taught this basic writing class any differently than the courses I had taught previously for high school juniors. I saturated my students in writing experiences, and I encouraged them to write about what they knew and to make connections between their lives and the texts they were reading. I also emphasized the importance of correctness because I still felt the same pressures to make sure that my students were aware of their own mistakes.

The faculty talk I heard at the community college was similar to that at the high school; instructors felt that student error was a definite weakness that reflected student inability to write. And I still believed that this emphasis on correctness often hindered their ability to think critically and thoughtfully. I have read enough to know that there are theorists who support the idea that students need to make mistakes if they are going to improve their writing, yet I was worried that if I could not get my students to focus on their own errors, I would be perceived as an incompetent teacher. I am still not sure of the best way to deal with this sensitive issue; I am well aware that students will always first be judged on how they use language at the surface level, but I also know that attending to that level will not help students increase their depth of thought or their willingness and ability to contend with more sophisticated thought in writing.

Because of the alliance seminar discussions and the work I was doing in my basic writing class, I did have one of those epiphanies that make you wonder why you didn't already know what you have just discovered. Unfortunately, what I came to know isn't something that will be accepted in most traditional high school classrooms. I was not giving any of my students enough time to talk about what they were reading, and this deficiency contributed to their inability to write effective papers reflecting sound analysis of what they had read. But the routine in most traditional high school classrooms is to assign reading, test for comprehension (test that they have actually done the reading), and then assign students the task of writing about the reading, with the teacher's analysis possibly being the only "discussion" of the text that occurs.

This now seems like something I should have known all along—my students, both high school and basic writers, need to talk, and talk a lot, about what they have read before I can expect them to write critically about text. While I had always wondered why most of my high school writers had little to say about the text beyond summarizing it, it took the experience in the basic writing class for me to understand that writers can't write about a topic or reading they haven't worked through by talking about it in a variety of ways with their peers and without pressure from a teacher to interpret a piece in a particular way.

Even after this experience, the way I teach juniors in high school will not be that different from the way I teach basic writers in college; both kinds of students need opportunities for writing in a safe environment in order to build their confidence. Both groups need to be shown that they have control over a text and that they can validate their opinions by going back to the text to figure out why they responded to it as they did. Both groups need to be allowed to wade through the complex process of turning "felt" experience into substantiated reality. I would hope that my juniors in high school get enough of this kind of "conditioning" in my classroom to prepare them to write well at the college level. But I still can't answer fully why so many enter college not yet ready to do so.

Richard Hoadley

Rich in theory and poor in experience, I, the novice of our group, saw the similarities and the differences between secondary and college education with the fresh eyes of the uninitiated. I listened as my seminar colleagues from middle and high school, where I intend to teach one day, talked about the limitations of standards-based curricula and standardized tests while I reveled in the freedom and autonomy I found in my college classroom. All of this served mainly to reinforce my belief in student-centered learning and to make a career in higher education look more and more attractive.

It is not difficult for a bunch of teachers to get bogged down in the negativity of standardization and the increasing number of limitations imposed on teachers these days that force them to teach to the tests and do other things that go against our professional knowledge and teacher's instincts. Our conversations headed down that road more than once, but we did try to stay focused on the positives, on finding solutions, many of which I was immediately able to use in my teaching. The freedom I had in the college teaching experience to practice what I knew to be good pedagogy might spoil me as a public school teacher. But the knowledge I gained from the seminar has made me want to hang on to the practices I have acquired.

As a beginning college teacher of beginning college students, I was surprised by the number of high school graduates enrolling in basic writing courses because they could not pass the placement tests that would have allowed them take regular first-year writing courses. To my amazement, Truckee Meadows Community College was running about twenty sections of English 090, all full, with waiting lists for most of the classes. Even many of those who do get into the regular entry-level course, English 101, struggle to write effectively.

Helping these first-year college students who arrived on campus often with debilitating deficiencies in the ability to write, deficiencies both real and imagined, is no easy task. In planning a curriculum, I had to look realistically at what could be accomplished in a single semester, in a few hours each week. I certainly wasn't going to "fix" all the problems twelve years of public school education could not. But I realized I could do much to set my students on the right path, mainly through practice and some well-timed help from me. Mostly what I was able to offer were coping strategies—Band-Aids, if you will—but strategies that could serve students well in their effort to succeed in college writing.

Perhaps the most important initial coping strategy teachers can offer is a change in habits, such as getting an early start on assignments and involving others in reviewing and proofing papers. The last minute, single-draft habit is most likely the root cause of most unsuccessful attempts at college writing. Instilling a new *writing ethic*, a commitment to stick with each paper until it is truly *good enough*, was a focus of my course throughout the semester.

In our area's secondary schools, the steps of the writing process model are a regularly repeated element in the curriculum. Yet it is clear that many of the students in the basic writing course do not understand what *process* means, or choose to avoid entering into a process when developing papers. They are unfamiliar with or don't understand the common sense of Barry Lane's revised version of the process model, which consists of revision followed by revision followed by revision followed by revision. Teaching students that good writing is indeed a process of multiple revisions must be a part of any good course for basic writers.

Many of the writers in the English 090 course are content to hand in their first efforts— to hand in something, anything, just to be done. This is, of course, an effective way to avoid rewriting but also a good way to avoid success. Those who are competent, reflective writers— including many writing instructors—may not be aware that fear drives this behavior. A person who sees him- or herself as incompetent is often reluctant to share work with others who might help the writer see the writing more objectively and precipitate revision. If these writers are asked to have someone else look at their work, they often do so grudgingly. Breaking down this fear is a real challenge.

One of the most interesting, and most distressing, aspects of the basic writing course is the pressure from the outside to enforce correctness. Most of those who complain do not themselves have the insight or patience to untangle and interpret illogical and ungrammatical work. I knew I would have to address issues of language mechanics but believed that lectures and exercises on faulty sentences were probably what turned off a majority of my students in the first place. And it was apparent from the first diagnostic papers they wrote that the range of problems was so wide as to make lessons on all pertinent issues impossible. Instead, I arranged for conferences in which I could address individual needs. I also devised a plan that allowed me to address correctness without making all involved hate the classes.

I asked my students to write in journals, with a page or two devoted to compiling errors that they were to transcribe from returned papers. This practice allowed them to focus on mistakes in the context of their own writing and served as a reference when they were developing final drafts. At the same time, I encouraged students to use every resource available for helping writers clean up final drafts: spellchecking and grammar checking programs, the college writing center, tutors, classmates, friends, and parents. To encourage editing and revision, mistakes did not count until the *final* final draft.

I noticed that surface-level errors tended to increase with the difficulty of the writing task, but I did not want to scare students away from attempts to put sophisticated thought on paper. Focusing on the recursive process of moving ever closer to writing that reflected real depth of thought and sophisticated thinking gave students an opportunity to create *real* essays that meant something—to them and to those who would read them. Separating error checking from reasoning and the structuring of ideas in text allowed students to write papers that were more substantial than the safe but shallow themes many had written to earn passing grades in high school English courses.

Frank Smith separates composition from transcription and considers composition the more important and more difficult of the two. Transcription, he says, is a skill that involves memorization of a set of rules that can and will be learned with practice and some guidance. The more a person writes, the better he or she becomes at using the rules to achieve correctness. Most of my students identify themselves as poor spellers, poor users of correct English grammar, and poor users of proper English mechanics. But these problems pale in significance to their inability to read closely, analyze, draw conclusions, and organize thought into logical, readable pieces of writing. These are the real problems and this is where our attention as writing teachers needs to be focused.

In the classes I taught, we wrote a lot and revised papers together until they were truly good enough, holding them up to high and authentic standards. We spent a considerable amount of time proudly sharing these perfected products. And I was quite honest about my shortcomings as a writer, about the fact that I was still learning and by no means an expert. I shared my writings with my students and even assigned myself their projects, drafting and composing alongside them to get a feel for the difficulties and frustrations they might have as they practiced to become effective college writers.

I also realized early on, from the seminar and from a survey I took of my classes, that these students weren't just preparing for college writing but were already being asked to write in the other courses they were taking. The same students who were struggling in my classroom were being asked in their psychology, business, and Western civilization courses to write the papers my course was intended to help them learn to write. They are expected to demonstrate proficiency before they are proficient. As long as colleges fail to understand the consequences of writing-across-the-curriculum (WAC) initiatives for basic writing students, writing at the college level will continue to discourage a good many intellectually competent students from continuing with their college careers.

The seminar discussions constantly came back to issues of what the goal of writing instruction at the different levels should be. The WAC issue suggests that college instructors from different disciplines need to consider who their students are and what expectations they can have for entry-level students who are struggling to find their way through the difficult process of learning to write effectively as thinking adults. Further, teachers of English at all levels need to seriously consider their mission. A simple survey will show that most of the students in any given course are not and will not become English majors. Therefore, to what ends do we teach literary analysis and writing that shows the results of deep reading of text? We need to consider whether and how the teaching in our courses helps or hinders students when they meet the writing tasks set in courses other than English. Can our work help students derive meaning from nonliterary texts? Does our work help students write the kinds of papers that WAC-oriented, non-English teachers want them to write? What adjustments might we make to our writing courses with goals such as these in mind? And what conversations do we need to have with our WAC recruits to save them from damaging the confidence of the fledgling writers who populate our developmental writing courses?

Terry DeBarger

The seminar was a refreshing introduction to the world of composition education. As the only participant teaching at the middle school level, I had a tremendous opportunity to examine my role in a community of professionals with whom I had had little opportunity for contact, and the opportunity to share with them the perspective I had developed through my work with middle school students. The commonality of our concerns was striking, as was the variation in approaches we'd taken in our teaching of writing. With the development of student writing as a central point of reference, we probed some of the questions all teachers of writing seem to have. We all wanted to know, for example, the types of writing that students should expect to write at higher levels. This was one of the seemingly simple but highly complex questions that seminar participants considered with a range of students in mind. At a basic level, I discovered, college students in basic composition courses are expected to read one or more texts and write something "smart" about them. Some postsecondary students arrive ready and willing to do this, but an alarming number are not able to convey their thoughts adequately on paper, let alone in a manner that would signify "smart." Indeed, those who had worked with students in the basic writing courses said that many of these students could not read the texts they were assigned in an "adequate" manner. "Shouldn't they have learned this in high school?" I wondered. "Or earlier?" I was forced to wonder what these students had been asked to read and to write before they got to college.

In middle school, as in high school, writing instruction responds to the demands and limitations of district standards, state standards, approved texts, state- and district-sanctioned assessment programs, and department policies. The school board, parents, and the community at large expect middle school to be preparatory training for high school. They expect high school to provide preparatory training for college, which they assume to be the training ground for professional careers. To meet perceived demands, dutiful teachers revert to the few "tried and true" approaches available. If it is November, time for the five-paragraph essay. December? Compare and contrast. January . . . introduce the business letter. And so on. Yet this sort of instruction, repeated with limited variation over six years of postelementary schooling, has failed to enable large numbers of students, many of them college-bound, to read and write smartly. I have come to believe that formulaic writing is hobbling, often preventing students from becoming engaged with complex material and attempting to respond to these complexities in writing. Thus, I have been forced to ask, "What should students be expected to write?"—a question that has nagged at me throughout the semester.

It is too simplistic to label any curriculum or part of a curriculum as an essential rung on the ladder that leads to competent college writing and/or writing that is acceptable to the business world. Given that over one-fourth of my middle school students will not complete high school, it is wholly unreasonable to build my middle school writing program around college and business expectations. But if not college or business demands, what should shape objectives for middle and high school writing instruction? While I would not presume to speak for all middle school educators, I believe that middle school language arts teachers differ more from high school teachers in their approach to teaching than high school teachers do from their college counterparts. College and high school teachers are, or at least seem to be, tied to English as a discipline, as a course of study. They share a common link to literature as an area of study. Though their work situations are different, they share their connection to subject. Middle school teachers are more loosely tied to subject, more tightly bound up in the awkwardness of early adolescent students. We middle school teachers teach "English," but we do not always have degrees in English. We are just as likely to be trained as elementary school educators as literary critics. Our attention is directed less toward the subject than to the learner.

Thus, we have been willing to experiment with writing workshops and literacy workshops. These approaches have been discussed in works by Nancie Atwell, Linda Rief, Janet Allen, and others who write for middle school English educators. They advocate for classrooms in which students have choice in reading and choice in writing with support from teachers in developing skills. Students often, though not always, write in the personal voice and often, though not always, read young adult fiction. Choice in reading and writing activities provides a powerful incentive to write meaningfully. The intent of middle school teachers is to encourage children to join the *literacy club,* to become willing readers and writers. This approach stands in contrast to traditional programs that are built on a body of canonical literature and the study of specific academic forms of writing. By addressing the needs of *students* before the needs of the *discipline,* middle school teachers believe they are helping students develop attitudes essential to the development of skills that will allow them to become smart readers and smart writers.

None of this would sound unfamiliar to my middle school colleagues; however, a number of people in the seminar were as unfamiliar with Nancie Atwell and Linda Rief as I was with Wayne Booth and David Bartholomae. Yet I was struck by the relevance of the readings and discussions that were not tailored to teachers of early adolescents. As the class examined writing and composition instruction, it quickly became clear to me that there is need for discussion between college, high school, and middle school teachers. I would not argue that Atwell's approach can be directly translated into sound curriculum for college composition courses, but her ideas may lead instructors in interesting directions, just as Joseph Williams's "Phenomenology of Error" has taken me in new directions. As we examine our particular circumstances, we can benefit from the expertise of those who are not usually a part of our regular discussions.

April Sawyer

I have been struggling with my section of this chapter, believing that if I did enough prethinking about our class, the Seminar in the Teaching of Writing, I would come up with a focus. But I didn't. What persists is the same confusion about the teaching of writing that I felt while taking this class last semester.

In spite of my confusion and that of other seminar participants, or perhaps because of it, two issues seem to stand out in our minds. One major concern is the different levels and types of motivation we find in students at various stages of their education. Students below the age of seventeen are *forced* to be in school, while students enrolled in courses at institutions of higher education are there by *choice*. For me, the resulting difference in attitude cannot be overstated. The goal of students who are forced to be in school is, quite simply, to get out of school. For many, this means concentrating primarily on passing classes and jumping through the hoops—meeting the minimum standards. Students often ask, "What do I have to do to pass this class?" On the other hand, students enrolled in higher education classes have various reasons for being there, none of which involves the enforcement of a law. Teachers must recognize and address this essential distinction in their classrooms.

It is true that many teachers do identify this difference in motivation, but the question remains: how do we address this difference? Teachers in our seminar seemed to have no answers and instead pursued another, but related, query—the purpose of writing courses. Are we preparing students to express themselves or to write as they need to for instructors they will meet in various college departments? This was the second matter that dominated discussion in the seminar.

It was simultaneously reassuring and disconcerting to discover that among college English teachers there is no consistency of purpose. Differences can be found both among colleges and within colleges; some professors prepare students as writers and others prepare students to write for professors. This was valuable information since high school English teachers face the same dilemma and are not consistent about their expectations for students.

High school teachers in our seminar expressed doubt that their assignments actually address the needs of students with varied futures. Some students will seek an advanced education while others will pursue a job to support themselves or their families. This raises the question of how any individual course will work to promote the well-being of any particular student. Our doubt about the purpose of writing was soon joined by doubt concerning the teaching of language mechanics. In order to write for self-expression or for college professors, do students need to concern themselves first with mechanical correctness or do students need to grapple first with analysis, connection making, and the discovery of hidden meanings in texts?

Seminar teachers seemed to agree that perhaps these purposes do not have to interfere with one another. In order to write for self-expression, the student must question and search unhindered by a concern for mechanics. This process is not so different from that required for writing meant to demonstrate an understanding of material covered in a college course: students first need to synthesize the material by getting messy with their thinking and then with their writing. In both cases, correct mechanics will follow and are important insofar as they promote reader comprehension.

In the end, we arrived at no solid conclusions. This is ambiguity in its most acute manifestation, and like many teachers who demand order and form in what we do and ask others to do, the seminar teachers found this uncertainty challenging, perhaps too challenging to endure. Consequently, the seminar continues, not for college credit, but because we seek and desire answers—which, perchance, do not exist—to our questions, which are many.

Conclusion

Perhaps the level of ambiguity the course generated was too much for all involved, because everyone who attended the seminar walked out of class on more than one day frustrated by the group's inability to draw conclusions, solutions that would lead to a clear and orderly pedagogy that would lead students to success in writing. But effective writing pedagogy is as difficult for teachers to come by as clarity and order in writing is for students involved in authentic writing activities. Good writing is often about that which is complex, not easy to understand or make understandable to others. It is about ideas the writer has mulled over in order to make them sensible for self and for others. Good writing is not easy, nor is it easy to teach. Teaching effective writing is extremely complex because it involves the complexity of complex minds dealing with complex subjects. Effective writing instruction helps students understand that complex topics are worthy of study, that they are capable of studying complicated issues, and that they themselves have complex minds and therefore their writing is worthy of study by others.

What is good about the seminar and the Nevada Writing Alliance project as a whole is that they are not orderly. They are, in a word, messy. And they are messy because they are concerned with the messy process of writing and the messier process of helping students become competent, effective writers.

Perhaps the seminar experience will allow those who have participated to give themselves some room for experimentation. Perhaps it will give them courage to become participants in the discourse about the teaching of writing, to assert themselves by arguing their own positions and listening deeply to the assertions others make about proper pedagogy. Maybe the messiness of the topic is a messiness that needs to be experienced to be understood, and perhaps the ramifications of that understanding are critical to the development of classrooms that grow good writers, good thinkers who can write. Thirty students thinking in thirty different ways makes for a healthy environment in which to learn how to write. Thirty students thinking in thirty different ways trying to be understood by twenty-nine others who think differently than they do is a messy classroom indeed. Managing so many voices while trying to *get something done* can be a daunting task. The seminar leaders had at most fifteen voices to manage, and even so the classroom was a messy one—but one in which much did get done.

Works Cited

Lane, Barry. *After the End: Teaching and Learning Creative Revision.* Portsmouth, NH: Heinemann, 1993.

Smith, Frank. *Writing and the Writer.* 2nd ed. Hillsdale, NJ: Erlbaum, 1994.

Williams, Joseph M. "The Phenomenology of Error." *College Composition and Communication* 32 (1981): 152–68.

IV High School to College: How Smooth a Transition?

The previous chapters demonstrate that teachers from different grade levels can learn from each other even when they disagree. In Chapter 8, Janet Alsup, a former high school teacher, and Michael Bernard-Donals, a college writing program administrator, engage in one of their many friendly disagreements about writing, this time about whether the move from high school writing to college writing could—or even should—be considered a transition.

In Chapter 9, college professor Wendy Strachan asks a group of high school teachers what they see as their responsibilities as English teachers. Their answers, and the conversations that follow, highlight some of the differences in contexts and goals for high school teachers and their college counterparts—differences that explain why the "transition" can be so difficult.

8 The Fantasy of the "Seamless Transition"

Janet Alsup
Purdue University

Michael Bernard-Donals
University of Wisconsin

Janet and Mike have been arguing about teaching for over five years now. Janet, trained as a teacher educator with an expertise in the teaching of writing, and Mike, trained as a rhetorical theorist with experience as a writing program administrator, have taught courses and participated together on conference panels about what writing can and can't do. What follows is the beginning of another argument: is it possible to provide a seamless transition from high school to college writing?

Janet: I met Mike in the winter semester of 1997 at the University of Missouri–Columbia. I was in my first year of graduate school in a Ph.D. program in English education, and I had signed up for Mike's Rhetoric and Pedagogy of the Holocaust course, a graduate-level seminar in rhetoric and composition, a discipline I had chosen as a support area on my program of study. I was still a little unsure about my future success in graduate school and more than a little intimidated by my university professors who all seemed so smart, and Mike was no exception. I was fascinated by the reading and discussion in the class, and I was pleasantly surprised by the emphasis Mike put on teaching—not only a concern for how we, his students, were experiencing his course, but also a concern for how undergraduate courses about the Holocaust might most effectively be taught. Mike even allowed the final seminar paper to take the form of a course plan that would devise and lay out a writing course based on Holocaust texts and the idea of Holocaust representation. Of course, being a former high school teacher and a current graduate student in education, I took Mike up on his offer. I created a course plan for an intermediate university-level writing course that revolved around the reading and discussion of Holocaust fiction, poetry, memoir, film, and history. To my surprise, Mike asked if I wanted to implement the class the following fall. I accepted with much excitement, and we began planning to teach English 120, Writing the Holocaust.

Mike: Janet was one of two graduate students from English education in the graduate seminar, and the two of them together really held my feet to the fire of teaching, particularly the teaching of writing. That's why I wanted so much to give Janet a chance to teach the course, with me if possible: I wanted to see whether the theoretical foundations of writing would bear out in practice, and the course Janet proposed would allow us to test this. She paired an interest in pedagogies that worked, from her experience teaching high school, with a critically acute sense that even if something worked, if it didn't originate from a sound position—call it epistemology if you like, or call it a sense of how writing hooks onto the world, in Eugene Garver's term—we shouldn't be doing it. This was an especially important issue in this course. We had thirty-eight students who were "prepared" as writers in high school and by the compulsory first-year writing course, but who were put profoundly ill at ease when asked to wrestle with difficult questions and take positions on controversial issues. Through teaching this course with Janet, I became more than just passingly interested in how high school and first-year writing both does and doesn't prepare college students for the writing they're likely to do both in the academy and outside of it.

Janet: Since that class, Mike and I have collaborated on several teaching and writing projects. Our mutual respect for the other's knowledge has enabled us to learn from and with the other. To date, Mike and I have co-presented on five conference panels or presentations and co-written two essays (including this one). One topic of discussion to which we often return, whether officially on a panel or over drinks afterward, is writing pedagogy. Mike and I have expressed some basic differences in pedagogical philosophy over the years, although our thinking has also influenced the other in positive ways. I know that my beliefs about teaching have changed due to Mike's influence. I often, for example, argue for student-centered pedagogies, pedagogies that privilege student choice and risk taking. Mike, while not resistant to these ideas, sees them in a different context: a rhetorical context. Mike's emphasis on the language of argument and rhetoric is sometimes hard for me to swallow, perhaps because I was not trained in classical rhetoric or perhaps because the language seems so inaccessible that I can't imagine using such an approach with adolescents. At the same time, Mike and I tend to balance each other: when I argue for a "safe environment" for unencumbered student expression, and Mike argues that writing is an ethical act that requires taking a stance, we often find a middle ground that balances safety with rigor, or what could be called my brand of "social epistemic expressivism" with Mike's "social epistemic rhetoricism."

As Mike noted, a recent topic of discussion between us has been how to prepare high school students for college writing. At the fall 2000 NCTE Annual Convention in Milwaukee, we presented as part of a roundtable panel (along with two other educators) called "Toward a Seamless High School-to-College Writing Curriculum." One of the things we discovered during this presentation is that "seamlessness" may not be an appropriate or realistic goal. This isn't to say that progress can't be made, however, or that communication between high school teachers, teacher educators, and university writing faculty can't improve student writing skills and subsequent academic success. But how should we approach this conversation? How can secondary and university writing teachers best communicate about college writing?

Mike: What, exactly, is "college writing?" Depending on which first-year writing director you ask, you'll get a variety of answers. I've now taught at four different colleges, each with the same stated mission—to prepare its students for the intellectual work of the world and to do it in a way that stresses the inquiry over the answer—and yet "college writing" at each couldn't have been more different. At one, writing was seen as the accurate communication of ideas, and the pedagogy was straight out of the Royal Society; at another, writing was seen as the expression of an individual's relation with the world, and the pedagogy was informed by a constructivist-flecked expressivism that could have come straight out of a self-help manual. One reason the seamless transition from high school to college writing is a fantasy is that there's no such thing as "college writing."

Another reason is that, as I've seen from my own experience at state-sponsored research-oriented universities of between 17,000 and 41,000 students, not all colleges are the same. They *don't* have the same mission, in part because their students come from remarkably varied backgrounds. It may be appropriate to use Corbett's *Classical Rhetoric for the Modern Student* in a university where most students won't have trouble understanding what an enthymeme is or the difference between induction and deduction; it may not be appropriate to do so with students whose high school English teachers didn't assign any writing, or with students who speak a language other than English at home or with friends. Andrea Lunsford's assessment of the changes that have occurred in the demography of the first-year college student—changes wrought by vast material, cultural, and ideological changes in notions of literacy, education, and writing—accounts for those students who make it to college.[1] But there exists an equal number of students who don't go on to college (and there are smaller numbers who do but who are woefully underprepared by elementary and secondary institutions) who complicate the idea of the seamless transition: does the fact that they don't make it mean that teachers aren't doing their jobs adequately?

Janet: That's a good question. As a former high school English teacher and a current teacher educator, I often think about how best to prepare secondary school students for life after high school. I want my current students, preservice high school English teachers, to know how to facilitate student growth and learning and ease the transition of their future students into college, technical education, the world of work, or whatever path they may choose. Of course, this is a huge instructional task. I find myself trying to teach something about which I'm unsure anyone can give definitive, one-size-fits-all advice. To make matters more difficult, my students, about to embark on their careers as English teachers, *want* me to give them such definitive advice. Semester after semester they ask, "How do I motivate my students to write?"; "How do I get students to revise and not just respond to my corrections?"; and "How do I grade and evaluate student writing in the fairest, most just, way?" These are tough questions that I can (and do) address with my students—but give definitive answers? Only in my dreams! The home and school lives; socioeconomic status; and racial, ethnic, and gender identities of secondary school students are so varied that it is difficult to know how any one class or student will respond to instruction. In addition, no common future awaits these students, for their futures will vary as greatly as their present lives do. We know that not all will attend or complete college, for example. But what will they do instead? The answers range from technical school to a life of crime.

Mike: Well, then, let me talk about the question of transition for those students who do go on to college. My comments question the notion of seamlessness because the first-year curriculum we've just implemented at Wisconsin shows some ragged seams. That is, it demonstrates what sorts of things are *not* learned in high school, or maybe what sorts of things are learned there that are made more complicated once students get to college. Nevertheless, what holds high school and college writing together—and what holds it together in our curriculum at Wisconsin—is understanding argument and invention as ethical acts: that in writing, we create (for better or worse) the future in which we're fated to act.

First, why rhetoric? Or, given the rise of postprocess theories founded on constructivist models of thought or on studies of culture or literacy, why would we want to resurrect this old-fashioned term that, in the wake of the 2000 presidential election, sounds like another term for the spin that results from contested ballots? In fact, far from being a catalog of style, or a formal system of language and thought sucked dry by most textbooks (including some good ones), rhetoric is simply another term for argumentative discourse. If being rhetorical is what we have to be in the face of a contingent world—a world ruled not by the laws of nature but by human behavior that is often unpredictable even when the humans in question like and understand one another—then argument is how we make sense of those contingencies. By argument I don't mean the kind of disagreement a high school student has with a parent or sibling; it doesn't involve shouting or name-calling. Argument is the instrument people use to probe, in a principled way, one another's statements about who they are, what they know, and how they understand the circumstances in which they live and communicate with one another. Rhetoric is finding the available means of persuasion in any given case; argument is what you do once you've found them. To argue, you not only need to know something about the given case and about the people with whom you're arguing, but you also need to use that knowledge to change the nature of the case and the people involved.

Janet: I'm not so sure that the principles connecting high school and college writing curricula need to be explicitly rhetorical, though I don't believe they're necessarily exclusive of rhetoric. Regardless, I have specific ideas about what I think should be included in a high school writing curriculum and the philosophical/theoretical principles on which an effective curriculum should rest. I believe, for example, that students and teachers should understand writing as a process of inquiry. Many English education texts include discussions of writing (and reading) as a process of inquiry, stretching back to John Dewey in the 1930s, moving through the work of Emig and Berthoff in the 1970s and 1980s, and culminating in contemporary texts such as George Hillocks's *Teaching Writing as Reflective Practice* (1995). Inquiry can be analogous to "critical thinking," "analysis," and even "argument." When applied to the teaching of writing, a process of inquiry includes the following stages: development of interest in a topic; exploration of this interest through reading, talk, and prewriting; crystallization of a question or issue to be explored; drafting of a text; discussion of text with peers and instructor; revision; asking new questions; revision again; editing; and finally sharing with an audience. Of course, writers could revise, discuss, and reformulate questions and texts indefinitely, until they have to stop because of time or audience demands. The point is that inquiry is a thinking process in addition to being a writing process. That is why the discussion and definition of topic sentences, paragraph structure, thesis statements, and the like can be troubling. These terms, and often the modes of teaching them, imply that there are discrete bits of knowledge about writing, facts that are applicable to any writing process or task, that can be learned in isolation from a real writing project and real inquiry.

Mike: But what you've said sounds a lot like rhetoric, or maybe more specifically, argument. Argument involves taking a position on a topic or subject on which reasonable people may disagree. This statement has several implications. One is that ideally writing is not merely expository. Describing the position you take on abortion, say, or on whether English should be the country's official language doesn't help you engage or argue with someone who takes the opposing position. The research paper, the bane of first-year writing teachers, is a case in point: laying out a thorough description of what Napster is (to use an example I've seen recently in writing classes at Wisconsin), or what the legal debates surrounding it have been, is great fun. But (and I know this from experience) knowing those positions, or even how cool the technology is, doesn't help if you're not willing to explain why you think it's a good idea for this technology to proliferate. In order to take a position on an issue about which reasonable people disagree, a writer needs to understand the foundation of the argument, the more general claims—what Toulmin called "warrants"—to which all parties have to agree in order for the argument to proceed. Argument involves widening the intellectual context in which arguments are made, and that means giving writers an opportunity to explore not just the "opinions" and "facts" of the case, but also where "opinion" and "fact" bleed into one another depending on which party in the argument you're listening to. Making an argument means not just laying out what you know about an issue (going to the library, mining your own experience), but also finding out what your interlocutor knows and figuring out what common ground you share, what assumptions bind you together, and how opinion and received facts are shaped (and not just "found").

Part of the problem is that "audience analysis" of the writing textbook variety often devolves into dreadful tautology: the answer to the question of who might be the audience for an essay on the presidential election in *Time* magazine is often "people who read *Time* magazine." Knowledge, in other words, is built in communities that share assumptions, but those assumptions often go unexamined. Sometimes those assumptions are products of a culture or a discourse, but sometimes they're not. Sometimes those assumptions are the products of conditions or civic circumstances that aren't reducible to knowledge. It's one thing to know the demographics of the group likely to read *Time* magazine, or to vote for Ralph Nader, or to be affected by certain kinds of advertising campaigns; it's another to see beneath the language, the discourse, and the arguments to get a glimpse of the structures of the polis that gives those arguments shape. One place where Richard Rorty's pragmatism falls down is in his insistence that language goes all the way down—that there are no material foundations we can access without the mediation of language—and that by changing the way people describe things, we can change circumstances. We may be able to change how people see the abortion debate by asking them to investigate how that knowledge is shaped; but given the choice of what to do in the face of an unexpected pregnancy, the material constraints placed on single mothers—the scarcity of abortion clinics, the dynamics of one's family, the dozens of people holding placards in the street—have palpable but often unreasonable effects, effects that shape what can and can't be argued. Argument is important because it forces writers to understand how what we know sometimes butts heads with circumstances that seem beyond our control, and it forces writers to consider not just audience but also the real circumstances that constrain audiences and the civic communities in which they live and work.

My last point is that argument is inextricably tied to ethics. Something high school students successfully take away from their English classes is that clear, critical writing helps them analyze and interpret literature successfully. What's less clear is whether students understand what good this ability is outside the school or classroom (short of getting them into a good college). If we understand ethics as the analysis of one's circumstances and the ways in which those circumstances determine what we can do and how we can act, then every argument has ethical consequences, consequences that may not be precisely what the writer might have imagined.[2] Recognizing that individuals live in a polis, in which all members are responsible for the welfare of all the others, means that one understands some constraints as inexorable and beyond one's control. Taking and arguing a position requires that you know how your fellows may arrive at the same, or a very different, position and how what you advocate affects members of your own community and—perhaps more profoundly—those outside it. In other words, it requires an ethical orientation toward others. Now, in some cases, you're just not going to change another person's mind for the same reasons that it's exceedingly hard to change the law of gravity or to challenge some scientific paradigms: there are circumstances—and other individuals—that act in ways you can't account for beforehand. One result of this recognition is that the writer needs to be humble even when he or she is the most certain: although compromise isn't always required, some things about your audience and about the world you and they share simply aren't easily knowable.

So what does all this have to do with the transition from high school to college writing? What I've just described as the principles of argument meet and constructively complicate the criteria Janet set out for inquiry. First, argument is a mode of inquiry *par excellence* so long as you don't see it as a substitute for wangling a deal or see its aim as "winning." If Toulmin and Perelman have taught us anything, it's that we should understand argument as "a process of inquiry with others," a way of reaching decisions on sometimes difficult issues in ways that involve others on whom those decisions impinge. The formulation of a claim is more complicated than "finding a topic," in that claims involve narrowing a topic of invention to a statement of ethical obligation. Rather than take Napster as a topic—which would involve exploring all of the issues involved, such as its origins, the controversy surrounding it, the differences of opinion on patent and copyright law that have arisen—a writer should situate the topic much more locally and take a position on one of those more local issues (Does Napster violate copyright law? Does it involve intellectual property? Do Napster and related software programs outstrip the law?). Exploration and research would then involve gathering data to support the claim, data that aren't simply cumulative but that require an ability to sort the relevant from the irrelevant, the related from the unrelated. But it also involves understanding how data that support a claim counter to the one chosen need to be integrated into the argument and argued against. To know this, students also need to understand the concept of "warrants," the more general claim that underwrites the more particular one they've chosen to make. So to argue that Napster is illegal because it violates copyright law, students need to know how copyright law works and what it protects, because the warrant "the violation of copyright is a violation of law" needs to be made part of the argument and needs to be researched—and understood—as such. As students do so—as they explore not just the Napster issue but also the warrant on which it is founded (issues of copyright law and the idea of intellectual property), their claims may change, their emphases may shift, and the positions they take may become more complicated or fraught. What is most important here is that students realize the complexity of the intellectual process of inquiry, that it involves more than fact-finding, and that as the process continues there's an equal chance that their claims will become strained as that they will become stronger.

Janet: I agree. Central to an understanding that writing is a process of inquiry is the fact that writing is also often used for critical purposes. I don't mean that students should write through a critical (i.e., theoretical) lens, such as feminist or Marxist, but I do mean that students should be critical, and they should write analytically about topics they want to investigate. Writing critically necessitates writing about topics important to the student writer's life and sociocultural, ethnic, or family realities. Robert Yagelski's *Literacy Matters: Writing and Reading the Social Self* addresses the concept of "local literacies," or literacy acts that are relevant and meaningful to the individual student. Viewed this way, literacy becomes more than a set of skills to be learned; it becomes "at heart an effort to construct a self within ever-shifting discourses" (9). Yagelski resists oversimplification of the act of writing as learning discrete subsets of skills such as punctuation, paragraph structure, and spelling. Instead, he exposes literacy learning, which includes reading and speaking as well as writing, for the culturally determined and institutionally defined experience that it is. Instead of simply being a process of decoding and encoding symbols, literacy is at the center of human development and essential to intellectual and ethical growth.

Critical writing is often a component of critical pedagogy, introduced to Western educators by Paulo Freire and elaborated on by Ira Shor, Peter McLaren, and Henry Giroux, among others. Critical pedagogy is often called pedagogy for the "process of freedom" or for the intellectual (and sometimes material) liberation of students. Students are asked to examine their own subject positions as well as those of their peers and think critically about social and political issues that affect these positions. They are asked to be active thinkers and to use writing (and other literacy acts such as talking and reading) as a tool to facilitate the critical examination of their world. The goal is to become more adept language users and also to become more aware of their place in modern society and how to actively respond to inequities within it. Amy Lee writes in *Composing Critical Pedagogies: Teaching Writing as Revision* that critical pedagogy "suggests that having a political, critical conception of one's teaching will necessarily produce liberatory effects in the classroom that, in turn, will produce better citizens" (6).

What does teaching for liberation have to do with learning to write? Lee states that being a "better" citizen is dependent on being critical about dominant discourses and being able to produce discourse in response that expresses these critical views for others. I would go even further to say that the very act of writing, and to a lesser extent talking, helps would-be critical citizens understand issues of ideology and oppression that permeate society and affect their role within it. This increased understanding leads to more appropriate interactions with fellow citizens of the world.

Let me provide an extended example to illustrate my point. Pretend I am teaching Homer's *Odyssey* to tenth-grade students in central Indiana. After they've read the work, I want students to write an essay that explores and analyzes a theme or issue from Homer's text—make an argument, if you will, a literary argument about the epic poem. Instead of giving a blanket assignment that might ask students to "discuss Odysseus's hubris and how it leads to many of his problems" or "defend *The Odyssey* as prototypical of the 'hero quest' genre," I ask students to comb through their reading journals or literature logs for possible topics of interest. With appropriate prompting, students could find some kernel of an idea worthy of their continued exploration. Then I could ask students to relate this chosen topic first to the text *(The Odyssey)* and then to their present life experience in some way. This series of connections ideally forms a sort of triad of personal response, textual analysis, and sociotextual criticism. If a student chooses to write about the story of the Cyclops and how it seems to represent Odysseus's struggle with his own arrogance, then he might see the relation between that and recent election rhetoric and the refusal of Gore to "concede," hostile letters to the editor in the *Lafayette Journal Courier,* or perhaps even his own stormy relationship with his father and the discussion they had last night. The point is that even the most critical, the most analytical, of essays can become even more intellectually stimulating if it integrates the author's intellectual and emotional experience with the text at hand. These two points on the triad tend to produce the third point: true criticism or evaluation of the text in relation to other texts, other readers, and other events in the world.

Mike: What Janet has just described is the process of intellectual inquiry. But I want to make something of a disclaimer here. Maybe because we've all taken the process (and now the postprocess) pedagogies of the last thirty years to heart, we don't think much about this part of the work of writing. While it's important to teach students that one begins with prewriting and moves to the articulation of a point, gathers material, drafts the material, revises it in a community of peers, and so on in a recursive process, teachers in high school and often in college frequently superimpose these steps onto the content or aim of the course: the final paper(s). I see the most insidious result of this superimposition in first-year college writing classes as the "participation grade": students dutifully making changes in their papers, or following up on suggestions from peers or teachers for further research, or following peer review guidelines to make marginal notes on one another's papers, with their papers changing barely at all. The dutiful completion of these tasks—revision—is meant to earn that portion of their total grade, often a fairly small portion, that might bump their borderline grade (the one based on the final draft) up to the next rung. One of the advantages of seeing writing as argument, as a process of critical inquiry that moves students from claims and data to warrants and grounds, is that students don't see "the process" as something forced. In fact, it's something they have to do in order to successfully argue a point. Of course, this is sometimes excruciatingly frustrating for students, who often see finding a topic and writing a paper on that topic *as* primarily expository and the research process as fact-finding. And yet what I see time and again as the director of a writing program is that the most successful teachers—and by that I mean the teachers whose students seem to be most engaged in the intellectual endeavor entailed by argument as displayed by their papers and their other writing—are those who encourage students to see the blind alleys and the contradictions they find as they explore the rough terrain of claims, warrants, and grounds as opportunities to change their minds or to engage in spirited disagreement with peers or teachers.

Janet: I think we both agree that a writing process needs to be more than isolated tasks that students complete; it needs to require critical thinking and be intellectually rigorous and socially aware. But can this kind of intellectual and discursive work take place only when writing the academic essay? What about asking students to write in other genres? Many secondary English teachers routinely ask their students to write not only expository prose but also stories, poems, plays, and more. Often, first-year college composition courses emphasize expository or argumentative writing to the exclusion of creative genres. I don't believe this exclusion is because university instructors don't value creative writing; I think it's because it is a commonplace that most students will spend the majority of their college and professional lives writing non-fiction, expository prose, and consequently instructors are preparing students more effectively if they ask them to write primarily in this genre. While this may or may not be true for individual students, more bothersome is the assumption that argumentative writing teaches a mental process or intellectual skill that other types of writing don't. Tom Romano has gone so far as to recommend the "multigenre" paper, a combination of many genres, including but not limited to autobiographical narrative, exposition, poetry, fiction, drama, and even drawings. Romano defines the multigenre paper as

> arising from research, experience, and imagination. It is not an uninterrupted, expository monologue nor a seamless narrative nor a collection of poems. A multigenre paper is composed of many genres and subgenres, each piece self-contained, making a point of its own, yet connected by theme or topic and sometimes by language, images, and content. In addition to many genres, a multigenre paper may also contain many voices, not just the author's. The trick is to make such a paper hang together. (x)

This "hanging together," I believe, is where critical thinking, or inquiry, can occur. The multigenre paper in its totality must have a point, a theme, or an argument. It is not just a collection of unconnected writings placed together in no particular order. It must say something in its completeness larger than the individual parts could achieve and larger than any one genre could accomplish alone. Often, such a paper speaks not only to the logical side of an argument, but also to the affective, aesthetic dimension. It uses and appeals to both brain hemispheres. Consequently, Romano asserts, multigenre papers are more persuasive, more powerful, and more effective than traditional, single-genre ones.

Many college students may very well have to write far more expository essays than any other kind, unless they choose to be creative writing majors. But I don't believe that creative genres necessarily ignore analytical thought, and I don't think that every kind of writing students do in high school has to explicitly prepare them for college. Creative writing can be intellectually rigorous. A story, a poem, a one-act play, all should say something, should have a point that is created and reinforced in subtle, difficult-to-accomplish ways: dialogue, character development, description, setting, conflict, and so forth. I admit that at times creative writing is assigned to high schoolers as a kind of "fun activity" with few demands or expectations. Students like to do it, so they actually write. There's nothing wrong with that, of course. At least they're putting pencil to page. But thinking back to stories that my own high school students wrote, I can't say that I encouraged or enabled them to think very hard about them because I didn't know *how* to teach these genres effectively. These stories were often weak and frustrating for me to evaluate because they fell into two camps: either they went on and on forever with no point and no center of gravity (to use Elbow's phrase), or they were so short that there was simply no opportunity for any point to be made. When taken seriously and taught effectively, however, creative writing is rigorous and requires much analytical thought, as well as advanced writing skill. Perhaps this is an area of writing instruction teacher educators should explore more carefully. It's not that creative writing—Britton's "poetic" side of the language continuum—can't be intellectually rigorous and instructive about language, but instead that teachers don't usually teach it that way.

Mike: Much of what I've said here seems to work against the multiple-genres criterion, the idea that high school and college writing should not only be argumentative or persuasive, but also expository, imaginative, fictional/poetic. I do think there is a place for any number of different genres in both the high school and the college writing classroom. But these forms of written expression need to be understood in the broader (critical) context that sees writing as ethical action, action that effectively changes how people act to and with one another. The multigenre paper, as described by Romano, is important insofar as it "hangs together" and is interwoven with reference to a theme or topic. More important than having the paper "hang together" is having the student understand *how* and *why* it hangs together and for what purpose. As Janet says, it's not necessarily the case that creative genres ignore analytical thought; in my experience, though, teachers who deploy such genres often do—partly due to lack of training and partly because students seem to enjoy writing fiction far more than they do arguments since they have been writing fiction since grade school and it comes far more easily. But if we see the task of writing instruction in high school and college as helping students understand the responsibility that writing involves, then any writing task in whatever genre should be tied to a broader ethical problem: how does writing as a creative act have consequences for how I and others live our lives, and what are those consequences insofar as I can determine them? Whether we tie *The Odyssey* to the local newspaper, or freewriting to an essay about politics or economics, seeing the writing as staking out a position is of paramount importance.

Janet: So perhaps the issue is not so much what genre we ask our students to write in, but more how they engage with their writing topics in whatever genre they have chosen or been assigned. Many high school and college writing classes, for example, use peer groups for response to writing. I also know from talking to teachers at all levels that peer response is one pedagogical practice that creates headaches. Often teachers don't think students are giving valuable feedback to each other—instead they are chatting or talking about spelling and commas. But if students are instructed in methods of peer review and collaborative work and are held accountable for this work, group collaboration can teach valuable lessons about writing and the intellectual process. Experiencing your ideas as received by a real audience, and then asking that audience questions about this reception, is invaluable to the writer.

Lev Vygotsky, the Russian linguist and psychologist, wrote much about social interaction with peers and how such interaction can lead to language development and cognitive growth. His theory of the "zone of proximal development" (see *Thought and Language*) asserted that learners learn through association with and instruction by those developmentally more sophisticated. In other words, there is a "zone" of possible learner growth, and teachers (or peers) can "bump" students to the uppermost point of this zone through modeling and direct instruction. If, however, we attempt to instruct to a point more advanced than is contained in this zone, the students will see no benefit. The same is true if we teach below the student's zone of growth because in effect we are teaching them what they already know. Consequently, working with a peer who can give feedback that is even a trifle more sophisticated than the student writer's perception can help the writer grow.

To reiterate, one question high school teachers (and those who educate them) should ask is "How can we better prepare students for college writing?" Answers to this question are many and varied, but one thing is clear: high school and college students are readers and writers of texts on a daily basis. Textual arguments surround and affect their world at every turn, on billboards, on television, on the radio, in novels, in the newspaper, and even in their school textbooks. The texts students read are becoming more diverse, more varied, and, dare I say, more subversive all the time. High school teachers, university teachers, and teacher educators must keep pace with these changes and continue to expand and complicate their understanding of rhetoric and writing to make it applicable to the present and future lives of students. In short, the complexities of our assignments, the ways we evaluate student writing, and the processes of writing we ask students to engage in must reflect the increasing complexity of postmodern communication.

Mike: What this increasingly complex postmodern situation suggests— or, in terms I prefer, what this complicated rhetorical situation suggests—about writing and critical inquiry is that it involves more than just collaboration, and it means that we need to move beyond Vygotsky's idea of the zone of proximal development. To see writing as primarily argumentative is to see it as an ethical act: writing doesn't just say, it *does*. To engage in an argument means to engage in a process of changing how you and other persons live their lives. The argument about Napster might be seen as a good example: to propose the imposition of early twentieth-century copyright laws on a late twentieth-century technology is to advocate whether and how information changes hands, and may involve broader implications not just for whether you can download music onto your hard drive, but whether you can download intellectual property protected as belonging to someone else, so that even visiting a Web site and printing what you find there might land you in jail, or at least incur a hefty fine. To make an argument like this means arguing with individuals who don't want to land in jail, or who like a marketplace of ideas that's free and unencumbered. To make this argument means taking your interlocutor seriously and writing your argument so that he or she will take you seriously. The other writers with whom one collaborates in a writing classroom aren't just other sets of eyes to catch faulty reasoning or errors the spellchecker missed; they are members of a broader community who potentially have a stake in the issue on which the writer takes a position.

One way to play out this ethical dimension of argument is to understand audience as something more than a demographic set of like-minded individuals who will read an essay and react to it in stereotypically predetermined ways. This involves bringing the extralogical elements of argument to the surface, and one of the best ways to do so is to see the ethical or policy implications of a proposed course of action in terms of their effects on real individuals. This can be done through collaboration in the classroom by providing criteria for peer review that don't concentrate on the structure of the essays brought to the group but on their implications: To whose advantage, and to whose disadvantage, will it be to see virtual music (or texts) as private property, and in what ways does the writer's argument imply an answer? Who should be punished for the proliferation of music—the software designer or the poor schmuck who's caught downloading a Green Day CD? Questions like these might get at the more visceral, less "logical" problems inherent in a position, and may lead to questions of knowledge even though they don't start from them.

Another way to play out the ethical dimension, though, is to worry less about collaboration and to concentrate instead on *consequences*. This means seeing audience as something real and greater than its representatives (members of the peer group) in the classroom. One way to make the focus on consequences palpable is to bring an argument to an actual, flesh-and-blood audience that may (and in some cases may not) be the one intended by the writer. Part of the work involved will be to identify a community or polis different from one's own and to begin to make contact with one or several of its members. A point of entry here might be classmates who themselves are members of a community not readily identifiable for "school" purposes (a social or religious organization, an ethnic or cultural affiliation, or a gender identification are only a few that readily come to mind). Students can also be encouraged to find campus or community groups whose constituents might entertain an argument on an issue close to its mission or interest. But regardless of how one identifies members of a community with whom to argue, the idea here is to understand that the consequences of an argument are both real and often not what one would expect if one were simply to map them rationally or enthymematically. Members of an audience outside the classroom are constrained not just by the "marketplace of ideas," but also by the scarcity of resources; the religious, cultural, and political ideologies of workplace and family; and the prejudices and fears that sometimes get overlooked in "intellectual" debate. A pedagogy of argument makes real not just the rational but also the irrational element of discourse that makes itself evident when the writer stakes out a position, and it allows students to confront the irrational critically (if not to ameliorate or dissolve it). Such a pedagogy is critical not (only) in the sense that it is politically motivated, but (also) in the sense that it sees language as having effects that are often invisible to the logical apparatus of argument but palpable and very real to those with whom the writer is arguing. It's a critical pedagogy that sees audience as polis rather than classroom and that sees language as having material and ethical, and not just "meaningful," effects.

Janet: Will a "seamless transition from high school to college" writing ever happen for any student? Possibly not. And we may not want to smooth out all the bumps, even if we could. Being pushed out of one's comfort zone and challenged intellectually can be frightening but also conducive to personal growth. So while seamlessness may not be a realistic or desirable goal, I do think that working to increase "readiness" for college writing is quite valid. The question is how to achieve this increased readiness. Perhaps step one is improved communication between university and high school writing teachers, which is, of course, one of the goals of this essay and of this book.

While I'm still not completely convinced that the language of rhetoric and argument is the best way to frame a high school writing class, I do understand Mike's point of view that it can be the most effective way to teach a college writing class. Regardless, I think the criteria I've discussed for a high school English class can be compatible with such a college curriculum. For the record, I don't think high school and college writing (or writing classes) will ever, or should ever, be exactly the same. They are different classes, taught in different contexts, to students at different cognitive and developmental (not to mention emotional) levels. To conflate the two would be unfair and inaccurate. Devising high school and writing curricula so that they are compatible, however, seems only logical and desirable for our students who are planning to attend college. So maybe that should be our goal when high school and college writing teachers communicate: an increased sense of compatibility, not the creation of a false seamlessness between our respective curricula.

Mike: That's right; seamlessness is probably the wrong metaphor. It's a metaphor that comes from the anxious feeling college and high school writing teachers have that the best they can do is give their students a working vocabulary for how language works and a set of practices that will come in handy down the road. So while it's true that Janet's criteria are valuable to the first-year college writing class too, they may not be as easily transferable as we've made them seem. In fact, one could argue that though the criteria are the same, the way they're "operationalized" is quite different. This operational difference is possibly unavoidable (and even desirable) since the high school and the university are obviously diverse kinds of institutions, and teachers in each are instructing students at different developmental and intellectual levels. One principal difference is this: students in the first-year college classroom are introduced to how fraught argument is, how necessary it is to inquiry but how difficult it is to use, particularly if seen as a way of forging consensus. The political notion of argument laid out in the second part of this essay, based on the criteria outlined in the first part, is a lot messier in practice than it sounds (if our first-year writing program is any indication), though it's just this messiness that makes the college writing classroom unique.

And yet in spite of this caveat, we both see in these criteria, and in their practice in a course on argument, a way to tie high school and college writing curricula together. The most critical ingredient is for teachers in both places to understand writing as an ethical activity and as a way to change the circumstances of those who engage in argument, sometimes for the better and sometimes for the worse. It's important for students to understand that what they do when they write is make an argument—take a position among other positions—and that by writing they are establishing themselves as members of a community, a polis, a discipline. It's sometimes not an especially lovely realization for students—in fact, it can be seen as risky to step out on a limb. But to view writing this way is to better prepare students for the kind of principled and critical work they will face not just in their high school or first-year college writing classes, but also as members of a democracy.

Janet: Mike's and my collaboration, as well as our continuing conversation, has been infinitely helpful to me as a teacher educator. It has required that I articulate what I believe about teaching high school writing and preparing new teachers. Mike's point of view has also often prompted me to rethink my positions, and such rethinking has had positive effects on my teaching. Therefore, I would encourage others to collaborate in similar and even more extensive ways. Recently, I've learned of a project in the Milwaukee area that encourages high school and college teachers to meet and discuss teaching on a regular basis. Called the Milwaukee Area Academic Alliance in English, it bills itself as

> a gathering of teachers of English from throughout southeastern Wisconsin who come together periodically to share ideas, information, problems, and possible solutions concerning the teaching of English. Established in 1988, the Alliance now serves high school and college English teachers and middle school language arts teachers in a six-county metropolitan Milwaukee area. (Maris)

The alliance organizes and presents three programs a year about teaching and invites teachers and administrators from all levels to attend. The university provides funding, mostly for mailing and copying costs. During the 2000–01 academic year, workshops were offered based on the theme Teaching Matters and included presentations about censorship and gender equality. Maris states that forty to ninety teachers regularly attend the workshops from a variety of secondary and postsecondary institutions.

Parks and Goldblatt describe a similar program in the May 2000 *College English*. Called The Institute for the Study of Literature, Literacy, and Culture at Temple University, it is described as "an alliance of university, public school, and community educators." The goals of the institute include sponsoring "courses, seminars, workshops, and lectures designed to bring together the educational community surrounding Temple University" (593). Like the Wisconsin alliance, the institute offers informal presentations and workshops that allow secondary teachers, English education specialists, and university English faculty to communicate about their respective concerns and even work together to tackle literacy problems and issues in their community.

Mike: This conversation, which began in 1997 and continued through the 2000 NCTE Annual Convention and this essay, has convinced me that we need to do a much better job of fostering collaborations between secondary schools and universities. When I queried a department administrator about this kind of collaboration—involving workshops for school and college writing teachers, occasional joint professional development opportunities, discussions about curriculum, and so on—I was told that it wasn't my job as the first-year writing administrator to foster these collaborations. Leave it to the College of Education, I was told. What this means is that in order to understand how a "rhetorical" college writing curriculum might work better as a continuation or complication of high school writing curricula, I need to work through other organizations: NCTE, the Conference on College Composition and Communication, and National Writing Project sites, and more informally (I was about to say "surreptitiously") through meetings with local district teachers, teachers in the College of Education, city school administrators, and parents of both college and high school students. As a writing program administrator, all of this seems mightily daunting—after all, the demands on my time are as great as those placed on other teachers and administrators. But to return to that seminar in 1997, what impressed me then—and what continues to impress me now—is the wealth of practical and theoretical knowledge about writing, argument, and ethics that high school writing teachers have and that is practically invisible to many if not most college and university writing teachers and administrators.

Janet: Alliances and institutes (both institutionally sanctioned and "surreptitious") such as these are examples of institutional collaborations that can occur among literacy educators at various levels. Even if your community or institution does not yet have such a communicative forum in place, there are ways for secondary-university conversations to occur. Collaborative writing, research, and conference presentations, for example, can examine and report on successful communication and encourage other educators to look beyond the four walls of their own institutions and take note of the system of education in which their students will function throughout their lives as students. The professional collaboration between Mike and me is one example of a positive cross-disciplinary and cross-contextual working relationship that can serve as a model for other educators who are seeking such communication. I'm not implying that dialogue such as ours, a snippet of which we've shared in this essay, is a cure-all for an often-tense working relationship between high schools (and teacher educators) and university English departments. Of course problems remain, and just as our students may never experience a seamless transition from high school to college writing, there may also never be a seamless working relationship between English education specialists and university composition specialists. But the argument Mike and I have made that seamlessness in the transition from high school to college writing may not be the most desirable path to seek applies equally well to communication between our disciplines. While mutual respect is essential and seeing eye-to-eye gratifying, part of what makes collaboration and conversation useful is the tension, the articulation of differences that we continue to hash out in stimulating, intellectual exchanges.

Notes

1. I'm thinking of Andrea Lunsford's essay, "The Nature of Composition Studies," in *An Introduction to Composition Studies*, edited by Erika Lindemann and Gary Tate (New York: Oxford UP, 1991), but could just as easily cite James A. Berlin's work in *Writing Instruction in Nineteenth-Century American Colleges* (Carbondale: Southern Illinois UP, 1984), Shirley Brice Heath's *Ways with Words* (Cambridge: Cambridge UP, 1983), or Mike Rose's *Lives on the Boundary* (New York: Free Press, 1989) for different examples of the changes in writing education and their consequences.

2. I'm using the term "ethics" in a way perhaps different from Aristotle's. If Aristotle used ethics to refer to a systematic notion of how one should act in accordance with the good, I'd revise the term slightly to suggest that ethics is a way of describing the tension between acting as one believes will accord with others' beliefs, and at the same time knowing that those others are completely irreducible to oneself. In other words, ethics refers to the vertigo associated with the thought that even with the best systems of knowledge available to humans (yourself and the others with whom you're trying to make policy decisions or even just mundane ones), there's an irrational element to human behavior, and to the language we think we can use to domesticate behavior to

knowledge, that we simply can't account for, and that makes us and others behave in ways we can't account for. So ethics is at once a system of behaviors and actions available to us *and* a description of what happens when we forgo all but one possibility and go down that road—a very dark one—without so much as a flashlight. Ethics is a precarious notion, which is what I think Perelman would suggest. See Geoffrey Galt Harpham's very smart and readable essay "Ethics" in Frank Lentricchia and Thomas McLaughlin's *Critical Terms for Literary Study* (Chicago: U Chicago P, 1995).

Works Cited

Britton, James, et al. *The Development of Writing Abilities (11–18)*. Schools Council Research Studies Series. London: Macmillan Education, 1975.

Corbett, Edward P. J. *Classical Rhetoric for the Modern Student*. 2nd ed. New York: Oxford UP, 1971.

Elbow, Peter. *Writing without Teachers*. New York: Oxford UP, 1973.

Garver, Eugene. "Aristotle's Rhetoric as a Work of Philosophy." *Philosophy and Rhetoric* 19.1 (1986): 1–22.

Hillocks, George Jr. *Teaching Writing as Reflective Practice*. New York: Teachers College, 1995.

Lee, Amy. *Composing Critical Pedagogies: Teaching Writing as Revision*. Urbana, IL: National Council of Teachers of English, 2000.

Maris, Mariann. "Milwaukee Area Academic Alliance in English." University of Wisconsin–Milwaukee document, Oct. 2000.

Parks, Steve, and Eli Goldblatt. "Writing beyond the Curriculum: Fostering New Collaborations in Literacy." *College English* 62 (2000): 584–606.

Perelman, Chaim. *The Realm of Rhetoric*. Notre Dame: U of Notre Dame P, 1982.

Romano, Tom. *Blending Genre, Altering Style: Writing Multigenre Papers*. Portsmouth, NH: Heinemann, 2000.

Rorty, Richard. *Philosophy and the Mirror of Nature*. Princeton: Princeton UP, 1979.

Toulmin, Stephen. *The Uses of Argument*. Cambridge: Cambridge UP, 1958.

Vygotsky, Lev. *Thought and Language*. Cambridge: MIT P, 1962.

Yagelski, Robert P. *Literacy Matters: Writing and Reading the Social Self*. New York: Teachers College, 2000.

9 Talking about the Transition: Dialogues between High School and University Teachers

Wendy Strachan
Western Washington University

When Wendy, a university writing teacher, met with high school teachers to discuss "good writing" and "good teaching," she initiated what has become an ongoing dialogue with surprises and insights for all. The following account of those conversations points out the need for—and the value of— such cross-grade encounters.

"I think I ended up with a C after coming from high school with always an A."

"Last semester, grades on my writing assignments ranged from poor to just mediocre. I have not been used to such grades."

When they sign up for my first-year course in academic writing, students have already had at least a semester of university course work. They've discovered that what they thought is "good" writing often isn't and, further, that it's quite difficult to determine what is expected of them. They commonly voice despair at being unable to grasp "what the professor wanted" in their writing. As first-year students with B or better averages from high school, they enter our prestigious institution from among a pool of the most academically successful students in British Columbia. While they are likely to come from diverse linguistic backgrounds, English is not a major impediment in their learning. So what is it, I wondered, that makes the transition from high school writing to university writing such a letdown, so bewildering, and so difficult?

The author acknowledges and thanks the core group of teachers from Sir Winston Churchill Secondary School in Vancouver, British Columbia, who participated in the discussions cited in this chapter: Starla Anderson, Elizabeth Barthel, Muriel Dunsford, Tom Henderson, James Hill, Louise Howard, and Kim Parrish.

I was sure that high school teachers are no more likely to award undeserved A's for writing than their university counterparts. I was also sure that their expectations for student writing would take account of what seems developmentally appropriate as well as what is required for success in externally imposed standardized examinations. But I am no longer a high school English teacher; I've been teaching at the postsecondary level for the past fifteen years and in an English department for the past five and have little collegial contact with secondary teachers. I am clearly not alone in this respect, for as the introduction to Chapter 14 notes, "it is an unacknowledged truism that high school English teachers and professors of English in colleges and universities have all too little to say to one another" (p. 214). During a fall conference conversation over coffee, however—a conference at which, paradoxically but typically, I was in my role as presenter to teachers—Starla Anderson, a veteran teacher at a local city high school, suggested that we set a time to meet with members of her department.

In my conference presentation, I had been identifying what I saw students experiencing as writers at the university, information based on five years of teaching a first-year academic writing course and of meeting with students in one-on-one consultations in our Writing Centre. Starla and I agreed that an exchange about what we do might enable us to develop some shared understandings of our different contexts for teaching writing and perhaps identify ways to mitigate the problems of transition. Over a period of about eight weeks, I met after school with a core group of seven teachers at Starla's school and also with two other groups of senior-level English teachers to discuss these same issues for periods of one to four hours in roundtable-type sessions during professional development days. These latter sessions provided a larger context for interpreting the insights that came through the smaller core group exchanges. Each session was audiotaped and transcribed.

I approached these various meetings as a learner, eager to bridge the divide; I found myself met more than halfway by equally eager secondary teachers who had both practices and views to share and questions to ask. Through e-mail and telephone calls, we identified specific topics to focus on in our discussions: teachers' goals and expectations for writing, problems with student writing, desirable habits and attitudes toward writing, and criteria for assessment. The core group of seven gathered around a table on a Monday afternoon after school for the first session, a tape recorder in the centre with the tea and cookies. We all leaned inward. After the introductions, I asked, "Well, shall we begin with some talk about what you see to be your responsibilities as English teachers?"

There was a moment of silence, broken by a male voice to my left. "Are you serious? You really want to know?" Everyone laughed.

"Yes, really. What's real? What's workable?" I asked.

"[Students getting] a good mark on the provincial exam. That's very important, high scores. That's what we have to do."

Murmurs of agreement around the table were echoed in similar comments and expressions of concern about this responsibility.

"I am kind of 'mentioning' the grade 12 exam when I teach them expository writing."

"I find that the climate, because of the provincial exam, seems to favour mostly in-class writing." Teachers give students practice in the kinds of writing they will be asked to do on the grade 12 final exam, such as the fifty-minute timed writing on a given topic that is usually phrased as a single word: *remembering, manners, searching.* Students must write spontaneously in the given time. The directions tell them to "draw on any aspect of your life: your reading, your own experiences, the experiences of others, and so on."

"What this means," said Starla, "is that they have an open topic and are encouraged to blend different genres—to blend narrative, expository, and descriptive methods—so I help them to develop descriptive narrative they can use as illustrations in the expository essay. Having marked a lot of English 12 finals, I see those are the essays that get the best marks."

The outcomes of this kind of focused effort are evident in the results: "We have very high standards, and in fact our kids graduate with good solid B averages in this school. Even though 80 percent are coming out of ESL [English as a Second Language], we bring out the best in these kids, and they show very good results province wide." Muriel reported a student who got 100 percent in English 12 even though English is not his first language.

These accounts are confirmed by my university students, who recall spending time in high school getting "weekly writing tests. There would be a topic and we would have fifty minutes to write three pages." I realize how different the situation is for the university professor, who answers to no one about choice of genre or length of writing assignments. Students' success or failure in university courses is attributed not to the teacher but to the learner. For the grade 11 and 12 teachers, the need for students to do well on final, external exams is a responsibility and constraint that weighs heavily. I no longer raise my eyebrows at the thought of these fifty-minute training sessions! The exam results determine students' future opportunities for further education and for job opportunities, and the teachers are embedding exam preparation within a context that accommodates multiple purposes. The exam, its nature and form, and the criteria it sets for success necessarily influence decisions about what kind of writing to assign, how to assess it, and how much time to spend on it.

Identifying the exam as a priority, however, prompted some questioning of what taking such a stance entails. Many, perhaps most, teachers are under no illusions about the limitations and implications of simply preparing students for the type of writing expected on the final exams. The structure of the open-topic "expository writing" requirement conforms, not surprisingly, to the traditional five-paragraph essay. Among the core group of seven, as well as among teachers from other groups, there were varied opinions about the value of teaching this structure, and people expressed strong views.

"We are all going to encourage [students] to be creative and to come forward . . . to find their own voice and try to be honest with it; don't write what you think any of us want and simply follow the formula. Sometimes they get knocked down for it. But that's what we want, those distinctive voices."

"With that structure, you get 'sandwiches' and 'hamburger' snippets rather than a sustained argument of any sort, whether it is expository writing or a creative story. The writing I have them do beyond journals, which is a paragraph or two, would be more sustained—it would be either essays or their own version of a story, but definitely multiparagraph."

On the other hand, some believe equally strongly that "the way to get started is with a structure from which to work and then when you become skilled you can remove yourself from that structure, but until you have it . . . . In the early years, there has to be something that they can start from. Otherwise, by the time they reach grade 10 or 12 they don't have that organizational framework. That's what I see as the primary need."

In response to that comment, I suggested, "Well, from our point of view, I'm not sure that's necessarily the case. You can't simply apply a set of fixed rules to university writing. It's not the case that an essay has to be five paragraphs or that a thesis has three things. Students run into difficulty if that is the only [structure] they know. We have to unteach the five-paragraph essay. So they do need to learn how to write longer pieces, because five paragraphs won't work for a 2000-word paper."

We laughed at that idea, imagining such a paper, but someone pointed out that the problem exists at the other end of the spectrum as well.

"I was just going to say that I think some of my students had a real problem last year in the English 12 exam with writing a 300-word composition that was supposed to be an expository essay. Taking the form of the old five-paragraph essay—that's a 60-word paragraph! It gets so choppy. As the kids said, 'What are we supposed to do? Are we supposed to write a 300-word paragraph?' I don't think so. That whole thing was really unsettling for a lot of the students because they have been taught certain things since grade 8."

There were nods around the room and some discomfort, perhaps as thoughtful colleagues indirectly challenged each other's beliefs and practices. But this was what we came for—to hear each other and explore some of the territory we inhabit. I had put some students' comments on an overhead, and we looked at these. Students recognize the limitations of having only one structure to rely on for all "expository writing," and they recognize too the ways in which university writing asks something different of them:

> In university, I need to learn different styles of writing academically that are suitable for different situations. Last semester, I wrote two papers my marker did not like but I didn't know how to write the second one any differently.

> I am comfortable when I write the classic five-paragraph structured essay. The only problem is that my paper turns out quite limp.

> In my opinion, university writing heavily involves researching and critical thinking. In high school, teachers are emphasizing format—the hamburger style.

The need for "different styles of writing academically" was illustrated as I showed teachers successful samples of the variety of writing a first-year university student might be expected to produce over the course of the first two semesters. Just in the opening few sentences of each of these essay samples, we could see different expectations about organization, voice, and discourse conventions. How the writers establish their own position and role, for instance, is evident in different ways of wording and is more and less explicit and relevant in each piece: in the philosophy sample, the writer is summarizing and stays in the background; in the political science opening, the writer explicitly introduces his argument, position, and purpose in the paper but refers not to himself but to "the paper"; in the fine arts piece, the writer is immediately visible and lets us know that she will be interpreting the topic from the point of view of a particular critical discourse. We don't find "grabber" openings here, nor "three things" that follow from a thesis.

Philosophy 100   **The Theaetetus**

In the passage from "The Theaetetus" by Plato, Theaetetus and Socrates try to define knowledge. By the end, Socrates shows Theaetetus that "true belief with the addition of an account [is] knowledge. . . ." (205). He also points out that knowledge has two facets, "the thing itself" and the objects of knowledge (205). Similarities and differences between "The Theaetetus" and Elliott Sober's passage will be discussed after the summary of "The Theaetetus."

Political Science 100

SINKING THE SENATE:
Abolishing What Cannot Be Reformed

Attempts to reform the Canadian Senate have spanned more than a century. From the 1887 Interprovincial Conference to the Charlottetown Accord of 1992, many proposals seeking modifications to the Senate have been presented. However, the problems of the Canadian Senate are not likely to be alleviated with reforms, which could simply create different (and sometimes greater) problems. Because no reform schemes without significant drawbacks have been posited, it is becoming clearer that the shortcomings of the Senate lie in the fundamental nature of the body itself. This essay intends to show, then, that a logical course of action would require the Senate's total abolition.

Fine Arts 100

I cried when watching Franco Zeffirelli's film of *La Traviata*, the classic opera by Guiseppe Verdi. I did not want to cry in class, I tried to hide my tears, but I could not seem to help it. The music, the rising, passionate voices, seduced me and brought tears to my eyes. I was angry with myself for being moved: part of me was saying, "this is a ridiculous romance, why are you crying?" I knew, as a feminist, that this movie was rife with misogyny from the very first image of Violetta, beautiful and ill.

Psychology 100   **Abstract**

This study examines the effect of colour on memory, colour serving as an attention and arousal factor. The prevailing view in research on the physiological and psychological effects of colours is that warm colours such as red are more arousing and attention enhancing than cool colours, such as blue and green, are. In the present experiment . . .

English 101—Introduction to the Novel

When John Willoughby dramatically enters the life of Marianne Dashwood, in *Sense and Sensibility*, he creates a first impression of a vibrant hero. When he sees Marianne struggling to rise from a fall that injured her ankle, Willoughby's quick thinking translates into swift action, and he "ran to [Marianne's] assistance . . . took her up in his arms without further delay, and carried her down the hill . . . he bore her directly into the house . . . and quitted not his hold till he had seated her in a chair in the parlour" (Austen 37).

Two lines of discussion followed from our reading of these extracts: first, the use of the first-person pronoun "I" and the paper's reference to itself in the political science sample and, second, the implications for English teachers of the diversity of these writings.

Two of the "rules" students consistently report being given by their high school teachers are not to refer to the paper and not to use "I" in their formal writing. The introduction to the political science paper attracted strong and generally negative response from these teachers.

"I would consider that very poor writing."

"I have a problem with simplistic introductions of that sort . . . 'I will begin to write' and that sort of thing. I tend to regard those as weak introductions and kind of an easy start for a first draft but not very artful for a finished project."

"That last sentence: 'This essay intends to show, then, that the only logical course of action requires the Senate's total abolition' would be much stronger and more forceful if it left out the first words 'This essay intends to show, then,' and simply stated the writer's thesis: 'the only logical course of action requires the Senate's total abolition.'"

"That's another way of saying 'I think,' and I was trained that you don't have to say 'I think.' It's embedded in the paper itself that you are thinking this—you signed your name to the paper."

As I listened to these objections and the reasoning the teachers offered, I could hear echoes of the students in my classes as well, and I wanted to tuck these comments away for future reference. They illustrated for me the difference in role that student writers must take on in their university writing, a difference reflected in these stylistic preferences.

"So, how is it for you?" I was asked. I acknowledged the logic of the teachers' thinking and the fact that wordings such as "I intend to show" could be seen as redundant. "But," I pointed out, "this use of explicit signals to the reader is very common in most disciplines. It's true it looks simple, but this example and others—which are more elaborate and set out the structure of the paper as well—are ways in which the writer makes it plain what position he or she is taking and how the paper will develop. In most of the social sciences, in women's studies, in some subfields of geography, and even in the introductions to physical sciences, you encounter these kinds of signals to the reader."

There were some nods of agreement.

"Equally, if not more importantly," I went on, " is the fact that the writer in this political science paper is simulating the role of someone participating in a conversation among colleagues. He foregrounds the paper rather than the writer, however, and while it's true the second half of the sentence indicates the writer's position, the modalized phrasing also implies that this is not necessarily a fixed position. It indicates that this paper may or may not make a contribution in a setting where people are in the business of [the] making of knowledge. It offers a way of looking and an argument that asks to be taken seriously but expects critical reading and response. So this is unlike a confrontational or debating stance—it wants to convince or persuade but it manifests a different relationship, one that is characteristically academic; the writer is participating in a social activity—this is writing as sociocultural participation—so it isn't simply a matter of having his or her own opinion."

"Well, the rule I recall from university days went something like this," responded the teacher to my left. "When you have become somewhat of an expert in the field . . . then it may be appropriate to contrast your position with the positions of others that you may also be discussing in your paper. But your discussion is not generally going to be about your position in relation to the general discourse on this particular subject. It is going to be about the work of others. So I have a problem with this."

I realized, as I reflected later, that the difference in view may reflect a difference in perception of the relationship of students to their subject matter and, perhaps, in perceptions of learning and knowing. Students observe that "in university, I need to use more of my judgment, critical thinking and analysis in writing, whereas in high school, writings were more from books and involved less critical thinking." Such an observation echoes this teacher's characterization of the student as not yet expert enough to be critical and express a view. When we moved on in our group discussion to the related matter of using first person, we raised more issues and questions that appear to be about stylistic conventions but that I think are actually about stance and relation to the subject matter. Although I have long challenged what I regard as an obsession with rules, I had not really understood until then how the concern for rules makes it possible to overlook the nature of stance and relation.

"Can I ask you a question? Everybody else in my department except me has this obsession with 'never use "I,"' and it just irritates the hell out of me. So would you say something about that? I say sometimes you can say 'I.' When they come into my class, I tell them they can use 'I' as long as they don't say, 'in my opinion, I.'"

One of the teachers shook her head and expressed what appeared to be a common frustration. "At the junior level and the senior level, [students] are very much into response. How do you teach them that they need to be learning a process of social-cultural participation? I don't see them doing that when they use 'I.' As soon as they start saying 'I' in their essays, they are just responding, they are not arguing anymore. They are not developed to the point where they are making those kinds of distinctions. They think if they can say 'I,' they are being asked to give opinions and that means response. How do you teach that and how can you say, 'Oh yeah, go ahead, say "I" all you like?'"

We seemed to agree that this was not an issue easily dealt with. I suggested they might make distinctions between the personal "I" of "I really loved this book" and the discursive "I," which indicates not concrete but textual action, the "I" of the introduction that tells us how the writer plans to sequence the arguments and what is to be included. I said that I tell my students, "We don't care that you loved it!"

"I say that to them, too," someone quickly responded.

We all laughed but recognized we were dealing with more significant issues than simply whether there was a rule to be applied and under what conditions: one obvious issue was what implications we could draw for the high school English teacher about the diversity in university writing. The examples I had shown were from several different disciplines, only one from English. But these were English teachers, responsible for teaching English language and literature and, as they were quick to point out, it is not up to them to try to assign and teach the conventions for writing in all the other disciplines.

"My experience," suggested one of the veterans in the group, "is that writing, the teaching of writing, is seen as the exclusive domain of the English teacher. You have mentioned history and psychology, and I am sure they do writing in the sciences at the university level. But in the high school, there is a reluctance on the part of our colleagues from the other disciplines to undertake to teach the kind of writing that their disciplines demand. That's why they may assign a research paper in social studies and you get a pastiche of thoughts. It's all nicely put together, but it really doesn't say much. It doesn't form an argument. In many cases, it doesn't even express an opinion; it's just there. And now the problem somehow becomes the English teacher's—it's her fault: 'You are not teaching them how to write.' I spent years thinking about it, participating in discussions about writing across the curriculum. It is still not happening in a way that makes our job easier—not to try to make our jobs any easier, but to share the notion that writing is something that occurs in every discipline."

Others voiced similar experiences: "When I talk to people in the sciences or even socials [social studies] and I talk to them about teaching writing—teach how to write about your subject—I just hit a blank wall. What they want is to get these nodules of information plugged in there somewhere, and that's what they look for. I feel sometimes that, you know, I'm the voice crying in the wilderness. Like I am the only one who is asking for a developed argument. When certainly the social studies teacher ought to be asking as well. . . ."

"After teaching a bit of socials too, I was amazed to realize you were not responsible for marking grammar in social studies papers, Canadian history, and so forth. Most teachers don't bother with any of that. A lot of projects are full of errors. You would only have to look at some rooms with posters and stuff, and it's full of grammatical errors. We are the only ones who work on it. They don't believe it is truly necessary."

Starla summarized the issue for us: "On the one hand, it's English teachers who are given this task of helping kids develop expository essays, and on the other hand, up at the university all these disciplines all have their own unique rules about how they want these essays written. It seems to me that we have identified the crux of the problem. That first of all there has to be some training of teachers in all these disciplines to get busy in grades 11 and 12 and help the kids write the kind of essays they are going to be expected to write when they enter university. English teachers cannot do it all."

We all knew we were going over familiar ground, and the perceptions were as accurate now as they had ever been: English teachers cannot take on the task of teaching the discourses of other disciplines. I suggested, however, that what they might do is demonstrate and teach attitudes toward writing that unseat notions about writing as rule-governed practice and replace those notions with ideas about function and situation and the social nature of writing. The examples we had looked at did not conform to many of the "rules" that students have internalized.

"The students I see are preoccupied with certain beliefs and rules about what good writing is, and that does have to be challenged. Their assumptions are not generalizable to all situations. But the most important thing it seems to me is attitude. Attitude towards what writing is and what it can do and what is good. Rigid regulations about what is good and what works are difficult to dislodge because they get very deeply embedded. Students have remarkably strong memories. Consistently they will say, 'Stay away from jargon.' But I will teach them to use jargon—jargon in the sense that you have got to use the technical language of the subject. They say, 'Don't start sentences with *but* or *and*' and 'Always write an outline.' But outlines can be extremely constraining, and often [students] stop thinking when they have an outline. They tend not to listen to their own meanings and reasoning as they write because they are just following the outline. Not that outlines are always a bad thing!"

"They also say they try to avoid the passive voice, and some students attribute their 'dull writing' to overuse of the passive. And maybe they are right—but the passive voice is typical of the methods sections of science reports and of lab reports. So we need to encourage them to be aware of differences in style and purpose and to examine their own writing as well as that of others in terms of purposes. They do that in their reading of literature—so perhaps extend that kind of analysis and awareness to other genres and discourses. What this kind of practice implies is that there is time for some sort of process during writing and response to drafts."

I explained our practice in my first-year academic writing course of response, which is based on the think-aloud protocol. The responder reads the paper aloud to the writer and stops to report what she is thinking as she reads; that is, the reader reports how she is constructing meaning, phrase by phrase or sentence by sentence, following the reasoning of the text. When something makes her stop and reread, that stopping is reported and sometimes an explanation given of what the reader thought or wondered. First-year writing instructors emphasize that every sentence should lead to the next—the reader should be able to predict what is coming, so if I read a sentence and expect X to come next but it doesn't, something may have misled me. I acknowledged to these teachers that this is a time-consuming process, and the sample we looked at affirmed the general response in the room that if I was proposing a similar approach for high school classrooms, I was obviously out of touch with their realities!

"Our school has a philosophy that the grade 8s are supposed be doing lots of reading and creative writing, the grade 9s are supposed to focus on the writing process—we actually have a folder. I don't know how many grade 9 teachers use it anymore, but this has certainly been a big part, teaching writing as a process, and then there is the peer editing and the brainstorming, revision, and we do the whole process. That is supposed to be taught beginning in eighth [grade], focusing on the ninth and repeating in the tenth, so that by the time they get to the eleventh and twelfth grades they know how to do that process. They don't have any time to do process writing in class, but if they have had the training in the first three years, they are supposed to know how to do it, though I guess obviously they don't."

Others affirmed the difficulty of a process approach: "There is a reluctance to polish those first drafts. . . . There is a phenomenon that close enough is good enough. . . . We spend a lot of time talking about thesis statements and developing an introduction and argument, but we don't have time to read everything they write and provide feedback. . . . They do not have the background to recognize what's going on. . . . I give them at least ten days to two weeks to write an essay at home, and they still don't do any revision. I am not robbing them of the chance to do rewrites and to peer edit. . . . I simply don't have time to mark something twice."

Yet others adopt strategies to encourage process: using rubrics that identify criteria for each piece of writing; making time in class for students to read and respond to each other's papers; implementing flexible deadlines that result in some students handing in multiple drafts; recommending getting help from someone who will be an editor; and offering extra marks for rewriting graded drafts.

Lack of time isn't the only reason some teachers don't emphasize process; plagiarism is also a major problem. "I tend with regular classes—that is, not the international baccalaureate classes—not to give too many of those take-home assignments. Certainly not essays. Cheating and plagiarism are more and more of an issue. In an in-class essay, it's their pen and their brain and their heart and that's all there is."

"You see real discrepancies between take-homes and in-class writing."

"I find that, because of the provincial exam and the paranoia, . . . ESL students are getting essays written by tutors; most of the writing in high school is first draft in class. I would say that 50 percent to 70 percent of the writing that students do for me is in class."

My description of the response process had highlighted not only differences between high school and university practices but also, and even more clearly, the different conditions under which we teach. I work with two classes and thirty-five students; these teachers typically have seven classes a day and over two hundred students to see each week. A high percentage of their students do not speak English as a first language. While I do not *have* to be responsible for the difficulties such students may have with the English language, competence in English being a prerequisite for the writing course, the high school teachers are not able to select or exclude students. I have plenty of time allotted for preparation of class activities and detailed commentary on papers; theirs is very limited. While I know there is a massive essay market available on the Internet, I do not need to be too concerned about plagiarism: I supply a range of nonstandard readings to be used in class and have such an elaborate process of feedback that students would not be able to submit a purchased essay without attracting attention.

This exchange of views and practices has been richly rewarding for us all. Our conversations have illuminated the contrasts in the places we inhabit and the corresponding contrasts in our practices and goals. For me these conversations have become anchoring points for the comments students make in my class about their beliefs and assumptions about writing and themselves as writers. The conversations have contextualized and situated those comments and given me insight into their meaning and origin that I can use in practical ways in my teaching. I can better explain to my students why they have learned what they learned and why it made sense in the high school setting. I can encourage the development of a metalanguage for reflection on the differences in emphasis, on the differences in the roles they are to take on, and on the stances they need to assume toward their subject matter. I can better help them understand what they are doing when they write at the university now that I better understand what lies behind the attitudes and beliefs they report. Among the high school teachers, there seems to be a consensus on the constraints they encounter as they work to teach writing but no corresponding consensus on how to respond to them. They find multiple routes that suit their own personalities and judgments, but our conversations were an open forum for hearing what others do and how they do it, offering each person new perspectives to consider.

The discussions that provided the material for this description and analysis took place over a period of eight weeks with three different groups. The one I have labeled the "core group" met after school and the others during professional development days. The professional day sessions drew teachers from many city high schools and were titled "Making the Transition from High School to University." They were described as a conversation with a university instructor for the purpose of sharing perceptions and practices in teaching writing. Starla's observations about the sessions again seemed to summarize for all:

"What these conversations did was reinforce the sense that we are doing a great job by teaching writing. We spend a lot of time teaching and assessing writing and need to feel that it matters, that it's worth taking seriously and that it is worth caring about. It was great to see how many people showed up to talk about this. A lot of us feel that instructors at the university don't have a clue about the conditions of teachers at the high school, so these conversations are highly motivating—we can see that our work is respected and understood."

As we reviewed the outcomes of our sessions, we decided we would like to take a next step in the dialogue. We will try to set up a meeting on our university campus between a group of faculty in the English department, and perhaps other disciplines as well, and a group of ten to twelve teachers from the high school. I had e-mail addresses for those who came to the first sessions, and it seems likely that we can write a proposal and draw together a group from a few schools in the area. A cross-disciplinary committee is already established at the university to generate proposals for rethinking how we teach writing, so that would be a group to approach for our cross-institutional dialogue as well. Our first collaboration enabled us to develop some shared understandings of our different contexts for teaching writing and to compare our purposes and practices. In a second round of conversations, we anticipate developing not only understandings and awareness but also relationships with individuals who can actively pursue collaborations such as reciprocal observing in classrooms, collaborative teaching projects, and discussion and assessment of student writing. We emerged from this initial collaboration feeling that high school English teachers and professors of English in colleges and universities have much to say to each other if we construct the settings and raise the questions that are at the heart of our teaching.

V Starting College in High School

While most high schools try to prepare students for college writing, some schools also offer college writing courses for students during their senior year. Institutions can also bridge the divide by letting college students mentor high school students, or even by bringing college and high school teachers together for common training. The following chapters explore all three such programs.

Chapter 10 describes Susan Kapanke and Melissa Westemeier's experiences with a dual-enrollment course—a course offered at high school but following a college curriculum and for which students get college credit. Although the syllabus is the same as one from a college course, Susan and Melissa note that seventeen-year-olds who take such courses on high school campuses seem to differ significantly from the eighteen-year-olds who take the same courses on college campuses.

In Chapter 11, Kim Jaxon describes a program in which college students serve as mentors to high school students, coaching them on the same writing tasks given to first-year college students. Though not a dual-enrollment course, the program does offer one credit hour as an incentive to participate. The course is also unusual in that most of the mentoring takes place online rather than in person.

When Chris Jennings (a community college instructor) and Jane Hunn (a high school teacher) saw students satisfactorily complete high school writing programs only to be placed in remedial courses at the college level, they suspected that the problem might lie not with the students but with the differing goals and expectations of the high school and the college writing programs. In Chapter 12, they explain how they used a survey to identify differences and then brought high school and community college teachers together for a series of workshops to help create some shared expectations.

The dual-enrollment program described in Chapter 10 has been in place for years; the projects described in Chapters 11 and 12 are both still developing. All three, however, offer workable models of collaboration between high schools and colleges.

10 The University of Wisconsin Oshkosh and Area High Schools Strike a Partnership

Susan Kapanke
Elkhorn High School

Melissa Westemeier
Kaukauna High School

Susan and Melissa teach college-level English composition to high school seniors through a partnership with the University of Wisconsin Oshkosh, enabling their students to earn dual credit. The following dialogue explores their curriculum and experiences as teachers in this program and some of the unique challenges and opportunities that accompany teaching college English to high school seniors.

The Cooperative Academic Partnership Program (CAPP) offers high school students the opportunity to earn dual credit for various courses before they graduate from high school. Wisconsin high schools offer CAPP courses in areas such as English composition, American literature, art history, and Spanish. CAPP students pay reduced tuition rates to the University of Wisconsin Oshkosh and earn college credits as well as appropriate high school credits. UW Oshkosh approves the CAPP courses offered and ensures that the instructors meet the requirements of both institutions.

One reason high schools embraced CAPP courses is that more and more students began traveling to area colleges to earn college credits while in high school. Offering dual credits *in* high schools keeps students on high school campuses, thereby minimizing the liability, money, and time involved in commuting. CAPP benefits both the high schools and the parents as the students save hundreds in tuition. High schools break even because they use the returned tuition to pay staff; students end up paying half the regular university tuition.

Junior or senior CAPP students must have an ACT score of 24 or higher, have a cumulative grade point average of 3.25 or higher, or be in the top 25 percent of their class in order to take the course for dual credit. Occasionally, a promising student who does not meet the college requirements can enroll based on the instructor's recommendation. Typical CAPP students are high achieving, college-bound, and heavily involved in high school life. We find that their needs are quite different from a regular college student's, and the courses must consider those differences, in both curriculum and pedagogy.

The CAPP composition course fulfills the three-credit requirement for first-year composition at most colleges and universities. Students who earn a B or better in CAPP composition can enroll in sophomore-level English courses when they begin college. Most students easily transfer their CAPP credits to their colleges the following fall, occasionally as humanities credits but usually as fulfillment of English 101 requirements.

Both of us base our courses on the various rhetorical writing patterns that students will encounter in their academic careers as well as in their personal and professional lives. These patterns include writing narration, argumentation/persuasion, definition, classification, and literary analysis and research/position papers.

Curriculum

Susan: Although I do not want to assign busywork, I believe certain usage principles must be reviewed at the college English level. English teachers have a professional responsibility to teach certain skills, and not to do so because the particular concept is not "fun" to teach or too difficult to teach is abnegating our responsibility. We should, for example, teach pronoun-antecedent agreement, sentence structure, the use of coordination and subordination to show the relationship between ideas, parallel structure, and wordiness/conciseness in writing. While mastery of usage skills contributes to effective writing, I often tell my students that if they can understand and demonstrate parallel structure in their writing, their style will improve greatly; certainly they will be more successful in communicating the relationship between ideas.

I often tell my students, "Language is power!" We should make an amendment to our Constitution stating that every U.S. citizen has the right to know how his or her language works. Effective speaking and writing give a person a decided edge, an advantage in his or her personal and professional life. Using language well can bring wealth, authority or power, and popularity. Good communication skills are required in business, industry, law, government, national and international politics, education, medicine—in all professions. As I tell my students, quoting a trade publication brochure, "Talk is cheap, but good communication is priceless."

Melissa: Because teachers of most English language arts classes in our departments teach writing in relation to specific genres or literature, we spend little time on writing techniques. It is therefore unrealistic to expect every paper from the beginning of the semester to be written at a college level; students simply haven't had enough instruction.

I break down various writing techniques for my CAPP students throughout the semester so they can absorb and develop each one individually. For each paper I assign, my students also learn and apply a specific writing technique. As they move into the next paper, they have to apply previous techniques taught or reviewed, but I reinforce only as needed. For example, I first teach the narrative. The technical skill I focus on is using specific and vivid vocabulary choices, a natural match for what tends to be a descriptive genre of writing. Practice drills and focused peer editing and revision help students grasp this technique and apply it in their own writing. The next paper I assign includes not only the vocabulary emphasis but also a new skill, such as using active voice or sentence variety. By the final paper, the students find that most of these techniques have become second nature to them; they understand writing patterns and have the skills necessary to write for a wide variety of purposes.

The average high school student at both schools has not experienced the demanding expectations of a college course so, since this course both introduces and provides an actual experience with a college course, I have learned that I must be sensitive while grading. Most of the students in CAPP rank in the top 15th percentile of their graduating class, and when they take regular classes with other students whose abilities range from exceptionally skilled to exceptionally deficient, they earn A's with ease, particularly if graded on a curve. During their senior year, they can take a CAPP class, which pulls them out of a mixed grouping and into a place where all are quite able and talented.

Because these students set the standard in other classes, their A's reflect much natural ability combined with relatively little effort. Many of my students have told me that they sometimes purposely do poorly on an assignment in order to test the teachers grading their work. The result is nearly always an "A—Good Job!" They enter CAPP eager for a real challenge, as well as an awareness of their lack of accountability and critique thus far. Since many of these students quit developing their writing as ninth graders, they come to class genuinely unaware of how they might improve or change their style, which has always worked for them.

Consequently, the first grades I give are pretty tough. The first major paper I assign is worth 80 points, and each subsequent paper is 10 points higher until the research/position paper, which is worth 200 points. This progression ensures that as they "get it" and learn how to write effectively, their grades are worth more. Also, my revision policy allows students to learn from their mistakes and create a better paper in the process.

I grade the first major CAPP papers rigorously, writing all over the margins and following up with comments at the end that break down students' writing problems into two or three major areas. (Of course, some students' writing needs more work than others, but giving them a few specific directives rather than several is less intimidating.) While the rubric helps clarify specific problem areas for the students, the comments can address content, style, and technical issues beyond the rubric's design. Most students walk away from the initial paper aware of the work ahead, but the positive spin on the comments (for example, "I like the part about the cat; how can you explain its relevance to the day your aunt died?") keeps their frustration level to a minimum. Pointing out the positive elements of a paper, even things as trite as good organization, balances the criticism. I reinforce to them again and again: "If you already knew how to write, then you would not take this class. You are here to learn to write, and this is the beginning of that process."

I also use a book by Anne Lamott, *Bird by Bird,* to drive this point home. She reminds us that we write one word and one sentence at a time. Yes, the initial drafts are poor and not printworthy, but as we carefully go over students' drafts, we can glean from them what works. The stress is on revision and editing, not perfection the first time around. This is the writing practice that makes my students successful writers in college, but it is also the writing practice that many of my colleagues cannot or do not make time for when they teach a mixed-ability group of twenty-eight students a curriculum overflowing with state standards requirements.

Two Views of the College Application Essay Assignment

Susan: Ideally, students in a college composition class should freely explore primarily expository or persuasive topics of their choice using the considerations of purpose and audience to help determine which rhetorical pattern(s) to choose. When I think back on my own college course work, I do not recall a writing methods class in which these patterns were defined and briefly explained. As with so much of teaching, I learned these when I had to teach them, so I collected brief definitions when I had students of my own whose writing I was expected to evaluate and attempt to improve. I also urge my students to study Kathryn Lamm's *10,000 Ideas for Term Papers, Projects, Reports and Speeches* for topic ideas. Although it's important to review the rhetorical patterns, I also tailor the class to my students' topic choices.

As a form of introduction, the first short essay students write is in response to Langston Hughes's "Theme for English B" ("Go home and write / a page tonight / And let that page come out of you— / Then, it will be true"). I am always amused at some of their struggles to focus or limit what they can say about themselves to one page. The first major and weighted essay of the semester is the college application essay, certainly relevant at the high school level but unnecessary by the time the student enrolls in college English 101. Since the typical CAPP student is in the upper 25 percent of his or her class, active in extracurricular activities, and possibly working a part-time job, it is important to me that my students find the essay assignments relevant and provocative. Their time is precious and I don't want to burden them with busywork. In addition to the college application essay, I assign a causal analysis, exemplification/illustration, poetry comparison, classification/division, short story analysis, and persuasive researched essay as well as some timed writing activities. I have developed a rubric to help me teach and to assess the research essay. I do emphasize certain usage skills, either through review or, for some students, instruction for the first time.

Melissa: We both assign a college application essay because CAPP students spend much time during the school year applying to colleges and competing for scholarships. As described in the syllabus, reflective essays offer an opportunity for students to write about themselves, answering questions commonly asked of them on scholarship and college applications. Reflective essays provide a creative writing assignment that stresses coherence, unity, individuality, and reflectivity. My students generally do not write about themselves for such a specific purpose, so successfully writing these essays can be difficult: how does a student make sure his or her essay rises to the top of the stack of hundreds, sometimes thousands, of other essays?

Four times a semester students turn in a reflective essay. I provide nine questions at the back of the syllabus from which to choose a focus. These questions come from various application forms that the students will probably see sometime during the year. I also allow students to use other questions or prompts if they apply to an application on which they are currently working. The first essay follows a discussion of a model essay by a former student. The assignment focuses on the clarity, description, and uniqueness of the piece. Then students write their own essays and bring them in for revising once before they are due.

Students appreciate the practical nature of this assignment as well as the opportunity to write creatively and about themselves, especially when the other writing for the course tends to be quite dry and academic. They can use these essays for multiple applications, so they take them seriously. These are the papers most students will ask me to peer edit during workdays, the days students use to peer edit or write, using me as a resource.

Writing four different reflective essays throughout the semester obviously serves to broaden student portfolios and provide options when students have to select writing that best represents them to an unknown audience. They can see how to perfect this style of writing as they approach each assignment and learn from previous mistakes to become more efficient editors.

To be effective, the reflective essay must be unique. As a scholarship essay reader for a number of committees, I have felt frustrated by the lack of individuality in the essays. I stress to my students that they are *all* high achieving, hardworking, dedicated, and involved. To prove it, I have them stand in response to questions: "Do you have a job outside of school?"; "Are you in National Honor Society?"; "Are you a member of a school club or team?" When they see that every student in the room stands in response to these questions, it drives home the point that these are not the things to write about if they want to stand out in a pool of applicants.

From there we spend time discussing the sorts of details and information that would reveal all the positive things they want to share about themselves, but in a memorable way. For this we refer back to the student model essay and excerpts of other pieces. Each student is challenged to list things that are unique about him or her, experiences or qualities or talents that no one else in the room possesses.

The stress in these essays is also on coherence. Because the essays are only two to three pages long, the focus must be tight and reveal as much as possible about the writer, with examples that illustrate individual character and blend into a single theme. My students frequently struggle with writing examples that reveal something about them. Sometimes the lessons they learn about writing characters for fiction can help students develop this skill. For example, a quick study of what students carry in their wallets or backpacks or what can be found on the floors of their cars can reveal much about their lives. This brief activity helps them understand how inference can subtly reach the reader and interest the reader as much as or more than direct statements such as "I work at McDonald's."

Once students compile a list of possible things to write about, they can begin the first essay, confident that no one else will write one that resembles theirs. When grading these essays, I look for detail, clarity, and the author's presence. Usually these essays need more revision than the formal papers. My comments normally include questions such as "How did this make you feel?" or "Give an example of a time you showed determination." I find myself eliciting more detail and reflection from students in later drafts.

This assignment would not work as well for other students in other classes. First, not all high school students are college-bound. Second, few younger students have the maturity to write about themselves with much reflection. Third, most first-year college students, once accepted into the college of their choice, have little use for this type of assignment; they have achieved what this assignment is intended to facilitate.

For the high school senior planning to attend college, these essays address the upcoming transition. The assignment helps put into perspective the competition they will face when applying for colleges and scholarships. It helps them understand their unique traits and experiences, perhaps in the process fostering a better understanding of other people. Finally, these essays get students into college, with the extra boost in self-discovery from an assignment few college composition courses would offer.

The Differences High School Students Bring to a College Class

Susan: Maturity, extracurricular involvement, and the student's elective or required status in the course are some points to consider in contrasting a CAPP high school junior or senior with the typical first-year college student in English 101. The CAPP criteria and my school board's decision to allow only CAPP and AP classes to be weighted for college credit seem to set the tone for my CAPP composition and AP English literature and composition classes. One point of contrast between high school CAPP students and first-year college students may be the difference in attitude, which in turn may affect class performance. Because the CAPP high school student may have more external motivating pressures such as class rank, GPA, and scholarship money, not to mention the undue influence of some parents, CAPP students tend to be serious, conscientious, and motivated. This difference in attitude and possibly overall maturity was impressed on me when one of my CAPP classes and I had the opportunity to sit in on a UW Oshkosh CAPP English class several years ago. I was struck by how much more mature and serious my students were than the class of university first-years; my students made the same observation.

Another point of contrast is that CAPP teachers have a much better sense of the writing experience their students have had. The English department at Elkhorn High School recently adopted a writing rubric for all four grades to establish writing standards, so I know that ninth graders are taught primarily the literary analysis and comparison/contrast essays, while the sophomores write comparison/contrast essays, descriptions, personal narratives, definition essays, and a research-based essay. When I meet my CAPP students as juniors and seniors, the overriding purpose of the class is for them to choose topics about which they feel committed and enthusiastic, but I attempt to encourage those rhetorical patterns they may not have studied thus far.

If the purpose of college English 101 is to "level the playing field" to ensure that first-year students have the best chance for success in college writing, I perceive that my role is to help students do well academically in college. At my back, I hear, not "time's winged chariot running near," but the recurring refrain, "Aren't those high school English teachers teaching you anything?! #@*!#!" One of my fears is that when my students go out into the world, their writing will reflect negatively on my teaching.

I suspect most English teachers would agree that a few students' intelligence is verbal/linguistic; for these students, writing is effortless and produces flawless pieces of stylistic grace. Possibly there isn't a lot we teachers can do for such students beyond the encouragement of providing arresting, significant topic choices. But we can provide an audience of that student's peers. One of the most powerful tools for teaching writing is other students' work—having students read the best samples of their classmates' writing, something I've found to be a powerful motivator. The thinking among students is, "If he can write like that, so can I!" I collect the best pieces of student writing and use them to teach.

I would hope my CAPP students come to feel that the highest compliment I can give them is to ask for a "clean copy" for my teaching files, although to believe this reveals my gullibility, naiveté, and idealism even after twenty-plus years of teaching! The compliment they really want is an A grade, and for some students, nothing but an A will do.

So how do I accommodate the "grade grubber"? I must be nurturing, not only of the serious student under lots of external pressures, but also of the student whose pressure is internal—the perfectionist—for whom nothing less than an A will do. After peer editing and my evaluation, I allow students to revise for the first two six-week grading periods. Another way I help my students earn high grades is by clarifying the assessment criteria through rubrics that also help justify the grade they earned, since the CAPP students (and increasingly the parents) demand an accounting. Rubrics are a gauge by which students can measure their own writing quality and a tool to provide me with a justification for the grades the students earn.

Also, since the CAPP grade is cumulative, I make appointments with each student after the class is completed to go over the final exam, discuss the grades on the essay parts of the final, and inventory all the writing samples in the portfolio, as well as answer any questions the student may have about the individual scores that make up the cumulative grade.

Melissa: Despite their enrollment status with UW Oshkosh, CAPP students are still high school students. Their lives are filled with other upper-level course work such as calculus and AP history. In addition, they pour themselves into school life, participating in various clubs and organizations, playing on school athletic teams, and contributing community service hours. They live their lives in a high school context, in their hometowns, with their families and friends they have always known. A successful CAPP course recognizes their status while slowly nudging them toward their impending future as full-time college students.

One of the ways to reach CAPP students is to connect the ideas presented in class with their immediate surroundings. Grammar lessons use names of places and events familiar to them (i.e., "The Kaukauna Ghosts will defeat the Appleton North Lightning this weekend"). Encouraging students to pick topics close to home also honors their world, such as a definition paper that asks students to reflect on how their gender has been reinforced from childhood to the present. This allows them to write about their own experiences in a formal context, making the format, not the topic, the focus of their attention.

Another way to nurture CAPP students is through awareness of the school calendar as we schedule the year. To expect these very involved students to turn in a major paper the week of homecoming is to set them up for failure. Granted, creating a sensitive course schedule takes extra effort, but students appreciate the effort. Attendance policies are common on college campuses; many professors, for example, will allow three absences from a course before absence affects a grade. To help students become accustomed to such policies, I stipulate that students can have five non-school-sanctioned absences before their grade is affected. Field trips for other classes do not count, but students need to carefully allocate their sick days throughout the semester. It is inevitable that CAPP students will miss class occasionally for school-related activities, but it is equally important to teach them how to prioritize attendance for every class.

To help nurture CAPP students as they learn how to write at a college level, we develop a rubric before each major paper is due so that students can check off the various assignment components. We use at least two peer editing days for major papers; the peer editing groups use this time to look over content, structure, and style. As the semester progresses, students become aware of specific areas they should ask for help with in that editing time, as well as the areas in which their peers struggle. I also have a revision policy that is incredibly lenient compared to those of most of my university colleagues. Each paper may be revised if the initial grade is lower than an A. One learns to write through writing and revising, so this policy reinforces the idea that no writing is a finished product; there is always room for revision. Moreover, some students need the instructor's remarks and comments on their paper to guide them to a better final product. While this policy generates extra papers to grade, it can, if applied properly, effectively help the struggling student achieve better writing skills.

Through the revision policy and the frequent invitation to "see me," I try to help students understand that I grade not their personality nor their potential, but only their performance. Many students identify with their grade and so feel personally offended when they receive anything lower than an A. Some students challenge their grade until I show them an A paper and demonstrate the difference visually. Some students feel they have hit a wall and cannot ever become better writers. Other students grumble violently to their classmates. In this setting, compassion is a teacher's best friend, and a successful college writing teacher figures out how best to reach and soothe each frustrated student.

In the high school setting, it is far easier to seek out these students: I can talk to them casually in the hallway, catch them in study hall, or invite them in to talk before or after the school day. I also can use their parents and older siblings as allies in the process of encouraging their work and persistence. In addition, a high school teacher has conventions such as nominating a struggling student for Student of the Month or connecting over an interest or activity such as basketball or Key Club. I need to know my students well to become their cheerleader and instructor; if I don't connect with them on a personal level, they will shut down quickly and fail to learn.

In a high school setting, a teacher's reputation can precede him or her, which makes my job much easier. Having had many of these students in previous courses, or knowing them, their friends, or their siblings from extracurricular activities or classes, I can cultivate a relationship so that they know my expectations even before taking the class. As first-year college students, they will have no previous knowledge of their English 101 instructor and often have little control over how they will approach the course. Even if they hear of a specific instructor before taking the class, there is little chance they will have met that instructor before.

Nurturing CAPP students means taking them to new places, preparing them for the world they will soon enter as first-year college students. A day spent touring and using the UW Oshkosh library exemplifies this point. A three-story building housing a huge collection intimidates students who have used only a one-room library in their high school. Just understanding a different system of cataloging books can frustrate a novice. I require students to use the college library for the research/position paper, raising the bar in my expectation of the sources they will use, in addition to familiarizing them with a vast collection of resources. Many students have never even used a microfiche before this day. This requirement helps them realize the many places information can be found and gathered, regardless of its function.

Finally, I use days designated solely for discussion to reinforce the climate of a college course in which the students themselves must debate and create their own discourse. Discussion topics range from the purpose of the canon in the study of literature to Ebonics. We spend one day talking about what to bring and prepare for that first year of living on campus. Two classes a month is a small price for the information generated during these "break-away days," which create ownership over academic discussion in a nonthreatening setting.

Reflections on a University-High School Relationship

Susan: Pamela Gemin, who teaches creative writing, advanced composition, and English 101 (i.e., CAPP English) at UW Oshkosh and who is a published poet, is the liaison instructor for both Melissa and me. CAPP recommends but does not require that our students visit the UW Oshkosh campus.

In addition to sitting in on our English 101 counterpart on campus, CAPP students have the opportunity to do research for their assignments in the college library or be instructed by a college professor. One year during our campus visit Pam taught poetry by facilitating discussion among my students, a memorable experience for them. According to their positive comments afterward, they were excited at having met a published poet. In addition to their college course preparations, the liaisons also travel to member high schools to observe the adjunct faculty and students or to teach the CAPP classes for the day.

Melissa: When I began teaching CAPP, Bernard Hupperts, my former colleague and developer of the program at Kaukauna High School, became my first liaison. He helped immediately by addressing concerns I had about teaching students how to peer edit. He also came into my classes to teach some parts of the argumentation/persuasion process. After Bernie retired, Pamela Gemin became my new liaison and provided continued support from the university. Our relationship actually became collaborative when she invited me to speak on a panel to her secondary English education students. She recognized the practical experience a high school teacher can share with future teachers and prompted me to reflect further on my practice.

Pam's visit each semester provides feedback beyond that of my students, and she encourages me through e-mail and telephone discussions. I spent a day this spring following her around the UW Oshkosh campus, an opportunity that allowed me to ask a number of questions about the curriculum as well as the pedagogy. She shared some helpful resources on teaching reader response criticism, and we compared our experiences teaching CAPP English to motivated high school seniors and English 101 to a mixed bag of university students, mostly first-year students. I realized how fortunate I am to teach students who have established rapport with one another and volunteer much more freely to speak up in class.

Sitting in on Pam's English 101 class allowed me to observe a class discussion conducted on a Web discussion board, a technological possibility I had never explored. Her lecture on metaphors in her creative writing course gave me some new perspectives on how to approach a sometimes abstract idea with students who might struggle with it.

Our discussions have challenged both my pedagogy and my curriculum, providing much to reflect on as I return to teach another semester of CAPP. It makes my job easier knowing an instructor in the English department at Oshkosh is available to answer my questions about both the program and the subject area as they occur. I think the real collaboration is between faculty members within the program because it is the primary way we remain accountable and grow in our teaching practice.

Finally, having ties to UW Oshkosh benefits me professionally as I can use some money from the university to attend workshops and conferences. I have access to everything they offer their onsite faculty, a professional perk that many of my colleagues at Kaukauna lack. This access raises my level of expectation for myself and has been instrumental in pushing me as a writing teacher. CAPP instructors, the liaisons, and the adjuncts are invited to attend both fall and spring conferences, giving the content teachers opportunities to discuss curricular concerns. This past spring, for example, the conference offered workshops on detecting plagiarism, evaluating Web sites, and using PowerPoint.

Pam Gemin (University Liaison): For me, being a CAPP liaison has been a winning experience all around. My roles as observer and perennial student have long eclipsed any notion of "mentorship" I might have had at the start of my association with these gifted teachers, Melissa and Susan. A lot has changed in the U.S. high school since I got my secondary teaching certificate more than twenty years ago, and one thing a lot of folks forget and a lot of college students don't know is that many of us who teach in the university have had no formal teacher training, though even the best teacher training can't prepare a teacher as thoroughly as daily classroom experience and personal contact with actual, rather than theoretical, students. When I entered my first college composition classroom, I was handed a textbook and wished good luck. I'd done my student teaching and a little high school subbing, of course, but how I wish I'd known Melissa and Susan back then!

In the two years I've worked with CAPP, I've shamelessly taken full advantage of our high school teachers' expertise as well as their resources. Susan has provided me with a wealth of material for teaching both creative writing and research in College English I, material easily adaptable to my university classrooms. Observing Susan's class the day she took her students through an inspired critical analysis of "Hills Like White Elephants," Susan having just returned from a critical theory workshop, I was reminded of why I became a teacher. She was clearly excited about sharing what she'd learned, and the students responded in kind. Likewise, watching Melissa steer her students through a potentially deadly lecture on sentence structure was like watching a champion figure skater in practice. Her grace, flair, and expertise, combined with her enthusiasm and good humor, made for a memorable lesson, and using her students' own names in sample sentences was a brilliant touch. Melissa has visited my college classroom, too, as a guest speaker in my Advanced Composition for Secondary Education class. My students, most of them English majors, have felt free to ask Melissa a full range of questions about her own students, her classroom, and her career path, and have appreciated her "insider" perspectives on the challenges they are about to face and the rewards they have in store.

CAPP is cooperative in the truest sense of the word, as it provides both the incentives and the circumstances for a meaningful, professional exchange of resources, ideas, and inspiration.

Implications

Susan: Because the CAPP high school student and the first-year college student in English 101 have different pressures, the curriculum and pedagogy must reflect these differences. Certainly the writing we all teach must prepare students for life; we're teaching not just the writing process and usage concepts but, more important, the self-awareness that comes from personal narratives such as the reflective essay and the college admissions essay.

Melissa: The high school student enrolled in a CAPP class has a wonderful opportunity to experience the education college offers. These students can take the risk of attempting college-level work without all of the other new experiences first-year college students go through on campus. Finally, in the nurturing environment of a high school classroom, a college-bound senior can prepare for the transition with the safety net that time, instruction, and experiences allow.

Susan: I don't think that I have an outstanding writing ability, but I believe I can recognize it in others. I see myself as more of a coach, encouraging students when they have doubts about their abilities or, more specifically, about a particular essay assignment. I hope that after they have completed CAPP composition, my students will feel they have learned or that their writing has improved. And when one stops to consider the significance of helping young people become better communicators, few jobs are more rewarding.

Melissa: I agree, and I can add that I know of my students' continued success because alumni return to share their achievements in college. It feels great when I learn that former CAPP students receive good grades on writing assignments from college professors. It feels even better when they speak of specific things they learned, like the student who shared last fall that her history professor is really strict about using an active voice in writing, a skill I repeatedly hound my students to adopt. She e-mailed me to express gratitude that she did well in his class!

Susan: I am indebted to some of my coaches; besides Al Tripp, my cooperating teacher during my student teaching days, I am grateful to the high school teacher who inspired me to follow her career path, Mrs. Lynn Schlies. And finally, to the English teacher who began the CAPP courses at Elkhorn High School and who established high standards for CAPP composition, Dr. K Hutchinson. In the final analysis, we must consider the thousands (by now) of students and hundreds of teachers who have benefited from this unique program, the dream of Dr. Earl Hutchinson and Dr. Leflin, the co-founders. Their idea has thrived under the able administration of current directors Polly Montgomery and Steve Winters and former director, Mary Beth Petesch. This program requires a team approach; in addition to the adjunct faculty such as Melissa and me who teach the classes, the liaisons have the responsibility not only for teaching their own college classes but also for making onsite visits to surrounding high schools.

Melissa: We agree that this collaboration between high school and university is instructive not only for students but also for teachers, personally and professionally. CAPP high school students and first-year college students in English 101 have different pressures. We prepare our students for college writing, whereas college professors perhaps feel they must prepare their students for wider objectives. Increased communication between the levels can benefit both ends of the educational spectrum since we have so much to learn from one another.

Works Cited

Lamm, Kathryn. *10,000 Ideas for Term Papers, Projects, Reports & Speeches.* 4th ed. New York: Macmillan, 1995.

Lamott, Anne. *Bird by Bird: Some Instructions on Writing and Life.* New York: Pantheon, 1994.

11 Creating a Connected Space: Mentoring in the Zone of Proximal Development

Kim Jaxon
California State University, Chico

This university-high school collaboration involved the creation of an online mentoring program to help high school students improve their writing skills. Following is an account of how the program developed, what it entails, and how it seems to be working so far.

In the fall of 2000, composition faculty at California State University, Chico were approached by the director of the Precollegiate Academic Development (PAD) program[1] about the possibility of creating a writing program for high school students that would decrease the need for remediation at the college level. Specifically, we were asked if we would create a "test-prep workshop" for students taking the English Placement Test (EPT) with the goal of raising test scores, thereby reducing the need for remedial English classes. We said no. We said no because the EPT score is not a good indicator or predictor of student success in the first-year writing course, and we believe that "test-prep for the EPT" is not what high school students need if we truly want to help them navigate the writing tasks being asked of them at the university level. Instead of a test-prep program model, we offered to develop a writing program for high school students that would give them access and exposure to university-level writing tasks. The director of the PAD program agreed, so in the fall of 2000 I began to create the Online Mentoring Program for High School Scholars.

The Theory

The model we created for working with high school students reflects the work of CSU, Chico's first-year writing program, so I believe it is important to include a brief summary of the theories that inform the program. CSU, Chico's first-year writing program is based on theories of literacy that identify writing as a *practice* as opposed to a series of "skills" that must be mastered. Reading and writing are not seen as having an absolute value; the practice of writing changes as the task changes, so it is difficult, if not impossible, to assess writing ability in a general way. Further, the program is informed by Vygotsky's concept of "the zone of proximal development." Vygotsky states that the zone of proximal development is the difference between a student's "actual development as determined by independent problem solving" and the higher level of "potential development as determined through problem solving under adult guidance or in collaboration with more capable peers" (Wertsch 86). In other words, structured activities led by more capable peers may allow students who test at one level to reach higher levels than they would be capable of on their own. With this in mind, CSU, Chico developed a program to help students succeed in doing the work of first-year composition by actually *doing* the work of first-year composition, not by simply *preparing* to do it. An understanding of literacy theory, and student potential as outlined by Vygotsky, have moved the first-year writing program at CSU, Chico toward student access to first-year composition. At CSU, Chico, in place of a series of basic writing classes, all students take the same first-year composition course, called English 1. For this reason, it may be apparent why we were skeptical about providing "test-prep" for high school seniors—we know that these students need access to actual writing tasks, not preparation for something else.

The move toward placing all students in the first-year writing course does not mean that CSU, Chico abandons students who may need more support. In addition to English 1, some students will also be required to enroll in an adjunct workshop, English 1A. Their eligibility for enrolling in English 1A is determined by taking the English Placement Test, which is intended to assess the student's level of ability in reading and writing. The first-year writing program is required by the chancellor's office "to use placement test scores and to 'place' students, [and] all students with low scores are required to take an adjunct workshop while enrolled in English 1" (Rodby 110); therefore, students who test below 147 on the EPT at CSU, Chico take English 1A, along with the English 1 class, to support their work in the first-year composition course. This cutoff score for "remedial" designation is higher than that of other CSU campuses in order to meet English 1A program goals.

In addition to providing a "space" for students with low test scores, the English 1A workshop does provide additional support for students who need more scaffolding in English 1. While the program administrators would like to see the support available in the workshop offered for *all* English 1 students, currently the program can support only students who test below 147 on the EPT. Of the students who take English 1A along with English 1 (and therefore have been designated "remedial" by test scores), 84 percent pass first-year composition the first semester. The level of student success with the writing demanded of them in the academy, regardless of test scores, informed the decision to create a writing program for high school seniors that was based on the kinds of real writing tasks being asked of them in the university as opposed to a program that would help them prepare for a test that might have no bearing on their success or failure in English 1.

The success students demonstrated in completing the tasks asked of them in the first-year writing course, along with Vygotsky's "zone of proximal development," provide a theoretical foundation for understanding why we developed the Online Mentoring Program for high school seniors. Institutionally sanctioned settings (Wertsch) such as the Online Mentoring Program provide a site where structured activities led by more capable peers allow students who test at one level to reach higher levels than they would be capable of reaching on their own. Vygotsky developed the zone of proximal development as a way to discover "how a child can become 'what he not yet is'" (Wertsch 67). This theory allows us to create a program for high school students to evolve as writers, and it is why I set out to create a program that modeled the activities of CSU, Chico's first-year writing course.

The Online Mentoring Program: An Overview

As stated earlier, the goal of the program is to provide writing assistance and support for high school students in order to better prepare them for the kinds of writing tasks that will be required of them at the university level. High school students who are involved in the program have the opportunity to conduct their own research project. The research assignment is coordinated by the high school instructor and graduate student mentors and asks students to make an argument about an issue they are interested in researching. It allows students to work with an assignment that is very much like the writing assignments being asked of students at the university level. In fact, the assignment we used for the spring 2001 semester was adapted from an assignment currently being used in CSU, Chico's first-year writing course that focuses on academic writing for the public.

The students' work is supported both by face-to-face interaction and through online technology: students participate in four workshops (three held at the high school campus and one at the university campus) led by graduate student mentors, and also participate in online discussions with the mentors. The online discussions provide ongoing, weekly support for the students and are mediated by the use of a listserv, an online discussion forum that allows students to pose questions and post drafts of their essays for feedback from the graduate mentors. Unlike standard e-mail postings, all subscribers to the listserv are sent posts to the list at the same time.[2] This forum allows students to see and respond to each other's work as well as see each other's responses from the mentors. As a way to facilitate the students' understanding of this online space, the mentors created "listserv protocol" prior to our first postings. The protocol helped remind students that the list was a public space, and as such, they should be sensitive to language choices and remember to identify who they are and what they are responding to with each post.

The Participants

The High School Faculty

At CSU, Chico, I am fortunate to work with faculty such as Tom Fox, who heads the Northern California Writing Project. As director of NCWP, he collaborates with an amazing group of public school teachers, including high school English teachers. In order to create the Online Mentoring Program, he introduced me to Rochelle Ramay, a high school English teacher from Corning Union High School in Corning, California. Rochelle acts as a mentor to other high school English teachers and runs a variety of workshops for NCWP; she is truly an amazing teacher and researcher. Luckily for our program, she was excited by the possibility of connecting her seniors with college-level writing tasks. In December 2000, Rochelle and I met to discuss possible ideas for writing projects and for recruiting students. It is important to note here that this is a true collaboration between the high school instructor and this program. The writing tasks outlined here can be negotiated based on the high school teacher's knowledge of his or her students' needs.

The role of the high school teacher is extensive; he or she must be willing to work with the coordinator in developing and giving feedback on the writing assignments. In addition, the teacher must communicate with parents and high school administrators. During the spring 2001 term, for example, Rochelle wrote a thoughtful letter to parents and administrators requesting permission for students to engage with topics that might normally be considered taboo in a high school setting, such as the current abortion debate and same-sex marriage. She was able to get all parties to agree that students should be allowed to engage in current debates, even the issues that are controversial by high school standards. She wrote descriptions of each student's writing history, including a short assessment of the student's writing ability based on prior work for her class, and gave us access to the students' current curriculum and samples of their work. It was not uncommon for Rochelle and me to exchange three to four e-mails a week in order to keep each other informed on the students' progress in the program.

The Students

While the goal of the Online Mentoring Program is to provide writing assistance and support for high school students to better prepare them for the kinds of writing tasks that will be required of them in college, a key feature of this goal is to provide access to any student who chooses to participate. Rochelle and I agreed from our earliest meetings that this program would not be labeled either an "honors" course or a "remedial" course. In other words, we did not create a program based on a model of labeling "good" or "bad" writers. As stated earlier, theories of literacy frame the understanding that labels such as "honors," "basic," and "remedial" do not reflect what students can do when supported by more capable peers. For this reason, Rochelle set out to recruit students from the various levels represented in her four English sections at Corning Union High School. As an incentive to participate in the program, we offer students the opportunity to earn one unit of university credit through the High School Scholars Program at CSU, Chico. Students interested in earning credit pay a seven-dollar fee and fill out the appropriate paperwork, which includes an application to enroll at CSU, Chico, and a form signed by the high school counselor or English teacher. It is important to note, however, that students may opt to be involved in the program without enrolling in the High School Scholars component. We also offer a certificate of completion that is given to them during their senior awards banquet.

   During the spring 2001 term, twenty-five students from a variety of Rochelle's senior English classes chose to participate. Most of these students will be attending college in the fall, mainly at CSU campuses, including CSU, Chico. According to feedback from Rochelle, these students represent a range of abilities in writing, although the students have been asked to work mainly with analyzing and understanding literary texts, as required in most high school English programs.

The Mentors

While Rochelle was exploring student interest in the program, I was searching for graduate students to act as mentors for the high school students. (We chose the term "mentors" because we believe that the high school students are not "lacking"—the students do not require "tutors." The students, for the most part, have not been exposed to college-level writing tasks, so we are providing mentors, "more capable peers," who do understand the tasks being asked of these students.) The search for mentors was not difficult due to the extensive TA training provided in our program. I was able to hire two graduate mentors, both of whom had taken graduate courses in the theories and practice of tutoring and theories in teaching first-year writing. Both had taught our English 1 course and introductory literature courses for at least two semesters, so they were already familiar with the writing practices in our program. Therefore, they did not have to complete lots of training before working with the high school seniors. We met on a weekly basis to plan workshops and discuss the student writing and how we were responding to the writing. On average the mentors each worked five to ten hours a week.

Most of the mentors' work for the program involved designing workshops and responding to student writing. They also worked hard to find resources for individual student topics; since they were familiar with the topics students selected, it was not uncommon for the mentors to send an article on Napster or cloning, for example, to the listserv. The mentors adopted the attitude, "It's not that we know more, it's just that we got here first," as a way to think about their work with students—they believed students were capable of doing the work, especially if mentors could help scaffold the work for them.

The Online Program Coordinator

As the coordinator of the program, I am responsible for design, development, and assessment. While I spend most of my time working with the high school faculty and mentors to design the workshops and writing tasks, I also spend an enormous amount of time on a myriad of details: filling out timesheets, filling out paperwork for all participants to be fingerprinted in order to work in the high schools, reserving transportation to the high schools, reading student work, and keeping the PAD coordinator and provost's office informed of our progress. The needs change from day to day, and I have discovered the importance of remaining available and flexible.

The Workshops

Workshop 1—Presentation of Topic and Research Proposal

During the first workshop, mentors visited the high school campus and gave students strategies for working with an assignment and for generating topic ideas. Students were presented the major assignment for the semester, which asks them to write an extended research paper that:

- selects the most relevant research for discussion and then states clearly the relationship between the different approaches, points of view, or perspectives
- argues for a specific approach, point of view, or side to the question, even if it is tentative (i.e., "at this point in time, given the research I have read/conducted, I argue that . . .")
- is thoroughly and carefully documented (MLA format)

Students may rely on written sources (including Internet sources, which are discussed at a subsequent workshop) and film, interviews, surveys, and so forth, but they must cite from at least four sources, two of which must be written.

After presenting the assignment to the students, the mentors began to help students generate topic ideas. Mentors brought an array of sources—magazines, newspapers, journals—and led students through activities that helped them understand current issues in public discourse. Students were asked to think about what makes a good research topic, and they were given a set of criteria for topic selection. The topics needed to:

- be a question or problem being debated, discussed, or explored in public discourse
- be discussed in different ways for different audiences
- have a history that can be researched
- be interesting and relevant to the student
- be narrow enough that students can attain some expertise in four to five weeks of study

After explaining the criteria, mentors asked students to get into groups of three or four and to skim through the texts; as a group, the students needed to choose three issues for possible research stemming from issues being currently debated in the public sphere and using the criteria for topic selection to evaluate their choices. Then, as a group, they were asked to share with the entire class the following:

- What does your text choose to highlight?
- What seems to matter to the publishers of your text?
- Which three topics do you see as possible research issues for the class?
- How do your choices match the "criteria"?

During our first workshop, we were pleased by the level of complexity of students' topic selections. As a whole group, students discussed U.S. intervention in foreign policy, standardized testing, Napster, cloning, the portrayal of women in various media, exit exams, and hazing in Greek organizations. Students were able to articulate how the issues met the criteria outlined by the mentors, and they were engaged and enthusiastic about the variety of possibilities.

For the remainder of the first workshop, the mentors modeled how to write a proposal for the research topics. Students were asked to submit a proposal to the listserv during the week following the initial workshop. The proposal asked students to write a two-paragraph summary of the topic they had chosen. In this summary, they needed to include possible arguments that they thought might be a part of their chosen issue. They were asked to think about what they might uncover and what they thought the debate surrounding their topic was and to comment on at least three various perspectives/positions on the issue—students were told that it is okay to make guesses about what they think they might uncover by researching the topic. They were also told to include a research question—this would be a real question they did not already know the answer to, but one that could be answered by further research. Finally, they needed to include a short discussion of why this topic was relevant and important to them.

During the week following the workshop, the mentors and I were impressed by the student proposals. Students had chosen debatable, relevant topics, and they asked smart questions about the direction their research should take. The mentors' responses to the proposals focused on helping students narrow down topic ideas, and the mentors gave students suggestions for possible resources for their topics, including online sources the graduate students were aware of.

Workshop 2—Researching the Topics

The next face-to-face meeting with the high school students took place on the CSU, Chico campus in our English department computer lab. Students were invited to the campus to use the facilities to conduct their research. During the first half-hour of the workshop, students were directed through the variety of resources available through the university library's online research station. Specifically, we showed students how to use EBSCO and LexisNexis to find online journals, newspaper, and magazines sources, and we showed them how to send these documents to their own e-mail or print the documents in our computer lab. We also gave students a handout listing a variety of Internet sources such as cnn.com, nytimes.com, newsweek.com, wired.com, and greenpeace.org, as well as a variety of online campus newspapers such as those from Harvard, Stanford, UCLA, and CSU, Chico. Students spent the next two hours using the computer lab to search these various sources while the mentors helped answer questions and guide student searches.

After a short break, the final phase of this second workshop focused on helping students understand how outside sources are used to support an argument in an essay. Students read a model essay from the publication *Working Ideas*, which is put together by CSU, Chico's English 1 program. The publication consists of models of student essays, written for the English 1 course, which have been selected for inclusion by a panel of faculty judges outside the English department. After the students read an essay silently, the mentors asked students to get into groups of three or four to look at how sources were used in the student model. Students were then asked to report to the whole group; a thoughtful discussion followed about the variety of sources, how they were used and formatted, and how students could apply this understanding to their own essays.

For the remainder of the day, students had lunch on our campus and were given a campus tour. We also asked them to post feedback to the listserv; we asked them to comment in these reflections on what they understood the purpose of the campus visit to be. We asked the following questions:

- Was it clear to you what the goals were?
- What did you think went well? What was the most helpful?
- What would you have done differently? What improvements would you suggest for the next time we conduct this workshop with a group of students?

The feedback we received from students was incredibly positive. Most commented on the amount of research they were able to find and how helpful this was. Many discussed how they had used only search engines such as Yahoo! in the past and that they now realized how limiting this type of resource is in finding quality research. Students also addressed the helpfulness of working with the model essay; they believed they had a better understanding of how the sources would work in their essays. All mentioned how much they enjoyed being on campus and how excited they were about leaving for college in the fall. Students made suggestions about visiting the library for future workshops and asked that we include a visit to a "real" English 1 class.

Workshop 3—Drafting the Assignment

Mentors led students through prewriting and drafting exercises for this third workshop, held at the high school campus. We asked students to come to the workshop having read through their research and thought about the variety of perspectives represented in the research. During the workshop, we asked them to examine their sources by answering the following questions for each source:

- What is the main claim of the text? What is the text presenting or arguing? Is there more than one claim in the text?
- Who wrote the piece (doctor, teacher, reporter, consumer, etc.)? When?
- Why would the author of the article argue or present the topic in the way he or she does? What might be the underlying reasons for arguing this way?

After spending thirty to forty minutes answering the questions, students were asked to make a graph or drawing to visually chart their sources and their position in the argument. They were given the following directions:

- On a separate sheet of paper, write a two- to three-sentence summary of your sources (you may find that you can use the answers that you worked with in the previous exercise). Make a chart or graph that represents each summary; place opposing views opposite each other, for example, or show connections between similar arguments made by the various authors.
- After you've plotted your summaries, place your tentative argument on the graph. Where do you fit in the debate? Which parts of other arguments do you agree with? Disagree with? Why?
- Share your graphs in pairs, explaining the debate to your peer and where you think you fit in the debate.

Students in this workshop came up with a variety of ideas for charting their sources and began to make connections between a variety of arguments surrounding their issues and to discuss their tentative claims and arguments.

After a short break, the students were asked to come up with a variety of ideas for getting started on writing the paper. The mentors asked students to consider a variety of ways to write the introduction, and the mentors wrote ideas on the board solicited from the students; these strategies included starting with a short background on the history of the debate, an overview of the current debate, or a scenario (such as a current court case or a personal narrative), or by outlining the opposition argument. The mentors then modeled a variety of outlining/mapping techniques, and students spent the remainder of the workshop mapping their essays. Students were asked to post their mapping strategies or outlines to the listserv within the next week for mentor feedback.

Workshop 4—Editing and Citation

The final workshop, held at the high school, required students to bring a (mostly) final version of their essays. (Between the third and fourth workshops, students had posted a "best first effort" of their essays to the listserv and had received feedback on those drafts from the mentors. Students arrived at this workshop having revised their essays based on the feedback and subsequent discussions with the mentors on the listserv.) Mentors assisted students with editing and grammar concerns; the focus of the workshop was on using MLA format for in-text citations and creating a works cited page. Students were all given access to grammar handbooks and worked together to edit their texts.

Preliminary Conclusions

The feedback we are getting from students (we are still collecting feedback from the initial trial) and the level of work they are doing suggest that this program is working in the ways we hoped—students have access to and success with college-level writing tasks. Our plan is to track these students through their first-year college writing classes to see if we can make connections between their work in the Online Mentoring Program and their success in first-year writing courses.

In retrospect, the success to this point of the program comes from a variety of influences. First, the students self-select to participate in the program. They are not chosen based on their prior success or failure with writing assignments; instead, they volunteer to engage in the writing tasks we present to them and they receive college credit and recognition for their efforts. Second, we have a highly trained group of participants, including high school faculty who are engaged in ongoing scholarly research and stay informed about current writing pedagogy. Rochelle Ramay's students were familiar with mapping, drafting, revising, and making claims in their work with literary texts. In addition, the mentors are highly trained graduate students and teachers of record in first-year writing courses at CSU, Chico; they are prepared to respond to and assess student needs, and they have an understanding of the literacy research that informs the program. (In the future, I would like to consider hiring undergraduate mentors who are training to become high school English teachers, but these hires would need to be trained in responding to student work and in components of literacy theory.) Finally, we do not base the success of this program on the "products" produced by students. While we worked hard to move the students along in terms of their writing goals and abilities, and the students are producing thoughtful and well-researched essays, we are also interested in their exposure and access to university writing tasks and resources. For this reason, we see student involvement as a measure of success.

I would argue that in future seminars all workshops should be held on the university campus rather than the high school campus.[3] Part of the reason stems from student excitement and feedback about the campus workshop, but we also noticed a difference in student engagement with the tasks while in the university space. Workshops held at the high school were negotiated around rally posters, cheerleading uniforms, interruptions from "notes from the office," and dress-up days. The students viewed the work we did on the high school campus as "less scholarly"; one could argue that this is due to the space allowed by the high school setting. In student responses, they always asked for more exposure to the campus—the addition of another library day or being allowed to visit a "real" English 1 class—which seems a reasonable request. If part of our goal is to give students exposure to the university, obviously this is easier to do while on the university campus.

Our program is very much a work in progress; although we are finding the work to be valuable and engaging for both mentors and students, we are eager to explore further an understanding of the "space" we are creating. We are not always sure what to call it—it is never completely high school, or college, or online. But even if the physical and virtual space cannot yet be defined, we do know we've developed an institutionally sanctioned setting that creates a space in which writing matters.

Notes

1. According to PAD's published goals, "The Precollegiate Academic Development Program (PAD) funds CSU student interns to work in public schools to help K–12 students who need assistance in strengthening precollegiate English and mathematics skills. PAD is committed to working with local elementary and secondary institutions and with other segments of higher education in a comprehensive effort to promote the acquisition of basic academic skills." While I believe PAD acts as a valuable sponsor for collaborative programs, we differ in our interpretation of "basic skills" and what they may or may not include.

2. The listserv was made available through our campus resources; WebCT, Blackboard, HorizonLive, or other types of Web communication software could be easily substituted. We are considering using HorizonLive in future semesters because it allows for video and audio technology in the form of real time "chats."

3. The students' visit to the university campus was funded by "field trip" money made available to the high school through the local school district, not by the Precollegiate Academic Development program.

Works Cited

Rodby, Judith. "What's It Worth and What's It For? Revisions to Basic Writing Revisited." *College Composition and Communication* 47 (1996): 107–11.

Wertsch, James. *Vygotsky and the Social Formation of Mind*. Cambridge: Harvard UP, 1985.

12 "Why Do I Have to Take Remedial English?" A Collaborative Model to Solve a National Problem

Chris Jennings
Tidewater Community College

Jane Hunn
Salem High School

When students with good grades in high school English consistently scored poorly on a community college's assessment measure, Chris (a community college instructor) and Jane (a high school teacher) began to examine both the assessment process and the preparation being given those students in high school. By bringing secondary and postsecondary teachers together to talk, they identified several problems and found some solutions.

Mary, a typical senior from a typical high school, graduates with a B average in English. She registers at the local community college, takes a twenty-minute placement exam, and finds herself enrolled in a semester noncredit, four-hour, remedial composition course. She returns to visit her high school English teacher to share her news. The teacher is aghast: "What is wrong with the college placement instrument? What is the college testing?"

Mary begrudgingly enrolls in developmental composition at the community college where she sees classmates from high schools across the city who also wonder why they have to take remedial English. The instructor reads the students' first papers and is aghast: "What is being taught in the high school English class? Why are students unprepared for college composition?"

This scenario is being repeated across the nation. Educational reports reveal that high school students are graduating with deficient writing skills while college developmental programs are expanding.

National, state, and local reports emphasize the magnitude of the problem. Historically, according to the Virginia State Council of Higher Education, one in four Virginia public school graduates enrolls in remedial courses in state-supported colleges ("5,748 Incoming Freshmen").

Chris: Our college catalog has been adding more sections of developmental composition each semester to meet the needs of increasing numbers of students placing into remedial English. In 1996, 74.4 percent of area high school graduates attending Tidewater Community College (TCC) placed into developmental courses; 79.0 percent of Salem High School (SHS) students enrolled in developmental English, math, and reading classes. Data from 1997 through 2000 reveal that recent high school graduates from Virginia Beach City Public Schools have been placed in developmental English courses at an average rate of 45 percent; as a result of intervention strategies, however, students from SHS fell from a 1997 placement rate of 41 percent to a 2000 rate of 25 percent.

Jane: In 1996 I was teaching an English 11 (junior-level) class and a dual enrollment English 111-112 class at Salem High for college credit at TCC. At the end of the school year, when my English 11 students were tested by TCC for placement into the dual enrollment course, I noticed that students who were good writers were not testing into the senior-level course. Other teachers in our department noted the same problem. We contacted the English department at TCC to better understand their placement process.

Chris: I was asked by my division chair to investigate the issues of curriculum and placement with teachers from Salem High. As a college, we surveyed English 12 (senior-level) teachers and students to determine perceived strengths and weaknesses of the then-current teaching of composition and to ascertain teaching staff and student needs. Fourteen teachers and 415 students responded. Data showed that 36 percent of the students indicated their ability to write well was extremely important to them, 57 percent indicated it was important, and 7 percent indicated it was not important at all.

   When we asked students to choose one of five facial expressions indicative of their feelings about writing, 42 percent chose one labeled "indifferent," 34 percent selected "confident," 9 percent chose "anxious," 5 percent chose "lonely," and 10 percent chose "undecided." Of all the types of writing they did outside of class, letters were the most popular.

Students were asked to rank ten strategies for becoming better writers. Twenty-three selected "More group opportunities in class to discuss your drafts"; the next largest percentage selected "More informal writing assignments." Twelve percent responded, "More instructions from teachers." No one chose "More lectures."

Jane: When we surveyed the teachers about classroom activities, they reported spending an average of 7 percent of class time teaching grammar and punctuation usage. Although they allocated 13 percent of class time to writing and revising, they spent the majority of instructional time on lecturing, collaborative writing, journal writing, reading and oral discussion, and audiovisual presentations.

Twenty-three percent of the teachers wanted "Increased time for instruction in grammar and punctuation," and 30 percent believed "More group interaction in the writing process" would improve student writing. The teachers' most difficult challenge in the teaching of writing was "Teaching students correct structure, punctuation, and grammar." Surveyed about their attendance at recent professional development writing workshops, teachers responded that 62 percent of them had never attended any, 30 percent had attended one in 1997, and 8 percent had attended one in 1996.

Chris: After reviewing the surveys, talking to the teachers at the high school, and researching the literature on college-high school partnerships, I worked with faculty from TCC and SHS to prepare a grant application for monies from the Fund for the Improvement of Postsecondary Education (FIPSE) to develop a collaborative project. I had also been working with assessment issues and investigating the research on multiple indicators for placement testing; much of the literature proposed the use of portfolios for authentic assessment.

Jane: Somehow, out of all of this a team approach to improving students' ability to write at the college level was implemented at the high school with input from the college. Coincidentally, our language arts coordinator was emphasizing the use of portfolios in the classroom.

Chris: In August 1998, the U.S. Department of Education notified Tidewater Community College that a three-year grant award of approximately one-third of a million dollars had been awarded effective September 1, 1998. With many activities tentatively planned, all project personnel jumped into the fire with boots on and feet running.

The goal of the three-year project was to align twelfth-grade writing instruction at Salem High School with requirements of satisfactory placement in college composition at Tidewater Community College. The project goals were (1) to examine the placement procedure for entering students and (2) to improve students' placement in college writing courses.

Jane: The model was defined as a team of English 12 teachers and their students working with Chris, the grant director. Three English 12 teachers and I met with Chris weekly to plan activities and coordinate schedules. A study group of 150 to 200 students participated in the project each year. One college faculty member, the high school department chair, and three English 12 high school teachers implemented strategies to achieve project objectives:

1. To develop and disseminate a model for staff development in writing instruction
2. To improve student writing and increase the percentage of students competent to take college-level composition courses
3. To validate a multiple measures writing placement procedure

Chris: To determine the placement levels of senior English students at SHS, we used two of the traditional college placement instruments: COMPASS, a computer adaptive writing assessment instrument, and a twenty-minute timed writing sample. At the TCC Virginia Beach campus, where I teach, writing samples are read only for students whose scores are borderline according to predetermined cutoff scores for developmental courses.

Developmental courses include

- English 01 (four noncredit hours) "Preparing for College Writing I"
- English 03 (four noncredit hours) "Preparing for College Writing II"

The first-year college transfer courses are

- English 111 (three credit hours) "College Composition I"
- English 112 (three credit hours) "College Composition II"

Readers—experienced college faculty members—evaluate the writing samples holistically for recommended placement in developmental or college transfer courses. Prior to the grant, no rubrics had been developed for placement guidelines. Our counselors often asked for feedback on student placements based on writing samples.

Jane: We didn't understand the college placement process and questioned the validity of the process to predict student success in college-level composition. We also had concerns about the application of secondary school criteria from the Virginia Standards of Learning and Virginia Beach City Schools English objectives in creating alignment between high school and college expectations.

Chris: In the first year of the grant project, we bused the high school seniors to our campus for a full day of orientation and testing. Although the students enjoyed the opportunity to meet faculty and observe the college site, the full day was too disruptive to their schedules.

Jane: Many of the seniors who work or attend vocational education classes at another site are not at SHS for an entire day, so we looked for an alternative way of administering tests. In the second and third years of the grant project, the college came to us. To address the third objective—to validate a multiple measures writing placement procedure—COMPASS was administered as a post-test to the project group and to a control group of similar makeup in the same high school. Both groups also completed a timed writing sample.

Chris: With the help of our Assessment Office and technology personnel at the high school and college, we were able to test students in the high school computer lab during their regular English classes. This change also enabled us to test another group of students in the same school and obtain control group data for comparison purposes. As the project progressed, we brought high school and college faculty together for grading sessions to read writing samples and develop a language for evaluating the work. Gradually, a rubric has emerged to identify student levels of placement, one that we can share with students, teachers, and counselors.

A multifold approach was developed to incorporate increased communication about writing standards among high school teachers, high school students, and college instructors. Many partnerships between colleges and high schools have shown successful outcomes, but this project presented an opportunity for extensive collaboration to improve student writing and college placement procedures. Activities included pre- and postplacement testing, professional development for high school and college educators, creation of a writing center, exploration of innovative instructional strategies, portfolio instruction and assessment, and ongoing collaboration.

Chris: To address the first objective—to develop and disseminate a model for staff development—we invited high school and college English teachers to attend writing workshops on how to implement innovative teaching strategies in their composition classes. We purposely held the workshops at a neutral site in order to foster a spirit of collaboration. In addition, my college provided breakfast and lunch to allow teachers to talk informally with each other during breaks. We also contracted with Dr. Kathleen Blake Yancey, author of *Portfolios in the Writing Classroom,* to act as our advisor.

Jane: In year 1, our workshops focused on aligning public school curriculum with college writing practices. Participants were introduced to writing strategies using portfolios, letters, and reading/writing connections. (See Figure 12.1 for a list of speakers and topics in the year 1 workshops.)

Chris: Because teachers were unclear about the distinctions between writing folders and portfolios, our workshops in year 2 targeted the portfolio as both an instructional and an assessment tool. These workshops addressed the second objective, to improve student writing. (See Figure 12.2 for the topics and speakers in year 2 workshops.)

Jane: The writing consultant returned throughout the three years of the grant to work with the project teachers. In addition, she was contracted by our school system to work on a portfolio initiative with teachers in grades K–12.

Chris: In year 3, our workshops were designed to provide opportunities for project personnel to model project activities for teachers from other schools (see Figure 12.3). The first workshop demonstrated the value of writing conferences and encouraged participants to design, set up, and manage a high school writing center. As a follow-up to that workshop, two high school English departments created writing centers at their sites.

Response to workshop topics from participants has been positive; moreover, participants have valued the interaction with their colleagues, as evidenced by comments such as "Learning what colleges are looking for in their freshman writers," "Understanding high school teachers' position and methods," and "We don't have enough opportunity to talk together. Now I understand where my students are coming from."

Understanding the SOLs ■ Phyllis Ayers Virginia State Department of Education	An explanation of the Virginia Standards of Learning and how they are intended for use in Virginia's public school systems.
Descriptive and Prescriptive Elements of the Virginia Beach SOLs ■ Lorna Roberson Virginia Beach City Public Schools	The SOLs as defined for English teachers of the Virginia Beach City Public Schools system.
Development of Writing Instruction ■ Joe Antinarella Tidewater Community College	The use of the SOLs in developing the writing curriculum to reach goals.
Engaging Student Interest in Writing and Development of Writing Portfolios ■ Kathleen Blake Yancey University of North Carolina at Charlotte	Exploration of the composing process and portfolio instruction.
Teaching and Learning through Letters ■ Donna Reiss Tidewater Community College	Understanding the characteristics of letters and the students' enjoyment of writing them, and approaches to using them to foster writing in the classroom.
Peer Collaboration in Writing ■ Joe Antinarella Tidewater Community College	Exploration of group instruction and peer editing.
Evaluating Writing and Portfolio Assessment ■ Kathleen Blake Yancey University of North Carolina at Charlotte	Different types of portfolios and assessment using reflective pieces and a rubric.
The Reading and Writing Connection ■ Christopher Thaiss George Mason University	Development of strategies for improving student writing about literature.

Figure 12.1. Writing Workshops 1998–1999.

Chris: To provide more opportunities for students to receive feedback on their writing, my college sponsored a high school writing center at SHS in year 1 of the grant using our college writing center as a model. In the second and third years, the high school center became a pivotal part of the collaboration involving college and high school faculties and students. An innovative component of the high school center is the use of high school students as consultants. We visited high school dual en-

Motivating Students with Innovative Grammar and Revision Strategies ■ Kathleen Blake Yancey Clemson University	Exploration of revision strategies that enliven the writing process.
Portfolios ■ Kathleen Blake Yancey Clemson University	Portfolio assessment and what to do with it. Reading portfolios for college placement.
Writing Portfolio Assessment Project ■ Kathleen Blake Yancey Clemson University	Development of a portfolio system for the Virginia Beach City Public Schools.
Writing Sample Workshop ■ Sally Harrell Tidewater Community College	Development of a rubric to be used for writing samples in the placement process.

Figure 12.2. Writing Workshops 1999–2000.

A Model for Teacher Collaboration and Innovation ■ FIPSE Tidewater Community College/Salem High School Project Team	Introduction to partnership concept. Guide to setting up a writing center. Identification of and resources for teacher training. Strategies for writing instruction.
Refining the Portfolio Process/The Changing Role of the Instructor in the Composition Classroom ■ Kathleen Blake Yancey Clemson University	Refining the writing process. Exploring strategies for focusing on student change and growth in the composition classroom. Managing portfolio instruction. Providing meaningful feedback to the writer.
Using Portfolios for Evaluation and Assessment ■ Kathleen Blake Yancey Clemson University	Reading sample portfolios. Reviewing rubrics for evaluation. Using portfolio assessment/evaluation techniques.

Figure 12.3. Writing Workshops 2000–2001.

rollment and honors English classes to train students to work as volunteer consultants. In addition, my college donated materials and resources from our writing center. Faculty donated handbooks and college-level texts as well.

Jane: To staff the writing center, teachers were released from other non-teaching duties. Project teachers tutored voluntarily in the center before and after school and during lunch breaks. One teacher was designated as the center director. His duties included scheduling teachers to staff the center, obtaining and monitoring student consultants, coordinating student consultant training, overseeing and securing resources, scheduling bulletin board displays, tracking attendance, preparing presentations to showcase the center, and establishing a system of rewards to encourage students to frequent the center.

The mission of the high school writing center is to offer a place for all students to participate in a writing community where they may share and discuss their writing or ask for writing assistance. Teacher and volunteer student consultants encourage and support student writing. They provide practical assistance to help students understand how to interpret writing assignments, generate ideas, find a focus, organize information, develop support and evidence, revise, and proofread drafts. The center also provides free handouts and other writing resources. Service is available on a regular, first-come-first-served basis. The center offers varied audiences for student writers, cross-curricular instructional support, training for student tutors, and a reward system for student participants.

We have a motto for our writing center: "It's a Life Saver." When students complete a writing session, they receive a LifeSavers candy. They also receive valuable practice in understanding the writing process. Likewise, our student volunteers have discovered that when they help others, their own writing improves.

Chris: Teachers in our project group have also found added value in writing center activities. The experience has given them practice in reading rather than grading student work. Teachers have found their role changing from "red pencil" editor to writing coach. And this change has carried over into their classrooms.

Jane: College faculty and our high school textbook publisher donated handbooks for all students in the grant project and student consultants in the writing center. Students look forward to receiving their own copy of a college writing handbook. Who would ever have thought that a grammar book would be a carrot?

Project participants worked in partnership to identify common deficient skill areas in the student population and to develop appropriate strategies and activities for student remediation in writing. Having identified the portfolio model as an instructional tool that enables students to develop responsibility for their learning and demonstrate progress, the teachers implemented activities to assist students in preparing working and presentation portfolios. Many of the activities and strategies were the result of participating in workshops, researching professional texts, and adapting good practices of other instructors. Recognizing that alignment necessitates a mutual relationship of inquiry, research, and willingness to experiment, the project team explored and experimented with new instructional strategies.

Chris: One of the activities was a letter-writing exchange between students in the high school project group and community college English 111 students (see Figures 12.4 and 12.5 for sample letters). Each year the process was tweaked to better adjust to varying schedules of the separate institutions. By the third year, the process began with college students describing "What I wish I had known before I came to college" to their high school pen pals, who in turn requested specific information on how best to prepare for college composition.

Jane: Our high school students enjoyed the opportunity to communicate with the college students during the fall semester. Again, students commented on the value of writing for a specific audience and learning what college writing really requires.

Chris: To introduce another component of assessment, we developed a portfolio model for use in the classroom and for college placement. An important feature of the portfolio process is training students to reflect on their own work and to incorporate instructor response in their writing. To provide prompts for reflection, teachers and students have generated questions. The format has varied from a letter to the teacher, to answers to a series of questions, to self-assessment. Questions such as "What is the main idea?"; "What are the key points?"; "What problems are you having in writing this assignment?"; and "With what part of your paper are you most pleased?" have motivated students to react to their writing and make predictions about the reader's reaction to their writing.

   Peer review as a method of discovery and shared learning was incorporated to involve students in a collaborative assessment. A "talk back" format enabled students to discuss essential concepts of composition (see Figure 12.6).

Salem High School
1993 SunDevil Drive
Virginia Beach, VA 23464

October 20, 1998

Tidewater Community College
Virginia Beach Campus
1700 College Crescent
Virginia Beach, VA 23456

Dear TCC Student:

I am a senior at Salem High School. I am seventeen years old and an honors student. I am involved in two school clubs, which include: DECA (Distributive Education Clubs of America) and BCC (Black Cultural Club). I have resided in the Virginia Beach area for six years.

My future plans include going to college and finding a career. My top three college choices include: Hampton University, Clarke Atlanta University, and Old Dominion University. I plan to major in physical therapy or respiratory therapy.

What advice would you give to a high school student about writing strategies required to be successful in a college writing class? Please give me some good pointers or experiences that you have had in your writing class.

Sincerely,

SHS Student

Figure 12.4. Typical letter from a Salem High School student to a first-year Tidewater Community College student.

Jane: To encourage students to use teacher suggestions for revision, highlighter cues were used. In response to student drafts, the teacher wrote intertextual comments. Students applied the suggestions to their revisions and then highlighted the changes on resubmitted drafts. This technique prompted writers to identify and address problem areas in their revision process. An alternative method was to request students to submit their texts on disks. The teacher then read the draft and inserted intertextual comments. This process encouraged students to read and consider each teacher suggestion as they worked within the text. Multiple intelligence activities, based on the work of Dr. Howard Gardner, have been used to foster individual student strengths. After

---

Tidewater Community College
Virginia Beach Campus
1700 College Crescent
Virginia Beach, VA 23456

November 1, 1998

SHS Student
Salem High School
1993 SunDevil Drive
Virginia Beach, VA 23464

Dear SHS Student,

I am an English student at Tidewater Community College in Virginia Beach. I am majoring in Administration of Justice. Like you, I was a DECA member at Salem High School. A career in law enforcement is in my near future. Hopefully something in the federal government.

One bit of advice you should know upon entering college English is be prepared to write and write a lot. Most English professors require a student to write anywhere between five to seven papers a semester. The papers consist of five paragraphs that include an introduction with a clear and thought out thesis statement, three to four paragraphs with specific details supporting your thesis statement and finally a conclusion that reiterates your thesis statement. All these papers range from anywhere between five hundred to eight hundred words. Except when writing a research paper, the word count can jump to fifteen hundred to two thousand words.

The main strategies in becoming successful in college English are (1) go to all your classes (2) take excellent notes (3) write in a very clear style without "rambling" (4) be prepared to write a lot.

I hope these tips and strategies are helpful and I hope you enjoy English in college as much as I do.

Sincerely,
TCC Student

Figure 12.5. Typical letter from a first-year Tidewater Community College student to a Salem High School student.

identifying student learning styles through a multiple intelligence checklist, the teacher provided alternative assignments to the traditional written composition, such as a poster, Web page, diorama, picture book, newscast, dramatic scene, song lyrics, or flow chart.

```
┌─────────────────────────────────────────────────────────────┐
│                          Talk Back                            │
│                                                               │
│  Author's Name:                                               │
│                                                               │
│  Date:                                                        │
│                                                               │
│  Type of Writing Assignment:                                  │
│                                                               │
│  Listener's Name:                                             │
│                                                               │
│                                                               │
│  Directions:  Listen to the author read his or her essay, respond to these ques- │
│               tions, and orally explain your comments and suggestions.           │
│                                                               │
│  1. Does the writing **focus** on a specific incident or event? Explain what it is. │
│                                                               │
│  2. Does the **introduction** capture the reader's attention? Cite several examples. │
│                                                               │
│  3. Does the writing contain **effective** supporting details? Cite several examples. │
│                                                               │
│  4. Does the writing **flow** in an organized manner? Explain. (chronological,  │
│     spatial, etc.)                                            │
│                                                               │
│  5. Does the writer's conclusion answer the questions **So What?** and **Who Cares?** │
│     Explain the significance to you.                          │
└─────────────────────────────────────────────────────────────┘
```

Figure 12.6. A peer review sheet using the "talk back" format.

Chris: Portfolios have given teachers and students a format for sharing what they value in writing. To develop guidelines for the students, high school and college teachers discussed what should be in the portfolio, what processes should be apparent, and what rubrics should be used to evaluate the contents.

To assess the writing project, students were directed to prepare the portfolios as follows:

- Materials should be on one side.
- Materials should be either typewritten/word processed or in blue/black ink.
- Materials should not be stapled. (Binder clips will be provided by TCC.)
- Student and teacher names are to be removed from all items (black magic marker or white-out).
- TCC will supply a roster for each class section that will list code numbers for each student.
- Students will affix labels supplied by TCC to the portfolio covers.

- Covers or plastic protector sheets should not be used.
- All portfolios should be labeled as a group to indicate teacher and section. (Include an identifying sheet with your name and bell number.)

Each portfolio included an annotated table of contents, an opening piece, a personal narrative, a literary analysis, an in-class essay, a writer's selection piece, a process reflective letter for one item, and a closing reflective letter for the portfolio.

Evaluating the portfolio for placement in college writing courses brought faculties from both institutions together not only to design and implement portfolio rubrics but also to assess and use the portfolio as a tool for college composition placement (see Figure 12.7 on p. 197 for the placement portfolio scoring guide they developed). Teachers were trained in a series of workshops led by Dr. Yancey. Using anchor portfolios, participants discussed the traits of proficient writers and of those in need of remediation. Faculty discussed what students needed to know and demonstrate in order to progress smoothly from high school to college. They discussed issues of student and teacher diversity, incomplete portfolios, and student choice of selections. High school and college faculty who had attended portfolio workshops were hired as portfolio readers to assess the study group. The (portfolio) reading process featured an introductory dialogue (among faculty from other high school sites and the college) on the portfolio process, followed by dissemination of portfolios. Each portfolio was read by two readers; if needed, a third reader was included in the assessment. By the third year, the process had become so effective that only 6 portfolios out of 260 needed a third reading.

According to the year 1 evaluation report prepared by project evaluator, Dr. Barbara Bonham of Appalachian State University:

- The data clearly indicated improvement in writing skills of the high school seniors participating in the project. The discussions in the following sections summarize the data provided on students' writing skills, their achievement on performance measures, and placement recommendations.
- Projected placement of students based on the pre-test objective scores from the COMPASS revealed that 41.25% of the students in the Project Group would have placed in English 111, which is the Freshman level English class at Tidewater Community College, at the beginning of their senior year. At the conclusion of the senior year, 60% of the project students placed in English 111 after one year of participation in the project using the post-test objective scores from the COMPASS, the writing sample,

and portfolio. This obviously reflects a significant increase in the number of students placing in the freshman level English course.

- Of the students who originally had placed in English 03 (developmental level) based on the pre-test, 33.3% of them had improved to English 111. There was an increase of 31.9% of the students who had originally placed in English 01 (lower developmental level). There was an overall positive change of 33.75%.

- Using a placement system based on a writing sample evaluation, 70.3% of the students in the project group placed in English 111 and 51.4% of the students in the control group placed in English 111. Using the writing sample evaluations, there is also a difference in the percent of students who placed in the developmental courses. In the project group, 27.5% of the students were in English 03 while 44.8% of the control group student were in English 03. In other words, more students from the control group were in developmental courses using the writing sample evaluations than students from the project group.

- Use of the writing sample clearly places an increased number of students from the project group into English 111. It appears that the preparedness of students for English 111 is influenced by participation in the project. (Bonham 16)

Using TCC's placement system described earlier in this essay, 44.0 percent of the students in the project group placed in English 111, compared to 35.2 percent of the students in the control group. Of greater interest is that 57.1 percent of the project students placed in English 111 when the portfolio project outcomes were used for placement.

According to the Virginia Beach City Public Schools (VBCPS) Department of Accountability, a comparison of 1998–99 Salem and Virginia Beach high school graduates showed additional gains: Project students enrolled in four-year colleges at a rate of 50 percent whereas other graduates of Salem enrolled at a rate of 42 percent. The overall city rate was 48 percent. Project students enrolled in two-year colleges at a rate of 32 percent whereas other graduates of Salem enrolled at a rate of 31 percent; the overall city rate was 27 percent.

Final placement of project and control group students in year 2 using the traditional TCC placement system (COMPASS and writing sample) indicated that project students were placed in English 111 at a rate of 52.30 percent whereas control group students were placed in English 111 at a rate of 34.16 percent. Using portfolio assessment, the project group was placed in English 111 at a rate of 70.11 percent. One hundred and fifty-three students who participated in the project were present for the entire 1999–2000 academic year and participated in each

---

Placement Portfolio Scoring Guide

4   The texts demonstrate that the writer can successfully complete at least three kinds of writing tasks, and the student's reflective commentary confirms how the work was completed. This is a writer whose composing processes are visible. The writing is sophisticated and mature. The texts in the portfolio show that the writer is "coachable": able to take the response and feedback of peers and teachers and use it appropriately in developing texts. Standard English is used throughout the texts; the texts are relatively free of surface errors as well as major grammatical errors, though they may not be completely error-free.

3   The texts demonstrate that the writer can complete some essential writing tasks, though some are completed far better than others. The reflective commentary suggests that the writer's composing processes are still evolving; some process is visible. The writer is still learning how to be "coached." In general, the writing is error-free (i.e., in Standard Written English), but it is not sophisticated or mature in style or in attention to audience. (For example, writing is not substantial in content; there is little evidence of varied sentence patterns; there is little evidence of risk taking.)

2   The texts demonstrate that the writer can complete one essential writing task and can attempt others. The reflective commentary is emerging and underdeveloped. The writer can talk about the texts but is not willing or able to make essential changes; he or she has not learned to revise. The writing is not sophisticated and mature. (For example, writing is not substantial in content; there is little evidence of varied sentence patterns; there is little evidence of risk taking.) There is little evidence of a composing process. The texts frequently include errors interfering with meaning (such as syntactic errors or faulty predication).

1   The texts show an emerging writer. This writer can focus on a task and attempt completion in abbreviated (unelaborated) form but is not fluent and shows no evidence of composing process. Successive drafts are highly redundant (with no significant changes in drafts, no stronger voice, purpose, or attention to audience). The writing is not sophisticated and mature. (For example, writing is not substantial in content; there is little evidence of varied sentence patterns; there is little evidence of risk taking.) This writer writes very little reflective commentary, and the reflection that is included is oriented to surface features like spelling and capitalization. The writer does not seem to know how to improve writing. The texts frequently include errors interfering with meaning (such as syntactic errors and faulty predication). The writer is still learning to control written expression.

Figure 12.7. A sample placement portfolio scoring guide.

component of the pre- and post-testing process. Of the 118 who pretested as needing developmental writing, combined post-test results from COMPASS and the writing sample indicated that 38.1 percent could be placed into first-year composition at the close of their high school senior year; 59.3 percent indicated readiness for first-year composition on at least two of the three indicators used at the close of the senior year.

Four years later, we have data showing that our activities have improved student readiness for college composition. In the fall of 1999, 37 percent of the students from Salem High required developmental writing; in the fall of 2000, the number was down to 25 percent. Of the students who were placed in first-year college composition courses by portfolios, 87 percent were experiencing success as measured by a grade of A, B, or C in their courses; our traditional level of success is 70 percent. Collaboration is working.

Jane: Collaboration can be painful despite the results. Working in a partnership is not always easy, especially for teachers who have traditionally worked in isolation. We experienced problems with stress, time management, and communication. Like a family, we have learned to respect each other's differences and build on our strengths.

Progress has brought not only evidence of student success but also the need to address affective issues among project personnel. Taking a proactive stance on conflict resolution, project personnel agreed to participate in a professionally facilitated mediation retreat at the end of the first year. Personnel identified the strengths and weaknesses of team members based on a personality inventory. Personnel became more attuned to the individual needs of each staff member. In the second year, a series of sessions was facilitated by a city employee who assisted the group in negotiating a plan for working through conflict resolution. This is an ongoing need given the nature of collaboration between dissimilar institutions.

Chris: High school teachers working with college professors can make a difference in student achievement. Generated by teachers who recognized student needs, this teacher-centered model has demonstrated success for all participants. Performance objectives remain vital to the needs of teachers and students in secondary and postsecondary institutions.

Jane: We will continue to refine project activities at our school. The project has made a significant impact on how teachers teach writing. The writing center has continued to serve a growing number of students from all disciplines. More teachers are working with the college site, and there is definitely an increased understanding of each institution.

Chris: Recognizing the importance of partnerships, my college has extended additional opportunities for collaboration to regional high school sites. Portfolio placements will continue to be available to students in lieu of the traditional placement tools. Students from the project group now attending my college have wholeheartedly endorsed their high school senior-year experience and praised their English 12 teachers for preparing them for college success.

Aligning instruction, empowering students, decentralizing classrooms, and heightening attention to better serving the needs of the graduating high school student/incoming first-year college student, this model has made significant inroads into secondary and postsecondary institutions.

Works Cited

Bonham, Barbara S. *Aligning Writing Instruction in Secondary and Postsecondary Schools: FIPSE Project—Year One Evaluation Report*, 1999.

"5,748 Incoming Freshmen in Virginia Needed Remedial Classes." *The Virginian-Pilot* [Norfolk]. 12 Sept. 1997: B7.

Gardner, Howard. *Frames of Mind: The Theory of Multiple Intelligences.* New York: Basic, 1983.

Yancey, Kathleen Blake, ed. *Portfolios in the Writing Classroom: An Introduction.* Urbana, IL: National Council of Teachers of English, 1992.

VI Conversations about Collaboration

If conversations and collaborations between high school and college teachers can be productive, what happens if middle school and elementary school teachers join in? The teachers in Chapter 13, one from each of the four grade levels, offer an argument that such conversations and collaborations can be quite useful.

In Chapter 14, Richard Brantley and Diana Brantley offer a different perspective on why college and high school teachers don't talk more. Both English teachers, they have discussed their professional lives with each other regularly for over thirty years—but he teaches at a university and she teaches at a high school. In their discussion, they identify some obstacles to communication and offer suggestions for navigating those obstacles.

Chapter 15 offers a brief departure from collaborations about the teaching of writing to highlight a collaboration about the teaching of literature. When Mary Baron (a college instructor) and Denise Rambach (a high school teacher) shared some of their frustrations about teaching *Beowulf*, they discovered that while high school students and college students might be extremely different in some ways, they can be quite similar in their approach to (or fear of) difficult texts.

13 Crossing Levels: The Dynamics of K–16 Teachers' Collaboration

Diana Callahan
Parsons Elementary School

Charles Moran
University of Massachusetts Amherst

Mary-Ann DeVita Palmieri
Great Falls Middle School

Bruce M. Penniman
Amherst Regional High School

Drawing on their experiences with the Western Massachusetts Writing Project, four teachers from four different levels argue that teachers from every grade level have knowledge to share with teachers from every other grade level.

Many educators have argued that learning goes better in a heterogeneous, diversified classroom. Difference among students, they argue, is an asset, a resource in the classroom. They see this diversity as cultural and argue for it under the term "multiculturalism." Writers such as Juan Guerra find that by embracing the cultural differences among our students we make it possible to "explore the clash of discourses and ideas, of different viewpoints and world views" (260). Others see diversity among students in terms of ability, and there is a substantial literature that argues for heterogeneous grouping, as opposed to tracking, in our schools (e.g., Oakes; Wheelock). Finally, diversity can be understood in terms of age or grade level, and the literature argues for the multigrade, multi-age classroom, where, for example, third and fourth graders are mixed in the same class (Cushman; Gaustad).

As a result of our work with the Western Massachusetts Writing Project and our experience as inservice staff development providers to K–12 teachers in our area, we want to add to these three categories of diversity—range of culture, range of ability, and range of age/grade level—the category of teachers' "professional level," or "grade level taught." We argue that teachers, like students, learn best when there is diversity, in this particular case when they work with teachers who teach at different grade levels—when a first-grade teacher and a college professor, for instance, share tasks and in this sharing come to understand what it is to teach at a level far different from their own. We believe that the presence of difference in a learning situation facilitates reflection, an activity that scholars such as Donald Schön have seen as a prerequisite to the improvement of teaching. We understand that there are substantial advantages to professional stratification along the lines of grade level and that much staff development is appropriately conducted at grade level. But teachers should also have the opportunity to learn by working with teachers across grade levels.

The benefits of such collaboration seem to us to be practically self-evident. Yet we feel the need to argue this point because we so clearly divide along lines established by our buildings, by our administrative structures, by our professional associations, and by our journals. If we, like Diana Callahan, are first-grade teachers, we associate professionally with grades K–4 teachers in our building. We go to the International Reading Association (IRA) conference or, if we go to the National Council of Teachers of English (NCTE) or the New England Association of Teachers of English (NEATE) conventions, we attend workshops designated "elementary strand." If we subscribe to a professional journal, it is likely *Language Arts,* the NCTE journal addressed to elementary teachers. If, like Mary-Ann Palmieri, we are seventh-grade teachers, we associate with grades 7–8 teachers in our building. We attend workshops labeled "middle school strand" and we subscribe to *Voices in the Middle* or the *Journal of Adolescent and Adult Literacy.* If, like Bruce Penniman, we are high school teachers, we associate with colleagues in our building, we subscribe to *English Journal,* and at conferences have our sessions designated "secondary strand." If, like Charlie Moran, we are college teachers, we subscribe to *College English* and *PMLA* and *CCC,* we associate principally with members of our own department in our own building, and we go to the annual convention of the Conference on College Composition and Communication (CCCC) and, if we are hiring or being hired, to that of the Modern Language Association (MLA). In practically every situation in each of our institutions, staff development proceeds by grade level: inservice workshops are given to elementary, middle school, high school, or college/university teachers.

Regrettably, the divisions by level carry with them, in the United States, a vertical metaphor of prestige. Elementary teachers are lower than middle school teachers who are themselves lower than secondary teachers who are below college/university teachers. This vertical metaphor is instantiated in salary scale and in the blaming that is part of our personal and professional discourse: "If they'd only been properly taught in the level below *my* level, I could really do my job." We prefer the British naming of categories: early-grade education is called "primary," middle and secondary education is called "secondary," and postsecondary education is called "tertiary." This set of category names makes it possible to assume equal value at all levels and to make it less likely that first-grade teachers will feel ashamed that they are not functioning at a higher "level" or that college professors will feel that by virtue of their position they have subsumed the knowledge of K–12 teachers.

The four of us teach English language arts, so we are members of the same profession, engaged in the same activity: helping the students in our charge become better readers and writers. Yet during our work year, we are separated from one another by the physical, administrative, and professional structures described earlier. We are brought together in our work with the Western Massachusetts Writing Project (WMWP), a local site of the National Writing Project (NWP). The NWP model, unlike other staff development models, assumes that teachers' knowledge is valuable—all teachers, not just college/university teachers. NWP sites must be located at colleges or universities, and their site directors must be college/university persons, but sites must be cross-level in governance. Typically the local sites' invitational summer institutes are led by co-directors who are K–12 teachers. NWP does everything it can to keep these summer programs from becoming graduate courses delivered ex cathedra by professors to teachers—a genre that some of us think of as the "drive-by" inservice workshop. Although graduate credit may be part of the mix, the WMWP summer programs are truly cross-level. The expertise that K–12 participants bring with them is on a par with any expertise the site director may bring to the program.

In this cross-level working situation, the four of us have learned a great deal from one another and from the K–12 teachers who have been our colleagues. In the sections that follow, each of us attempts to describe this learning. We tell our stories in our own voices because the stories are so different. Given our different experiences as professionals, and given the different values and cultures that obtain at the different grade levels, each of us has experienced the cross-level collaboration differently. Yet there are common threads.

———————

Diana: When I began my association with WMWP, I was a twenty-year veteran of elementary classrooms, having spent most of my time teaching first graders. My experience with teachers who taught at other levels was limited to my participation on district curriculum committees. As the first-grade teacher on these committees, I often felt that I was being held responsible for students' lack of basic skills at upper levels. Upper-level teachers often intimated that if I were "smart" enough, I too would have been promoted along with my students. I began the WMWP summer institute with little confidence that I had anything to offer my colleagues who taught at upper levels. Despite feeling intimidated, I was committed to the summer institute, to working on my craft as a writer and as a teacher of writing.

From the outset, the WMWP co-directors set the expectation that we would learn about one another as professionals, reflect on our own strengths as teachers of writing, and identify ways to become resources for other participants. As we shared our interests and concerns about the teaching of writing, no one ever asked, "What grade level do you teach?" It was clear that we were all in this together and that we shared far more than I had expected.

One of the requirements of the summer institute is to present a ninety-minute workshop focused on some aspect of one's own classroom practice in the teaching of writing. This daunting task is exacerbated by the cross-level nature of the summer institute. Since the audience for these workshops was K–12, the workshops had to be designed to be relevant across grade levels. The implicit assumption behind each workshop was that good teaching practice transcends grade level taught. In the summer of 1993, the workshops included such titles as "Learning to Write from Writers," "Cooperative Learning/Cooperative Writing," "Writing, Reading, and the ESL Child," "Reading/Writing and Mathematics," "Integrating Technology in the Classroom," and "Peer Review and You: Making It Work." I was the only first-grade teacher in the group, so ideas from these workshops were never grade-specific to my own teaching practice. I could not take workshop handouts to the copy machine and use them "as is" in my classroom, nor could many of the other participating teachers. As we supported one another and participated in each other's workshops, however, we became learners, and grade-level differences were quickly forgotten.

As a result of the summer institute, my practice as a teacher of writing was forever changed. From my colleagues, I learned about collaborative writing, peer conferencing, holistic scoring, writing across the curriculum, and much more. Beyond these specific ideas, however, I took the experience of being a learner and of working with my peers to "construct" my own learning. I gained an understanding of process and the confidence that I could modify and adjust the knowledge shared by my colleagues to meet the needs of my young learners. Finally, I learned to think critically and to be reflective about my own classroom practice.

As a co-director of WMWP, I continue to work with teachers who have experienced the NWP model of collaborative learning. I see this phenomenon repeat itself year after year. Teachers who initially believed they needed to attend grade-level-specific inservice are eager to work in cross-level groups, knowing they have much to offer and much to share with their colleagues.

Bruce: I began teaching at the high school level more than thirty years ago, and from nearly the beginning I have been a student and partisan of the writing process movement, student-centered learning, and other positive reforms in education. Yet only in the six years that I have been deeply involved in WMWP has my teaching philosophy fully evolved and my teaching practice accurately reflected the ideals I have long espoused.

From my association with elementary and middle school colleagues such as Diana and Mary-Ann, I have expanded and continue to expand my repertoire of imaginative and effective teaching strategies, strategies I would otherwise never have tried at the high school level. Through my collaboration with university teachers such as Charlie and Anne Herrington and Peter Elbow, I have stretched and continue to stretch my understanding of educational theory, policy, and politics. By my observation of the energy and creativity that dozens of Writing Project teachers bring to their work, I have renewed and continue to renew my commitment to positive change in my own classroom, in my school district, and in all the school districts in our area.

A good example of my learning through collaboration with teachers at other levels is my growing understanding of the place and purpose of low-stakes writing in the curriculum—any curriculum—as a tool for learning. I had used some low-stakes writing activities—response journal writing primarily—in my classes before my association with WMWP, but I have learned dozens of new techniques from my colleagues, including strategies that involve meaningful collaboration between students. Adopting and adapting these approaches has given me a whole new outlook on pedagogy, particularly in literature classes, where the teacher-led large-group discussion is still the norm in high school. I have come to see low-stakes writing not merely as a prelude to high-stakes writing, but also as a pedagogical tool in its own right. I have also come to believe that low-stakes writing must be the foundation of any successful writing-across-the-curriculum program, and I now stress this point in every workshop I present.

Incidentally, another benefit I have gained from my experiences in WMWP is the confidence to share my ideas (and those I have borrowed from my colleagues) with a variety of audiences. My most recent gig was a workshop series for third- and fourth-grade teachers on strategies for improving the writing workshop. I never would have considered leading such a series just a few years ago, but now, knowing how much I have learned from elementary teachers, I feel much more certain that I have something to offer them in return.

Mary-Ann: When I found WMWP eight years ago, I was already committed to the idea that teachers from all grade levels had something to teach and learn from their colleagues at other grade levels and in disciplines other than their own. So my experience at WMWP was not as much of a revelation as it may have been for Diana, Bruce, and Charlie. In 1961, when I entered teaching straight from a master's in English program, I earned $5,200 teaching English in a grades 7–12 high school—a paltry sum, but still more than my elementary school colleagues received. Apparently I was considered more of an expert than they were. I learned early on, however, that I was no "expert" on teaching English. On the contrary, I had no idea how students learned to read and write. Those elementary school teachers who were paid less than I were teaching their students this magical act of reading and writing, and I had no idea how they did it.

This big hole in my background yawned in front of me the first time I was faced with a seventh grader who had trouble writing a lucid sentence and could barely read. I realized that I had no idea how to help him. After some course work and stints teaching second grade, fourth grade, sixth grade, first-year college, and finally middle school, I was not only comfortable learning from teachers at various grade levels, but

I saw it as a necessity. My mantra became, "Every high school teacher should take a turn teaching elementary school students, and vice versa."

When I discovered WMWP, I found an organization that agreed with me and was committed to the philosophy that teachers are their own best resources. Since the teachers in the 1993 summer institute I attended were from all grade levels, we were immersed in a culture that I already knew worked, as we all became members of a learning community who taught and learned from each other. My UMass colleagues helped me see the relevance of continued research, and I added the concept of teacher-as-researcher to my repertoire. After doing an inquiry project on assessing student writing at the summer institute, I went on to do my own classroom research on the best way to teach vocabulary; when my school was trying to justify the use of grades 7-8 multi-age classrooms, I immediately went into teacher-as-researcher mode. My elementary school colleagues showed me that writing workshops were useful not just to students "in the middle" but to first graders as well. I have since led writing workshops with parents in an after-school program and with fifth through twelfth graders at SummerWrite!, a summer camp run by WMWP. I have also learned many interactive workshop tools from my colleagues: carousel brainstorming, jigsaw groups, and pair/share, techniques that became standard procedures in my seventh-/eighth-grade classroom.

Charlie: At the university, we almost never talk about teaching. By "we" I mean the English department, but what I say about our department could be said about all other departments—except for the School of Education. One aspect of a four-year research institution is that it privileges research, and therefore, whatever its catalog may say, it deprivileges teaching. At a four-year research institution, talk about teaching is assigned to the School of Education, which is then marginalized by subject matter faculty as a nondiscipline, a quasi-academic unit without a subject to teach. This separation and marginalization of the School of Education makes it even less likely that faculty in subject matter disciplines will talk about teaching.

So if university professors are interested in teaching and talking about teaching, they are not likely to find this talk in their workplace—except the kind of faculty-room talk about students that is perhaps the least attractive aspect of our profession. So in my work in the Writing Project, which includes K–12 teachers who are not reluctant to talk about teaching, I find great relief and support.

From my K–12 colleagues I find myself "learning"—and by *learning* I mean *taking, stealing* teaching ideas. For example: from my colleagues, I have learned how important it is to have students think about a topic before it is introduced—to have them do an inventory of what they know or think about a topic before we get to work. This thinking activates the base knowledge to which new knowledge will be linked. Without this activation, no linking and no learning. This seems obvious, but for this university prof it is something I have to relearn each year. The university teaching structure, within which I am seen as the well-paid expert, leads me to devalue what students already know and to jump in to tell them what I think. The vertical metaphor that pervades our educational system, which runs from the bottom ("elementary," then "secondary") to the top ("higher" education), tells me that I am the subject matter expert. If not, why then my position at the top of this system? In the summers, I learn how little I know about teaching and learning. I learn how I must consider not just what I know but also what my students know. I learn that I must respect students' knowledge and build bridges between what they know and what I know. I learn about learning styles, about language acquisition, about invented spelling, about the relation between graphics and writing, about young adult fiction.

I have also learned how important it is to structure a class discussion. Pat Hunter, a middle school teacher and founding co-director of WMWP, brought to us what she termed the "medium-sized circle"—a discussion format in which speakers have to earn the right to speak by summarizing what has been said before. This changes the dynamics of seminar discussion, privileging not *speaking*, but *listening*. And once I have established these rules, I as seminar leader have to listen, too, and not do what I would otherwise do: think about what my next intervention will be. I've learned to think about the role I play in a discussion: strong moderator, enforcer of the rules, but not "leader" of the discussion, the person with the best or most ideas.

Finally, I have learned how to manage a project-based, or task-oriented, curriculum, one focus of Writing Project pedagogy. It is decreed that during the summer institute we will all have tasks to accomplish: our own writing, an inquiry project, and a demonstration workshop. Our role as leaders of the summer institute is to give teachers the time and resources they need to accomplish the tasks they have undertaken. When university teachers come into our program to give one-week workshops, I find myself spending long hours coaching them: "Don't fill all the time! Give the teachers real tasks; give them the time and the resources they need to complete these tasks."

Clearly, we have learned from one another and learned across grade levels. But what are the factors that make this learning possible? Some of the factors are structural and are explicit or implicit in the ethos of the National Writing Project as we have interpreted it locally. As we noted earlier, NWP values teachers' knowledge, and, to the extent that its local sites follow this dictum, the college-based site director is enjoined from being the authority, the sole person in charge. So shared authority, shared status, and real and deep mutual respect would seem to be necessary conditions for cross-level learning. In addition, NWP evaluates local sites in part according to their ability to encourage and develop leaders. We are asked each year for the number of teachers who have assumed leadership roles in WMWP. NWP recently discovered that the growth rate of any site is a function of the number of teacher-leaders at that site. So there is continuing pressure on us to delegate, to distribute authority, and to level hierarchies that begin to appear.

NWP also insists that the invitational summer institute be project based. Everyone, regardless of grade level, accomplishes a number of projects: one or more pieces of writing, an inquiry project, and a demonstration inservice workshop. We believe that a project-based curriculum, in which everyone has the same set of projects, also acts to level hierarchies and facilitate learning across grade levels.

Further, each of these common projects has an element of performance attached to it. The writing will be shared in response groups and published, the inquiry project will be demonstrated at a poster session, and the inservice workshop will be given to the full institute. Institute leaders also perform, giving their own workshops to the group. This element of performance, carrying with it the risks inherent in all performance, has a bonding effect on institute participants. We have all been through the experience and have survived. We think here of Outward Bound programs, in which participants face physical danger as part of their curriculum. Participants in our summer institute do not face physical danger, but they do face the risks of public performance, which may feel as great as the impending storm or the possible fall down the mountainside.

What we agree that we have learned in this multilevel environment is that *learning is a continuous process governed by principles that apply to all ages of students in all kinds of school situations.* Among these principles: (1) students can and should be given responsibility for their own learning, (2) they can and should use writing as a powerful tool for learning, and (3) they can and should learn with and from each other. By now these ideas may seem self-evident truths, even platitudes. We have learned to believe in them. But the structure and priorities of our educational systems militate against our truly seeing and believing in the universality of these ideas. Teachers of different grades in the same elementary school or of different teams in the same middle school or of different subjects in the same high school rarely have the opportunity to share with each other. They meet and learn together across levels even less often. Their contact with university faculty is usually limited to taking courses. And if, despite all odds, they find themselves working on a cross-level committee or study group, the agenda today is more likely to be how to help students pass the latest state-mandated test than how to create thoughtful, independent learners and learning communities.

To see such learners working together in communities every summer in the Writing Project institute and in other Writing Project programs is truly inspiring. To find common philosophical ground with teachers of many different backgrounds from across an entire region, to share one's own best practices with them and learn from theirs, is to renew one's faith in true educational reform.

This is not to say that Writing Project teachers discover that they are all the same. On the contrary, the second important lesson learned through participation in the Writing Project is that *teaching is a multifaceted enterprise with many legitimate purposes, processes, and practices.* Again, this is not a startling revelation, but the manner in which teachers discover this truth in the Writing Project setting is significant. We have all learned to apply teaching strategies designed by teachers of other levels to our own classrooms. But we also learn from the approaches that do not apply. Seeing other teachers demonstrate what they do and hearing them explain why they do it always helps us to reflect on and clarify our own goals and practices. So even when we don't borrow each other's ideas, the process of sharing is instructive.

How then do we learn to learn across levels? The mechanism involves both broad ideas and site-specific strategies, both group interaction and individual reflection, both collaboration and contrast. An imperfect but useful analogy is the process of detracking classes in schools, another kind of cross-level learning with which some of us have had a good deal of experience in the past several years. Creating a heterogeneous group does not erase differences in learning style, academic ability, or cultural background, but as students learn to negotiate these differences, they always gain perspective and usually discover that they have more in common than they previously imagined. The goal is not to homogenize, but to connect and to capitalize on diversity.

The cross-level learning we have described takes place within the structure of WMWP, arguably a special place whose special character makes what we have learned to a degree context-dependent. But we feel that the cross-level learning we have experienced and described can be replicated in public schools today once the basic premise is agreed on: that teachers are their own best resources. Public school systems are the perfect places for cross-level learning. District curriculum committees are a good example. Teachers from kindergarten through grade 12 are often brought together to develop or restructure curriculum. Too often, however, college professors are brought in to "train" the teachers, to show them what needs to be done, and administrative officials often chair the committees. Our experience with the WMWP is that teachers learn best when they are on an equal footing—experts at their own grade levels and learners of the techniques and philosophies of teachers at other grade levels. A district curriculum committee should include teachers from various grade levels as well as administrators, college faculty, and preschool teachers, the chair being chosen by the group. Such a committee would be governed by the three principles that shape the activities of our Writing Project site: (1) teachers are given responsibility for their own learning, (2) they use writing as a powerful tool, and (3) they learn from each other.

Works Cited

Cushman, Kathleen. "The Whys and Hows of the Multi-Age Primary Classroom." *American Educator* 14.2 (1990): 28–32, 39.

Gaustad, Joan. "Implementing the Multiage Classroom." *ERIC Digest* 97. Eugene: ERIC Clearinghouse, 1995.

Guerra, Juan C. "The Place of Intercultural Literacy in the Writing Classroom." *Writing in Multicultural Settings*. Ed. Carol Severino, Juan C. Guerra, and Johnnella E. Butler. New York: MLA, 1997. 248–60.

Oakes, Jeannie. *Keeping Track: How Schools Structure Inequality*. New Haven: Yale UP, 1985.

Schön, Donald A. *The Reflective Practitioner: How Professionals Think in Action*. New York: Basic, 1983.

Wheelock, Anne. *Crossing the Tracks: How "Untracking" Can Save America's Schools*. New York: New, 1992.

14 Sleeping with the Enemy: Communiqués from a Pedagogical Marriage

Richard E. Brantley
University of Florida

Diana R. Brantley
Eastside High School

Although Richard and Diana work with the same materials, try to teach similar skills, and encounter the same students as year follows year, he teaches college and she teaches high school—and it is an unacknowledged truism that high school English teachers and professors of English in colleges and universities have all too little to say to one another. In this chapter, they consider formally the relationship of college and university professors of English to high school teachers of the same subject, for their more than thirty-year marriage has spanned that divide on a daily basis.

Richard: To avoid a senior professor's rut of specialization, I want to experiment with how I teach writing. Sheridan Baker's *The Practical Stylist*, though, has always served me well. I distribute watchwords: "Get black on white" (De Maupassant); "Put proper words in proper places" (Swift); and "Translate time into space" (Brantley). I cherish Emerson's advice: "The way to write is to throw your body at the mark when your arrows are spent." And Pope's: "Snatch a grace beyond the reach of art." I tell my students, undergraduates and graduates alike, that it is better to write for a very bright ten-year-old than for lovers of academic jargon.

Diana: Nowadays I work with an international baccalaureate program as an assistant principal, which has pulled me away from composition per se. Nevertheless, the past year has been the occasion for that wonderful advantage called hindsight, or at least for some modest perspective on the role that the teaching of writing has played, and may even continue to play, in my career.

Richard: We met at Wake Forest University, where we were both English majors. I came to English through the example of the late Judson B. Allen, a beloved professor of medieval literature; Diana came to it kicking and screaming but giving in to its universality. We shared such mentors as Allen and Edwin G. Wilson, the first of whom emphasized a sense of rigor and the second of whom inspired a sense of wonder. We came to love language and literature as the means of bringing the disciplines together and of helping students find their own humane ways.

Ours, in other words, has been a rather old-fashioned experience. Our careers have been unusually traditional. In the uproarious sixties, we were sedately in grad school, watching from the sidelines. If that also means that we are now a bit out of date, then we're so far *out* we're coming back *in*. We remain, at any rate, enthusiastic about the discipline and its ever-changing variations. We are both lucky and blessed to be doing what we enjoy.

Diana: It is sad and ironic that teachers and professors of English choose the profession because we love working with beautiful language, yet we thereby spend a lifetime reading terrible student prose. Only F. Scott Fitzgerald's "infinite hope" can keep us going. But our jobs and our relationship have survived the paradox. Indeed, our most fruitful and happy times seem to come when we're discussing reading, writing, and pedagogy. Actually, we do not diagram sentences at the dinner table (though our children may say differently). I must say that I did not want to teach school. I've found in this traditional career, however, an opportunity for professional independence, even in Gainesville, Florida, the complete company town. In this context, I must add another mentor, Christine Croft, who taught me in high school that the field of English mixed hard work with pleasure. We learn how to teach by modeling our former teachers, after all.

Things We Do That Are Similar

Diana: Since we think of ourselves as political "radiclibs," we recognize with a shock that our profession is in many ways conservative at its core. When it comes to the *rules* of usage, we are hardliners, not in a political or moral sense, but more as a question of good manners for good communication. Perhaps it is not entirely healthy for us to fight the lost cause rearguard action of traditional usage with such relish. The "lie/lay" and "different from/different than" distinctions are gone. The selection of cases to use in personal pronouns seems to have become a

matter of individual preference. Perhaps this attention to language detail is the thing about English teachers that causes strangers to fall silent when we tell them what we do.

Richard: We recognize that language constantly changes as time passes,
but at what point do we capitulate to the ongoing flux of written usage? How much consistency is necessary for effective (and beautiful)
communication? Horace said that studies serve both to instruct—
prodesse—and to delight—*delectare.* Jonathan Swift's bees bring both
"sweetness and light." If we bear down very hard on the enlightenment
of students, we risk obscuring delight at any level of instruction. High
schoolers are often as mature as college students, and undergraduates
are often as callow as any high schooler. Diana might lean a bit toward
E. D. Hirsch's notion of inculcating a type of "cultural literacy"; I might
lean a bit toward Howard Gardner's progressivist focus on depth and
understanding and his call for a curriculum based on the ancient categories of the good, the beautiful, and the true. But the two of us agree
that we are trying to teach our students not only to think and write
clearly but also to apply a broad model of aesthetic appreciation to a
multiplicity of times, genres, and cultures.

Diana: I might frame the topic a little differently, placing "cultural literacy" advocates over against those who endorse "critical thinking
skills." Phrases like these highlight arguments about politics, money,
and hot-button topics, including such egregious shams as the "Nation
at Risk" movement. But, finally, we enjoy working with students, we
love the subject matter, and we care about clear and imaginative thinking reflected in good writing.

Things We Do That Are Different

Richard: Our jobs are structured differently day by day. We all assume
professors are writing away in an inaccessible ivory tower, free to set
an independent daily schedule. We all assume high school teachers are
constantly harried and in danger of being shot dead at any moment.

Diana: We are judged by different sets of expectations, frequently nowadays as a result of collective bargaining and political rhetoric.

Richard: We relate to students differently: classroom management is not
a big topic in university English departments, and deep discussions of
critical theory do not happen in high school. High school teachers worry

more and more about competency testing of students, and university professors worry about attracting majors and placing graduates in the job market.

Diana: We have different relationships with our subject matter. Works that live high in high school are rarely studied elsewhere: when was the last time the average college professor read *A Tale of Two Cities*, *Julius Caesar*, or *To Kill a Mockingbird*? The ongoing update of the literary canon among universities has been widely and invigoratingly discussed, even in the media. The high school canon makes the news mainly because of questions about banned books.

Richard: Our status in society is different. A salary comparison is merely the most obvious way of making this point. But the difference in remuneration reflects a difference in mindset. A professor works hard for an initial credential, usually a doctorate, and tenure, but then it is assumed that each professor is a professional who can maintain currency in the field.

Diana: Teachers' initial credentials and tenure are not enough to ensure their professionalism, apparently, since they must continually update their certification and receive "inservice" instruction on topics from ESOL to IDEA and other alphabet soup.

Richard: All of these differences make communicating difficult. We have years of resentment, condescension, isolation, and ignorance to bridge. As it is, we too often badmouth each other. I read Diana's poetry, when she lets me, but she doesn't read my stuff any more.

Diana: Except for the first four or five paragraphs, which I read about a thousand times while he's revising. Besides, my education is dated, and I don't dabble in hermeneutics.

Richard: A spouse who lives with a high school teacher learns not to hassle him or her. I don't make demands on her time. Across such gaps silence falls.

Diana: The problem is illustrated in the way we went about writing this. It's like the money conversation that couples have. It was the same conversation again and again, with little or no advancement from one conversation to another.

Richard: I would ask, "Don't you think we'd better start writing?"

Diana: And I would reply, "Don't worry, it'll be all right."

Richard: You can see which one had more time on his hands. Yet by picking around the assignment, and by picking at it, we began to get somewhere as the deadline approached. After all, we acknowledge that some of the best times of our marriage were when we mutually expressed our shared love of the discipline. Some of the best times were when we discussed each other's writing—despite the pain entailed by such discussion. So I try to take a leaf from Diana's book. . . .

Diana: . . . and I try to take a leaf from his. Each tries to cultivate respect for what the other is doing.

Richard: And in that spirit of mutuality, together we offer some concrete suggestions to help us all appreciate our colleagues who teach at different grade levels.

Suggestions for Making Things Better

Diana: We need to talk to each other, whatever the forum; for instance, the reading held for advanced placement examinations offers an opportunity to discuss standards and works, and to be paid for the privilege. Both NCTE and MLA—not to mention such newly formed groups as the Association of Literary Critics and Scholars—need to encourage communication between teachers and professors by programming specific sessions to make such discussion happen.

Richard: One result of such discussion could be a formal method for speeding up a kind of sharing that happens informally and by osmosis now. Diana and I and our daughter, who is a new teacher of English, have found that our discussions of pedagogical technique have been fruitful on all sides. I have received at least as many ideas for improving my classroom style as I've given.

Diana: A wonderful contribution that professors could make would be to help K–12 teachers enrich what we do. As it is, we spend more and more time teaching to tests such as Florida's FCAT, which does a disservice to most of our students. Classroom time is spent going over basic-level skills rather than plunging into the wealth of cultures that we claim as our traditional subject matter. We don't begin to bring theory or criticism to the students. But we should. One concrete way to further this effort would be to offer a college course that considers state-adopted standard high school English textbooks. Furthermore, we need professors to help us convince politicians and the public that schooling should be more than drilling in minimal-level skills aimed at the lowest common denominator. All students deserve opportunity.

Richard: This kind of collaboration would bring to colleges better students from a wider selection of the population. The state of Florida, for instance, does provide a place on professors' annual activities reports for us to indicate "service to high schools," but the traditional way of visiting—a one-period presentation—is inadequate, at best. One of my colleagues who is on the cutting edge of theory and technology talks about merging his undergraduate class with a high school class in order to conduct studies of the local area using the Web. This kind of project could eliminate the problem of reaching high school students who do not live close to a college.

Diana: Co-teaching between school and college might be a radical but useful idea. Richard could take over one of my classes; I could teach one of his. That way we would learn more about each other's worlds, and the exchange would give both the high school and the university faculties a good idea of our common pool of students.

Richard: The state might find it difficult to support a professor for a semester at a high school, but we just might contrive to support him or her with grants at the grassroots level. Would such an exchange fit in to Gainesville's acute town-versus-gown awareness nowadays? Could such exchanges blossom throughout the state?

Diana: Could summer retreats work? Say, over a weekend? Professors and teachers could discuss two selected books on theory or criticism. I went to an informal beach retreat sponsored by a new school board member a few years ago. The intense discussion and brainstorming about ways of improving the school system have led to concrete changes in the local district. As Wordsworth says, we can "build up great things from least suggestions." An idea starts with an individual.

Richard: Book groups have exploded in popularity; what about putting together professors and teachers? No one has time for more reading, but we always do what is important to us. Groups could be held not only in college towns but also in outlying communities. The book groups would have nothing to do with certification; they would not be about jumping through hoops. If they were fun, they would bloom.

Diana: What is my perspective after two years as an assistant principal for curriculum? *Ordering* books is not the relationship I ever wanted to have with them. Yet ordering textbooks, in the present scheme of things, is my reward for twenty-five years of successful teaching. What else might the reward for teaching be? *Sabbaticals.* At present, fifteen yearly sabbaticals are offered for the more than two thousand teachers in my district, but nowhere near that many are given out—because the year is at half pay; because takers have to write a report of the year's activity; and, worst of all, because takers have to be going to school in order to receive a sabbatical. Sabbaticals should be a means of offering a professional person an opportunity for independent research, for undertaking a focused reading program to develop curriculum, for writing/ painting/composing/building a contribution to our national culture.

Richard: In order to help any proposals along these lines come to fruition, individual teachers and professors need to initiate a change in the way their institutions relate to each other. That means principals need to confer with chairs of departments, deans with superintendents. Some crises of numbers are coming: many future forecasters predict a shortfall of both teachers and professors as the baby boomers retire. People who grew up in the technological revolution, who anticipate spending their careers at dot-coms, who think that a virtual human interaction will do, will be sorely pressed to educate their children if the humanity of teaching disappears at any level. In order to attract good people to this highly interactive, deeply personal, and labor-intensive profession, we need to make changes, to train a new generation, and to *talk to one another.*

15 Getting Out of the Way

Mary Baron
University of North Florida

Denise Rambach
Lee High School

Mary teaches at a university, Denise at a high school. Sharing their frustrations about trying to engage their respective students in the study of literature, they discovered the power of helping students make cultural connections, then getting out of the way while students learned. They also discovered the power of continuing to communicate across grade levels.

The Problems: Old Texts, Modern Students

Denise: I teach juniors and seniors, ages sixteen to nineteen, at an inner-city high school where 45 percent of the students are on free or reduced lunch, absenteeism is excessive, and we are on Florida's list of low-performing schools for the third year. A majority of my twelfth-grade British literature students come from lower-middle- to low-income families in which parental involvement in school activities is minimal. Most of my students read below grade level; ESOL (English for Speakers of Other Languages) and special education students are mainstreamed into my regular classroom, bringing with them a variety of learning behaviors. Teaching *Beowulf* or Shakespeare to this group requires me to adapt lessons to students' cultures and learning styles and to be willing to try new ideas.

In 1991 I was a fellow in the first invitational summer institute of Jaxwrite, the University of North Florida site of the National Writing Project (NWP). Working as a teacher consultant for Jaxwrite has kept me in touch with Mary Baron, director of the project. She and I have collaborated on programs—mine are Justread and Justwrite (sons of Jaxwrite)—and we often share frustrations and ideas by e-mail.

Mary: Working with Denise and with the other teachers who attended that first summer institute changed my teaching radically. Before that summer, I was a typical English professor, well trained in textual analysis and with no knowledge at all about teaching. Talk of best practice, higher-order thinking, collaborative learning, or multiple intelligences would have elicited from me the professional comment, "Huh?"

About twice a year I teach a college survey course inflicted on English and education majors; it covers literature in English from *Beowulf* to the seventeenth century. Students fear the texts, which one young woman described (before reading any) as "old, boring, and hard." Trying to awaken student interest is like trying to breathe life into a corpse. When I ask them why they are enrolled, the universal reply is, "I need it to graduate." Their preconceptions about the reading are illustrated in the following introduction to a student paper:

> Early on, I assumed that Surrey would fit the stereotype that most of us non-English majors assign to most sixteenth century English poets. They're all a bunch of prissy pale white guys resembling John Boy Walton who run around wearing tight big fluffy collars as they churn out mushy poems about love, death, the death of a love, or the love of death.

Finding Some Answers

Mary: When, as a result of my work with the K–12 teachers, I became interested in research on collaborative and active learning and in Howard Gardner's work on multiple intelligences, I decided to experiment with this course, which was my greatest challenge. I reasoned that if the collaborative method worked in this course, it would work anywhere. Besides, my lectures were beginning to bore me.

Previously I had structured the class as a survey, a series of "greatest hits." I introduced texts in chronological order, set them in historical context, lectured on the criticism, and capped each unit by assigning student writing. I responded to their writing and moved on. (I'm sure the students would have said, "and on and on and on.") I functioned primarily as a translator between text and students: telling them what the author was talking about, pointing out the meaning of words, elaborating on metaphor. I have come to see that I was a barrier, literally an obstacle, keeping students from the texts.

Now I do anything I can think of to get the students to read the text and revisit it, revisit it, revisit it—first for greater clarity, then for flavor, then to pose a question of it, then to prove their answer is correct. First I set the context with a minilecture, and then student groups experience, analyze, create, explore, and respond to the text in a "laboratory session." Only then do we read theory, because then theory makes sense.

I learned that when teaching a longer text such as *Beowulf* I need to break down the steps of reading, critical thinking, and analytical writing into carefully designed tasks. I start with a weathered copy of the facsimile first page of *Beowulf,* one for each student group. (The facsimiles are printed on parchment paper and have been gleefully torn and burned around the edges by my teenage sons. They are then aged in my garage. They look really, really old.)

I provide a modern translation on the overhead, and we listen to a CD of the text being read aloud. Then I focus on one passage or theme within the longer work and use this as the laboratory session text. We locate the passages dealing with Grendel, for example, and I assign one passage to each group. Next I show color transparencies (or Web pages) with Anglo-Saxon helmets and boats embellished with dragons and monsters. Then I pass out modeling clay. The first time I tried this, I admit I was afraid I'd be laughed out of the classroom. Instead, the response was "all right!" (Actually, "*Aw right*!!!") The task is to model Grendel or his mother based on the text's descriptions. Students work in groups and must be prepared at the end of the class period to exhibit and defend their model with evidence from the text.

Denise: My students, many of them low-achieving readers, have a difficult time understanding the text at all, never mind understanding the idea of using the text to prove their statements about it. Mary and I talked about the problems we both face teaching students who can't seem to grasp a complex text, and I decided to borrow the idea of clay modeling. I modified it to meet the needs of my students, who require more explicit structure than do college students and more "things that count for a grade" to keep them on task. I adapted the idea by developing a graphic organizer for the dragon and for Grendel. The organizer has three columns: details of appearance, line number, and page number.

I divide the class into groups of four or five and ask one member from each group to draw a slip of paper with *dragon* or *Grendel* written on it. Each group is to find as much information as they can about the dragon or Grendel and write that information, as well as the lines and page numbers, on the organizer. Each member's name is recorded on the graphic organizer, which is then turned in for a grade at the end of the sixty-minute period. I make sure to move around the classroom and observe participation for individual class work grades as well.

The next day students form the same groups and I return their graphic organizers. I tell students to clear all materials off their desks except their graphic organizers. Then I hand out two clumps of modeling clay to each group. Each group is to mold either the dragon or Grendel using only the information on their graphic organizers. I overheard one student say, "This class is off the chain." I later learned that meant the class was "cool." The dragons and Grendels are displayed in clear plastic cases in the classroom throughout the year. Students bring their friends in to see "their" monsters.

Research and Practice: Sculpting Dragons

Mary: Research on effective teaching, particularly Alexander Austin's national study of student outcomes, encouraged me to broaden the responsibilities of student groups. Austin determined that "two factors—interaction among students and interaction between faculty and students—carried by far the greatest weight and affected more general education outcomes than any other environmental variable studied, including curriculum content factors."

In my classroom, I replaced lectures with carefully designed tasks keyed to specific skills in reading, interpreting, and writing about literature. Group tasks must be pertinent, important, and achievable. I learned that groups must be accountable to the class as a whole and feel that they are contributing to everyone's learning. Like Denise, I walk throughout the classroom during group time, asking and answering questions and shamelessly eavesdropping. I require accountability, either orally or in writing, at the end of each task.

To make this approach work, I break down the material of the course into clearly defined units that I call "Ed.Bytes," each unit building on the previous one. I plan activities that build students' confidence in their abilities as readers and critics, and that require them to manipulate a text in many different ways, both individually and as members of their group. The intent is to give each student, no matter what his or her strongest learning style, a chance of success.

High school teachers tend to be much better at this careful course design than most college professors, who were given a book and told, "Here; teach it." I personally expect to spend time in purgatory for my feeble efforts to teach More's *Utopia* to first-year students at the University of Illinois. (Sorry, guys!)

While texts cannot always be made interdisciplinary, learning modalities can, allowing students to draw on individual strengths. Artistic and musical students, for example, shine as teachers and learners when allowed to use their talents to approach and interpret literature. I will never forget a rap on Greek tragedy with the refrain "Funky Cold

Medea" or a moving song on the death of race car driver Davey Allison patterned on "To an Athlete Dying Young," first performed with guitar accompaniment and then explicated for us. I have learned that well-structured group work increases interaction not only among students, but also between students and texts.

Denise: I begin my British literature unit with *Beowulf*. The abbreviated text I use is from *The Language of Literature* published by McDougal Littell. I give a brief background of the Anglo-Saxon period, discussing the times, the definition of an epic, and the characteristics of an epic hero. We use "jump in reading": I begin reading aloud to the class and then stop after a certain point. Volunteers then "jump in" to read until they want to stop. Then another student begins reading. I do not correct the students as they are reading, so their momentum keeps going. While the students are reading aloud, I underline in my text all mispronounced words. As we pause every few paragraphs to review what we've read, I make sure to pronounce all the words I've underlined. This strategy is a tactful way of teaching correct pronunciation. Because no student feels put down, I get more volunteer readers.

E-mail, Denise to Mary: Mary, I just had to tell you what a hoot today was! My seniors did their clay models of Grendel and the dragon. I had a ball watching seniors play—and they *all* had a good time. I took pictures as you suggested. The guys really got excited about this—the room wasn't even messy and no clay was thrown. Yesterday, I divided the class into groups, then had one member choose from a bag of slips which monster they were to focus on, Grendel or the dragon. I gave them a graphic organizer where they had to cite evidence of appearance, the page and line number! Then today, using only their organizers, they had to "mold" their characters. Tomorrow, we "bloom with Beowulf" as the kids are going to write the different level questions.

Connecting Critical Reading with Critical Thinking

Denise: On the day after we make our monsters, I divide the class into new groups of four or five and hand out examples of Bloom's taxonomy stems. We discuss his thinking levels by using key words to identify each one. We determine, for example, that knowledge is recall and that questions at this level use cue words such as *observe, name, define,* or *repeat.* After we do this for all of Bloom's levels, I model questions on *Beowulf* at each of the six levels, using appropriate cue words.

Each group develops two questions per stem using Bloom's taxonomy and *Beowulf.* Once students develop their questions, I give them a petal-shaped piece of paper on which to write their questions. Each petal has one of Bloom's stems on it. Finally, we paste the petals around a circle containing the word *Beowulf* to create a flower using Bloom's stems. We then display the Blooming *Beowulf* flowers around the classroom along with the Grendel and dragon models.

On another day, we play a modified version of *Jeopardy!* using the questions from our flowers. The six levels of Bloom's taxonomy are written on slips of paper and put into a bag. Each group picks a slip from the bag and must answer the questions for that particular stem. The group with the most correct answers wins.

Mary: I design my courses so that they incorporate individual work, work within a base group, and work that makes a contribution to the class as a whole. This structure grew out of student requests that individual responsibilities, along with group work, have a prominent role in the course.

A successful assignment that allows for this spread of accountability is what I call, with a nod to Ken Macrorie, the We-Search paper. I assign each group one author. Students in the group are to become experts on that person and his or her work. They define pertinent areas of research, such as the writer's genre, responses to his or her work, historical and social context—whatever topics seem appropriate and qualify as raising "real" questions. Students divide the work so that each becomes expert on one topic and shares information with the others. I schedule class time for this exchange of information and circulate among groups as they talk, offering hints about additional resources.

Each student then writes a paper on a different text by "his" or "her" author. They might each choose a different short story by Poe, for example. The papers are to be analytical, argue from the text, and make use of the group's research. They must answer higher-order questions about the text. I sometimes use Bloom's taxonomy here and sometimes Alan Purves's four levels of questioning. The papers are shared in draft form within the group, and then revised before being handed in to me.

Students working in this manner have the advantage of discussing and planning a paper with a small group of well-informed people. They have the freedom to use pooled information in developing an individual literary analysis. I sometimes combine this assignment with a group presentation on the author, in which students assign and teach yet another text to the class as a whole. If so, the papers are due first, and the presentation is planned with my input so that it helps move the class forward.

Denise: The success of the *Beowulf* lesson was overwhelming. My students brought their friends from other senior English classes into our room to show off their dragons and Grendels. Their friends commented to my students, "This class is tight." I checked with my students to make sure that "tight" was a compliment—it was.

   While using the modeling clay, many students commented that they hadn't had this much fun since kindergarten. They made comments like, "I didn't know that literature could be fun like this," and "I'm glad my group wrote down lots of detail." Students realized that the more detail provided or work they had done the day before, the easier the clay modeling assignment was.

   I was impressed with the higher levels of thinking from my students as they formed their Bloom's taxonomy questions. Students not only had to develop strong questions, but they had to know the answers, too. This was a challenge for the students as they tried to stump the other groups with what they determined to be higher-level or more difficult questions.

Spreading the Word

Mary: As director of Jaxwrite, I was asked to design and present an inservice to all faculty at Andrew Jackson High School, which has a student population much like the one at Lee High where Denise teaches. Four teacher consultants from the writing project planned a workshop that included practice in the use of Bloom's taxonomy to aid students in questioning texts across the curriculum. (Not incidentally, the new Florida statewide assessment test requires text-based writing.)

   After hearing about the success Denise had with her *Beowulf* unit, I asked her if she thought the students would be willing to come and talk about what they had learned. One young woman's response was, "I'm there!" Four students came to share their *Beowulf* experience. They told us later that they were scared, but at the time you couldn't tell. They faced a cafeteria full of teachers and calmly explained how the graphic organizers helped them locate detail and how they had to "have words" to prove that their dragon was like the one in the text. They explained the question stems in Bloom's taxonomy. All this was accompanied by visual aids, including several clay dragons. Then they circulated amongst the tables and answered questions from individual teachers. Their poise and understanding of the material were awesome—I can't think of another word.

Denise: After the students' presentation, I received several phone calls asking us to come teach *Beowulf* at Andrew Jackson using Bloom's taxonomy. Although time constraints would not allow us to go, the fact that teachers saw this as a useful tool in their classrooms is proof of the success of the presentation and of the students' understanding of *Beowulf.*

My students did present this activity to another teacher's class at Lee High. They distributed graphic organizers and explained the tasks involved with them; the following day they handed out modeling clay and gave the instructions. The other teacher's students participated and appeared to enjoy and learn from the activity. After the *Beowulf* presentation, we all went to lunch . . . and we then stayed in touch by e-mail.

Staying Connected

Our collaboration would have ended after the students presented their work were it not for e-mail. It was very difficult to find the time to collaborate. We both have teenagers at home as well as in the classroom; they are high maintenance. As we were working out the *Beowulf* lessons, however, we had gotten into the habit of sending each other electronic progress reports, and this continued. This section consists entirely of e-mail messages.

Denise to Mary: Mary, many thanks for all of the things you do! My kids said that they had so much fun yesterday. They were bragging that they were taken out to lunch by a university professor. They are so funny with their stereotypes of people. Zach said that before he met everyone he was so nervous and afraid he'd mess up. He commented several times how nice the ladies [the teacher consultants] were and that you didn't seem to mind being around high school kids. He doesn't realize that your children ARE high school kids.

Mary to Denise: Thank me! Do you realize that your students now are completely confident of themselves in the very scary arena of high school—and not even their own high school! Watching them teach the teachers was a highlight of my professional life. Students teaching other students and teaching teachers are students who have mastered the material well enough to question and manipulate it. They are scholars.

Denise to Mary: The positive experience yesterday will go so far with my kids. I'm anxious to move on with the *Canterbury Tales* this week. Zach (one of the student presenters) wants to e-mail you. I'll let him use my account.

Zachary to Mary: Hello Dr. Baron. I hope you are doing fine as yourself and with your assignment on *Beowulf.* [We told the students we planned to write about their work.] We just finish *Hamlet* and I didn't really like it but the movie was a little better and could have been better if they would have spoken English and not what they was speaken. And Mrs. Rambach showed us how to do PowerPoint and I really liked it a lot.

Mary to Denise: Hello Denise, I gave Zach a dare to translate *Hamlet* into street language and provide me with footnotes. I hope he decides to try it.

Denise to Mary: Zach asked for his *Hamlet* book back. He said "Dr. Baron emailed me and needs me to help in translating *Hamlet* into today's words . . . is she for real?"

Refining the Lessons

Denise: After the success with *Beowulf,* I was convinced that inner-city students could understand Shakespeare if it was presented at their level and on their terms, so I collaborated with another English teacher to develop a student guidebook for *Macbeth.* It contains quotes, act sum-

maries, graphic organizers, RAFT (role, audience, format, topic) assignments, vocabulary, and puzzles. Each student was given a copy of the
play and a guidebook.

After we read act 1, one student informed me that the guidebooks
were "straight" (helpful). Students read character parts aloud. We took
the reading slowly as I translated what each character was saying. My
students asked, "Why didn't Shakespeare just write this stuff in English
in the first place?" I explained that he was writing in the language of
his streets. After the first three scenes, students translated for themselves.

When I asked one of my low-achieving students to summarize
act 1 before we continued with act 2, he said:

> Macbeth be a scrub and his pigeon be Lady Macbeth. Their crib
> be Inverness, and they plotting to kill the king, but that on the
> down low. At the end of the ack, Macbeth crunk cuz he thinking
> about killin the king.

My first reaction was one of horror as other students laughed and encouraged him to use slang terms unfamiliar to me. Just when I was about
to reprimand the young man for his disrespect, other students began
to translate what he said. Sure enough,

> Macbeth is this guy and his wife is Lady Macbeth. They do live at
> Inverness and are secretly plotting to kill Duncan. Macbeth is
> anxious and distraught as he ponders killing Duncan.

The rest of the play went that well or better. My new vocabulary words
and their definitions adorn our classroom word board, which contains
any unfamiliar words we come across in our reading. I now have my
own column translating street talk into teacher talk.

The students were so excited about understanding Shakespeare
that I decided to keep the learning going by letting them work in groups
on their unit test. To get them to revisit the text, I assigned them to prepare PowerPoint presentations on the play. The five groups in each class
were each assigned one act. They were to create a PowerPoint presentation that included a summary, their favorite quotes, and examples of
foreshadowing, theme, and symbols. I used a rubric to assess each presentation, and then all classes voted on the best presentation of each act.
I knew this lesson was a success when a group of usually disinterested
boys finished their PowerPoint presentation, raised their arms, and in
unison shouted, "Score!"

The presentations were uploaded to our reading enhancement
Web site (http://www.justread.cjb.net), created and maintained by my
students. The pride and ownership the students have in their Web site

and presentations continue to grow as they give the address out to their friends so they too can understand *Macbeth.* Students in the school visiting our Web site e-mail us questions about *Hamlet,* another student-produced PowerPoint presentation on the site. My students have now attached a Web cam to the classroom video monitor so that their parents and other interested persons can view them in the classroom. Mary visits and leaves messages for the classes and the "teaching students." The site is so much a part of the classroom experience for students that when I was sick one day and logged on to check what the students were doing, I saw a sign on the blackboard: HELLO, MS. RAMBACH! They were expecting me.

This lesson turned out to be one of my favorites in my twenty-two years of teaching because I learned so much from my students. These inner-city, below-reading-level kids *did* read and understand Shakespeare! On completion of the play, one student commented, "*Macbeth* on time." I agree; *Macbeth* is a good play.

Unexpected Outcomes

Mary: Zach accepted my dare and chose to translate *Hamlet,* act 3, scene 1 into street talk. He worked on it for more than three weeks. A sample follows:

Hamlet:	"What should I do about what I know about my father's death? Since my father died I have been thinking about killing myself, but I don't know what to do. I'm so confused. And now that I know how my father died. [Zach labeled the actual beginning of the speech, "To be or not to be."]
Ophelia:	Hey, Hamlet, how are you doing today?
Hamlet:	I'm just fine and thank you for asking.
Ophelia:	I hope you don't forget the fun times me and you use to have together.
Hamlet:	Man quit playing with me, I don't know who you is.
Ophelia:	Why are you playing? You know me and we use to be close to one another.
Hamlet:	Lady you're tripping. You need to quit fantasizing and open your eyes.
Ophelia:	Like I said quit fantasizing, because I don't know you.
Hamlet:	Quit thinking that I'm one of your customers and get back to work on your corner. ["Get thee to a nunnery"]

What We Have Learned

Denise: We have learned that empowering students and giving them ownership of texts and of their own learning are vital strategies for success in the classroom. The confidence that has surfaced continues to build with each new adventure we share. Zach told me that he was glad he could help me get published. His whole attitude toward class is changed. He now thinks of himself as a teacher as well as a student. Teachers who collaborate become active learners, as do the students who participate in cooperative learning activities. Our own confidence grows along with our students' success.

Mary: E-mail turned out to be a wonderful option for us. We often sat down at our computers and fired off "you won't believe what happened" notes late at night. Something I would plan for next time is to send each other a HEADS UP! whenever something doesn't work. I think that's important. We all make mistakes. Sharing our failures leads us to new successes. I wouldn't recommend this sort of project unless both teachers are willing to share the good, the bad, and the ugly. It won't work, as Denise's students would say, "on the down low."

Denise: Since I am a National Board Certified teacher, I have the honor of mentoring National Board candidates. This allows for collaboration and the sharing of teaching strategies that have been successful in the classroom. One National Board candidate was extremely discouraged about her small-group video entry. We discussed several options, and then it occurred to me—share the *Beowulf* experience. She loved the idea of revisiting text through graphic organizers and then applying this information to clay models. She videotaped her seniors as they found support from the text to complete their graphic organizers and as they created their clay Grendels and dragons. The teacher was thrilled with the results and commented on how easy it was for her to write the commentary for the video entry.

Mary: Collaboration leads naturally into reflective practice. We evaluate what we have done as we tell each other about it. This may be the greatest benefit for the teachers involved. For students, it gets the classroom "off the chain," gets the teacher out of their way, and helps them learn to be teachers themselves—something that is unimaginable to many students in inner-city high schools

A final thought: we underestimated how motivating it is for a student to be taken seriously. Zach's hard work "translating" Shakespeare was done without any promise of credit or a grade. He, like any good teacher, was self-motivated to go back to the text.

Works Cited

Austin, Alexander. "What Really Matters in General Education: Provocative Finds from a National Study of Student Outcomes." Association of General and Liberal Studies. Seattle. 18 Oct. 1991.

Macrorie, Ken. *The I-Search Paper*. Portsmouth, NH: Boynton/Cook, 1988.

Purves, Alan C., and Victoria Rippere. *Elements of Writing about a Literary Work: A Study of Response to Literature*. Urbana, IL: National Council of Teachers of English, 1968.

235

Editor

 **Thomas C. Thompson** taught at two high schools and a community college before settling into his current position at The Citadel in Charleston, South Carolina, where he directs the Lowcountry Writing Project and teaches courses in composition and public speaking. He is the editor of *Most Excellent Differences: Essays on Using Type Theory in the Composition Classroom* (1996) and the author of articles that have appeared in *The Writing Center Journal*, *Assessing Writing*, and *Carolina English Teacher*. Inspired by Don Daiker's example, he will use his sabbatical leave this fall to teach high school. He enjoys watching his three children progress through school, and he stands in awe of stay-at-home moms (especially his wife Sharon) and elementary school teachers.

Contributors

Janet Alsup received her Ph.D. in English education from the University of Missouri–Columbia in May 2000, and she is currently assistant professor of English education at Purdue University, where she teaches pedagogy courses to preservice English teachers and conducts research on the topic of teacher development and professional identity formation. She is currently engaged in a longitudinal study of preservice teachers that focuses on the potential role of narrative and metaphor in teacher education. She has recently published in *English Education* and has book chapters forthcoming in *Witnessing the Disaster: Essays on Representation and the Holocaust* edited by Michael Bernard-Donals and Richard Glejzer and *Protean Ground: Critical Ethnography and the Postmodern Turn* edited by Sid Dobrin and Stephen Brown. She presents regularly at NCTE and CCCC conventions.

Mary Baron is professor of English at the University of North Florida. Learning from teachers in Jaxwrite, the National Writing Project site she directs, is the joy of her professional life. The author of two books of poetry as well as articles on teaching and on young adult literature, Baron teaches all over the curriculum.

Michael Bernard-Donals is professor of English and Jewish studies at the University of Wisconsin–Madison, where he also directs the English 100 program, the department's contribution to the university's first-year communication requirement. He also teaches undergraduate and graduate courses in rhetoric, literary theory, and representations of the Holocaust. Bernard-Donals is the author of articles on pedagogy and writing and recently coauthored *Between Witness and Testimony: The Holocaust and the Limits of Representation* (2001) with Richard Glejzer.

Diana R. Brantley's first job at Educational Testing Service included working at the readings held to score the advanced placement exams. Since then she has made a career of teaching English in the advanced placement and international baccalaureate programs. She has been a reader for AP, coming full circle to the ETS scoring sessions, and an IB coordinator for twelve years. For the last five years, she has worked with curriculum planning, scheduling, and textbook selection as an assistant principal.

Richard E. Brantley, alumni professor of English at the University of Florida, is the author of *Wordsworth's "Natural Methodism"* (1975) and *Locke, Wesley, and the Method of English Romanticism* (1984), which won the Conference on Christianity and Literature award for Best Book of 1984. He has also written *Coordinates of Anglo-American Romanticism: Wesley, Edwards, Carlyle, and Emerson* (1993) and *Anglo-American Antiphony: The Late Romanticism of Tennyson and Emerson* (1994). Currently he is reading and writing about Emily Dickinson.

Herb Budden teaches at Hamilton Southeastern High School in Fishers, Indiana, where he conducts classes in composition and AP literature. Herb is co-director of the Indiana Teachers of Writing Writing Project and serves on numerous language arts committees for which he focuses his energies on teacher action research projects. Budden has degrees in the teaching of English and in rhetoric and composition from the University of Illinois and Purdue University, respectively. His firm belief is that all real value in the teaching profession lies in the minds and actions of classroom teachers.

Diana Callahan has been a longtime elementary teacher in the public schools of Easthampton, Massachusetts. Currently she teaches a multi-age class of six-, seven-, and eight-year-olds who enjoy writing and getting published almost as much as their teacher does. In her spare time, Callahan works as a mentor teacher in her district and serves as co-director of the Western Massachusetts Writing Project, where she facilitates writing and response groups for teachers, presents inservice workshops, and co-leads the invitational summer institute. She has been published in *We Teach Them All: Teachers Writing about Diversity* (1996) and in numerous WMWP publications.

Don Daiker is professor of English at Miami University of Ohio, where he teaches courses in composition, American literature, the short story, travel, and the teaching of writing. He was the founding director of Miami University's first-in-the-nation portfolio writing assessment program, and he has written and edited books on sentence combining, teacher research, portfolio evaluation, and composition studies. Daiker grew up in Lyndhurst, New Jersey, majored in psychology at Rutgers University, and earned his Ph.D. in English at Indiana University, where he wrote his doctoral dissertation on the novels of Herman Melville.

Terry DeBarger teaches middle school English in Reno, Nevada. Before worrying about the traits of effective writing or students' process in learning them, he wrote at Vassar College effectively enough to graduate with a degree in sociology. He is working toward a master of arts, teacher of English degree at UNR.

Ron Fortune, chair of the Illinois State University English department, researches writing and literature on computers. He is the author of *School-College Collaborative Programs in English* (1986) and has been the leading author and director on four NEH grants relating to literature and writing. He has also published in *Computers and Writing* and coedited a guest edition of that journal. Fortune's research in hypertext has given direction to work on the use of computers in writing, being especially influential on computer instruction in ISU's English department. He has presented many conference sessions on computer instruction and serves as co-chair for the 2002 Computers and Writing conference.

Stephen L. Fox teaches at Indiana University–Purdue University Indianapolis (IUPUI) and is director of the Indiana Teachers of Writing Writing Project. He is coeditor of *Teaching Academic Literacy: The Uses of Teacher-Research in Developing a Writing Program* (1999), and his essays on teaching portfolios, non-tenure-track faculty, and teaching writing to working-class students will appear in forthcoming books.

Launie Gardner currently teaches social studies at Truckee Meadows Community College High School as well as basic writing courses and professional development courses and workshops for teachers at TMCC and the University of Nevada, Reno. She previously taught English in Reno area high schools for eleven years. Gardner first became involved with the dialogue between the three levels of public schools and higher education during her work with the Northern Nevada Writing Project in 1991. She has since served as director for the NNWP, and through this organization she continues to work toward greater communication with teachers at all levels.

Stuart Greene is associate professor and Frank O'Malley Director of the University Writing Program at the University of Notre Dame. His expertise is in rhetorical theory, writing in the disciplines, and literacy. Greene is the lead author of a textbook on written argument, *Inquiry and Argument: Entering the Conversation of Ideas* (in press), and coeditor of a number of books including *Reading, Writing, and Race: Classroom Inquiries for Racial Understanding* (in press), and *Teaching Academic Literacy* (1999). His research has also appeared in such journals as *Research in the Teaching of English* and in a number of edited collections on composition theory, research, and theory. He is past president of the NCTE Assembly for Research and is currently a member of the NCTE Commission on Composition.

Richard Hoadley, having spent the last fourteen years in the corporate world, is just beginning his career as an educator. He is both an instructor of first-year composition at Truckee Meadows Community College and a graduate student pursuing a master's degree in teaching writing at the University of Nevada, Reno.

Jane Hunn has a variety of experience in education both in the classroom and in curriculum development. Having taught for over twenty-four years in grades 9 through 12 in Alabama, Louisiana, California, and Mississippi, she is currently the English department chairperson at Salem High School in Virginia Beach, Virginia. She has taught all levels from basic English to first-year college composition and has worked on Virginia Beach City Public Schools' curriculum in various capacities for the past seven years. Hunn has been active in the development of Virginia Standards of Learning tests for the past six years as a member of the Standards of Learning English Assessment Content Review Committee, and she has been working with Chris Jennings and Tidewater Community College for the past three years in a FIPSE grant project to promote collaboration between secondary and postsecondary institutions.

Kim Jaxon teaches in the first-year writing program at California State University, Chico, where she was recently recognized as Outstanding Faculty by the Phi Eta Kappa Honor Society. She continues to co-coordinate academic writing programs for high school students and work with the Northern California Writing Project as a teacher-researcher. She plans to pursue a Ph.D. in education in the fall of 2002, focusing on teacher development.

Chris Jennings has been teaching composition at Tidewater Community College in Virginia Beach, Virginia, for fifteen years beginning as adjunct instructor and now as associate professor of English. Balancing adjunct work with a full-time position, she also served as English department chair and as a teacher in high schools in Virginia Beach and Richmond for twenty-eight years. An outgrowth of her secondary and postsecondary teaching experiences led her to cooperatively develop and direct a partnership model to improve student preparation for college writing that has received funding from the U.S. Department of Education's Fund for the Improvement of Postsecondary Education since 1998. Jennings is currently directing a half-million dollar FIPSE-funded national coalition of secondary and postsecondary institutions representing ten geographic areas of the United States. She has presented numerous workshops, published articles for national audiences, and coauthored *From the Beach to the Bay: An Illustrated History of Sandbridge in Virginia* (2000).

Susan Kapanke graduated from the University of Wisconsin–Eau Claire in 1977, taught high school English in Spring Grove, Minnesota, for two years, and has been teaching ninth-grade and upper-class electives, including AP and English literature, at Elkhorn High School ever since. In 1985 she earned her masters in English and education at the University of Wisconsin.

Stephen Lafer is associate professor of English education at the University of Nevada, Reno, where he has taught for the past fifteen years. He is co-director of the Nevada Writing Alliance and founder and co-director of the Reading and Writing the West summer institutes for teachers. His publications include *The Interdisciplinary Teacher's Handbook* (1996), coauthored with Stephen Tchudi.

Claire Lamonica, assistant director of writing programs at Illinois State University, works extensively with the teaching of writing, publishing in the *Illinois English Bulletin* and presenting at national and international conferences. Her work with collaboration in the writing classroom has led to research on learning groups and extensive work with the National Writing Project and NCATE. She has headed up Young Writers Workshops for NWP teachers and recently reviewed programs for NCATE. She is co-director of the Illinois State Writing Project.

Charles Moran is, with Diana Callahan, Mary-Ann DeVita Palmieri, and Bruce Penniman, co-director of the Western Massachusetts Writing Project. He is a member of the English department at the University of Massachusetts, where he has, with Anne Herrington, coedited *Writing,*

Teaching, and Learning in the Disciplines (1992); coauthored, with Gail Hawisher, Paul LeBlanc, and Cynthia Selfe, *Computers and the Teaching of Writing in American Higher Education, 1979–1994: A History* (1996); coedited, with Elizabeth Penfield, *Conversations: Contemporary Critical Theory and the Teaching of Literature* (1990); and coedited, with Pat Belanoff, Marcia Dickson, and Sheryl Fontaine, *Writing with Elbow* (2002).

Janice Neuleib, writing program administrator and professor of English, has published widely on the pedagogy of writing, including six textbooks (e.g., *Inside Out: A Guide to Writing* [1993], *Writing with the Masters I-III* [1994–1996], *Things Your Grammar Never Told You* [2001]), as well as coediting the *Mercury Reader.* She has also published on writing program administration and on research in language in journals such as *Writing on the Edge, College English, College Composition and Communication,* and *The Writing Center Journal,* and in chapters of numerous books. She is director of the Illinois State Writing Project and has participated as teacher coordinator in four NEH grants for teachers.

Mary B. Nicolini is Writing Center director and English content specialist at Penn, a high school of 3,000 students in Mishawaka, Indiana. She co-directs the Indiana Teachers of Writing Writing Project, works with preservice teachers in the Alliance for Catholic Education program at the University of Notre Dame, and teaches English methods at Indiana University South Bend. A graduate of Indiana University–Purdue University Indianapolis, Nicolini has received the Armstrong Teacher Educator Award from IU and is a trustee with the NCTE Research Foundation. She is especially interested in the creation and study of the personal narrative essay. Since 1998 her twelfth graders have participated in senior graduation exhibitions, oral exit projects based on the work of the Coalition of Essential Schools.

Mary-Ann DeVita Palmieri recently retired from teaching seventh and eighth graders at Great Falls Middle School in Turners Falls, Massachusetts. She continues to work with teachers and their students through the Western Massachusetts Writing Project where she is co-director along with Charles Moran, Diana Callahan, and Bruce Penniman. Her special interests include publishing student writing and mentoring new teachers.

Bruce M. Penniman, 1999 Massachusetts Teacher of the Year and National Teacher of the Year finalist, has taught writing, speech, and literature for thirty years at Amherst Regional High School, where he also advises the student newspaper. He is co-director of the Western Massachusetts Writing Project, president of the New England Association of Teachers of English, and newsletter editor of the NCTE Assembly on American Literature. Penniman has published over two dozen articles on topics ranging from American literature to writing instruction to educational policy. In May 2000, he received an honorary degree from the University of Massachusetts Amherst, his three-time alma mater.

Marguerite Quintelli-Neary is associate professor of English at Winthrop University, where she coordinates the English education program and teaches British and Celtic literature, English pedagogy, and writing. She is the author of *Folklore and the Fantastic in Twelve Modern Irish Novels* (1997), a study of Irish folklore and modern Irish fiction, and has published numerous articles on modern Irish literature and English pedagogy. She is currently at work on a study of Irish American frontier folklore and is coauthoring a work on Ives, Mahler, and Joyce. She spends her free time working with the NCTE student affiliate of Winthrop University, a group that focuses on literacy projects and support for new teachers. Having taught in New Jersey public schools for ten years, Quintelli-Neary values the liaisons between universities and schools and plans to involve as many local teachers as possible in projects that link high school students with higher education.

Denise Rambach graduated from Florida State University and has been teaching high school language arts for twenty-three years in Jacksonville. She is a National Board Certified teacher and charter member and co-director of Jaxwrite, Jacksonville's affiliate of the National Writing Project.

April Sawyer teaches at Procter Hug High School in Reno, Nevada, an urban high school of approximately 2,200 students representing diverse ethnic and racial groups. She has a master of arts in secondary education from the University of Nevada, Reno, where she studied education reform. As a volunteer for the Reading and Writing for Critical Thinking Project, she traveled throughout Romania presenting workshops for Romanian teachers. She is also a member of the Northern Nevada Writing Project, NCTE, and the International Reading Association, and she has served as both vice president and president of the Northern Nevada Teachers of English.

Wendy Strachan has a lifetime habit of being in transition and crossing boundaries: she was born and grew up in England, immigrated with her family to Canada at age twelve, and, after graduating from McGill University, married and set off to see the world. It took her seventeen years to return from prolonged stays in Malawi, Algeria, England, and finally Malaysia, where for eight years she taught at the American International School, started the East Asia Writing Project, and raised two children. Longing for the varied climate and landscape of the Northwest drew her back to Vancouver, British Columbia, but she continued traveling the world leading writing workshops while pursuing a Ph.D. at home. In 2000, for instance, she led a two-week summer workshop in Portugal for teachers from seven different countries. Strachan is again in transition, having taken a new position in elementary education at Western Washington University in Bellingham.

Nancy S. Tucker teaches English education, writing, and educational technology at the University of Michigan–Flint. She received her Ph.D. in English from Michigan State University in 1995. She has served on the steering committee of the Spring English Language Arts Conference of Michigan since 1989 and was coordinator of the conference for two of those years. Tucker has published articles about teaching, about writing and about the role of technology in education. When not writing academic articles, she works on her own poetry, essays, and short fiction.

Melissa Westemeier received a B.A. from the University of Wisconsin–Stevens Point and an M.S. from the University of Wisconsin–Madison. Her high school students have taught her much about writing over the past eight years. Westemeier teaches a graduate class on multicultural education through Viterbo University in addition to teaching composition through the CAPP program with UW Oshkosh and various literature courses at Kaukauna High School.

Betsy Wilson graduated from the College of Charleston, where she majored in business and education, and taught five years at Middleton High School, where she was awarded the Charleston County School District Sally Mae Award for most outstanding first-year teacher. For the past seven years, Wilson has taught accounting, computers, internship, and Teacher Cadet classes at Wando High School, where she also serves as the cheerleading sponsor. Her Teacher Cadet program has been cited as one of the most outstanding programs in South Carolina.

Leah A. Zuidema, a former high school English teacher, is a doctoral student in the Critical Studies in the Teaching of English program at Michigan State University. She is a National Writing Project teacher consultant, and her published work includes articles on teaching writing and literature and on teaching in technology-poor classrooms. She has presented at state and national conferences on the topic of incorporating technical writing into existing curricula. Zuidema is interested in working with preservice and practicing teachers, as well as continuing to teach composition and literature.

This book was typeset in Palatino and Helvetica by Electronic Imaging.
The typeface used on the cover was Goudy.
The book was printed on 50-lb. Husky Offset by IPC Communications.